A Naturalist
in Southern Florida

A
Naturalist
in Southern
Florida

by Charlotte Orr Gantz

University of Miami Press

Coral Gables, Florida

QH105
.F6
.G211

Designed by Mary Lipson

Manufactured in the United States of America

Illustration credits: Everglades National Park, p. 193;
Fairchild Tropical Garden, p. 71; Florida News Bureau:
pp. 54, 133; William M. Stephens: pp. 11, 12, 172, 194;
Dade Thornton: end sheets, pp. 42, 72, 134, 150, 232

15794

Contents

Illustrations

Preface

A love of nature in all its varied forms, from the mountain scenery of the West, to the pines and rocky coasts of Maine, to the cypress swamps and sandy beaches of the South is deeply embedded in most of us. It is joined with an immense curiosity about how birds, fishes, mammals, and even more lowly "critters" live—and finally in many of us with a great interest in names. Recently one of my friends was watching a striking black and yellow butterfly in the Everglades. I presented him with its name, the zebra, and his interest quickened immediately. He had been "introduced." This was no longer a stranger, but something he knew.

Today in the United States far too many people are confined to cities and suburban developments where wildlife and natural scenery are at a minimum. But our strong inheritance is hard to kill. Each year sees additional great chunks of our land set aside for parks and wildlife preserves, and still the public clamors for more. And as if in answer to a deep-seated urge, we pour out into the countryside in ever increasing swarms. Vacationers seeking our beaches, mountains, lakes, and woods clog the highways all through the summertime and flow down to Florida and other parts of the South in gigantic streams during both winter and summer months.

Having joined the southward-moving throng for many a year now, I know well the thousands upon thousands who walk the beaches of Florida. Inland the numbers may not be as great, but many thousands still follow the trails in the Everglades National Park, at Corkscrew

Swamp Sanctuary, and in many of the public gardens: Fairchild Tropical Garden at Miami, the Cypress Gardens, and Lake Wales Sanctuary, which includes the Bok Singing Tower, to name just a few. Walking may have become a lost art in our cities and suburbs—in fact for the average American at home. But on vacation he is venturing forth on foot again. And at this pace, once again he has time to look at birds and butterflies, to notice a lizard in his path or a pink periwinkle blooming by the roadside. And as he looks his interest mounts. What is that bird? That tree? That shell? Why is it here?

Field guides in many areas of natural history have a very disconcerting way of stopping in Virginia or at Cape Hatteras. Many books on marine life, when they do venture into southern waters, touch only fleetingly upon the world of the subtropics. I believe there is a real need for a comprehensive work on the wildlife of southern Florida, but to be of any value, such a work would have to run into many volumes. Because the area is small, it's a natural assumption that the number of species is limited. But this is not the case. Florida is a meeting ground for North and South, and the fauna and flora of temperate and tropic zones come together in the southern half of the state in numbers that are truly staggering. The normal field guide— even one limited to the more common forms—would be too heavy to carry around.

My solution is a guide in the form of walks showing what I have seen on a few beaches, on trails through some swamps, and on inland roads. The approach is not entirely subjective. Out of the great possible range I have tried to select that which the casual visitor is most likely to encounter and to notice. To take one example—forty warblers may be found in southern Florida, but the chances are almost nine in ten that the warbler most people will see during eight months of the year is the palm warbler. With this kind of aid, one has a chance of making a few identifications, and in that hope I offer this book.

Author's Note
and Acknowledgments

A word of explanation is due for the contents and form of the appendices. It seemed most unwise to burden the general text with scientific names (except where it was unavoidable). On the other hand, in some fields—plants and seashells are notable examples— general agreement on popular names is often lacking. Thus we have a "balsam apple" in the North which belongs to another genus than the one in the South. Half of the guides to trees refer to "mastic," the other half to "false mastic." In such a case scientific names are necessary in order to know what we are talking about. It's also true that sometimes there are no popular names, and a shortened form of the scientific name is then given.

In the case of birds, the American Ornithologists' Union decides what shall be the correct popular name and publishes this in the *Check-List of North American Birds*. As a result, scientific bird names are rarely used. Popular names for mammals and fishes are quite well established; there seemed little need for anything else, although I decided to include the scientific ones for reptiles and amphibians. Fossil species seldom have recognized popular names; scientific ones were needed here, and it seemed best to give the scientific names for marine life in general, as well as for insects.

This is a pragmatic solution. Where there was doubt, where popular names were missing, or where scientific names might be required for a shell, fossil, or plant display, they have been given. It is also common practice to include the name of the author—the person who first described the species and bestowed the name. In many cases this was Linnaeus, generally abbreviated to "L." Dr. R. Tucker Abbott, however, prefers "Linné" for marine mollusks, and so—even at the risk of seeming to be inconsistent—I have used "Linné" in that one field, "L." elsewhere.

In the reference lists, starred books are recommended for the general reader who may wish to go further. Other references are more technical or in some cases are out of print.

Common and scientific names and references are not repeated in more than one chapter, even though many are applicable throughout the text.

Thanks are due to the following for permission to quote briefly from the sources indicated: The Macmillan Company, for an excerpt from *Collected Poems* by John Masefield, and the Florida Audubon Society, for a quotation from "We'll Get What We Deserve" by the Florida Wilderness Committee, published in *The Florida Naturalist,* Vol. 42, No. 2, April 1969.

I am also indebted to Charles M. Brookfield, Joe Browder, and George Avery for reading parts of the manuscript and for helpful comments, and to Dr. R. Tucker Abbott, Dr. Marion Pettibone, and Dr. Alan H. Cheetham for answering questions and helping with identifications. Such errors as may have crept in are my own responsibility.

A Naturalist
in Southern Florida

Map of Southern Florida. Refer to highway and tourist maps for more specific locations. Adapted from the Florida Handbook, by Allen Morris.

Introduction: South Florida, Past and Present

The world of small wild things—be they plant or animal—needs a leisurely approach, the time to look carefully and closely at a spider crab, at a leaf covered with hairs, at a vivid butterfly clinging to a flower. Only in this way can their beauty or strangeness be savored to the full. But, having said this, I shall turn briefly to a very different view of southern Florida—a sweeping look at the country as a whole. For this, too, we must have if we are to understand the area in which we are to roam. Let me survey this lower half of the state from the soaring height of an eagle circling above the mangrove swamps, of a caracara mounting an updraft over the grassy plains, or of a swallow-tailed kite hanging motionless, a mere pinpoint in the sky, above Lake Okeechobee or the Everglades.

From the air South Florida is many things: cities such as Tampa, Saint Petersburg, Sarasota, Fort Myers, Naples, Miami, Fort Lauderdale, and West Palm Beach; highways and man-made canals crisscrossing the land; citrus groves, cattle ranches, fields of sugarcane and truck gardens; airports, race tracks, golf courses, and much else of man's making. But beyond and above all this it is still a land of wilderness: the world of the cypress swamp, of wet and dry prairies, of the Everglades, of slash pine and saw palmetto. Closer to the ground man's interference is sadly in evidence: we can see great areas that have been drained; we know that many of the forest giants have gone and that enormous tracts have been given over to cement and buildings. From an eagle's height, though, the overall view is of persisting vegetation. And this is much the way that the ecologist looks at it, too, for to him Collier County is still the Big Cypress Swamp in spite of invading truck gardens; Monroe, Dade, Broward, and Palm Beach counties are, in essence, the Everglades; and the Kissimmee Prairie, stretching north of Lake Okeechobee, is basically grassland, the nearest thing to the western prairies to be found east of the Mississippi. Looking southward again, the ecologist notes a mangrove forest, one of the greatest in the world, edging much of the shore from Tampa to Miami. Lagoons and barrier islands lie along both coasts, and in the south-central part of Florida, Lake Okeechobee can lay claim to being the second largest freshwater lake in our country. The area that I've selected for this book, that which lies south of a line drawn roughly between Tampa and Melbourne, may seem small in its sum of square miles, but it offers a quite astonishing variety of plant and animal habitats.

Looking down on all of the sprawling forests, lakes, swamps, and plains, fringed by sandy beaches and mangroves, we know little of what they rest upon. Nor can we tell what is beneath the blue waters of the Gulf and the Atlantic. Yet all of this is important to any natural history of this section, and, because of this, we must leave our airy perch and take note of the findings of geologists.

Half of the peninsula of Florida, like the legendary city of Ys, lies below the waves. The Florida Plateau is a big tongue of land, 500 miles long and 250 to 400 miles wide, or an area two to three times as large as that which is shown on the maps today. A small part extends out into the Atlantic, but the major portion lies below the waters of the Gulf, and this drowned half stretches for a hundred miles beyond the present coastline. Again and again in the past, the whole great land mass has emerged, been clothed with grass and trees, given shelter and food to hordes of animals, and then slowly has been swallowed up by the sea. Much of the area I am writing about was beneath the water a mere hundred to two hundred thousand years ago. Take away all of the east and west coast cities and towns and leave a much narrower tongue that ends in fingers above the present Lake Okeechobee with one finger stretching below the lake on the west side. This was Florida—geologically speaking—not too long ago.

What was the reason for all of this jigging up and down? What was Florida's role in North America? The truth is that Florida has lain below the sea for more time than it's been above it, although its basement rocks go back almost to the dawn of prehistory. For countless ages, while amphibians, reptiles, and mammals were developing on our continent, southern Florida was resting quietly at the bottom of the ocean, the home of corals, fishes, mollusks, and other sea creatures. Then, late in the Cretaceous, at the end of the long rule of the dinosaurs, a major uplift raised the central portion of the peninsula into a dome running north and south above Lake Okeechobee. In the Miocene, the land rose again and supported a flourishing group of land animals, among them many of the primitive ancestors of today's mammals. Then the seas washed over it during the early Pliocene, and it wasn't until late in that period that it bobbed up once more much like a jack-in-the-box.

During the million or two years of our most recent period, the Pleistocene, earth movements played a smaller part in Florida's alternate emergence from the waves and submergence under them. The great ice ages (we have had four of them during the last two million years) locked the water of our globe into huge ice masses. The sea level could fall as much as 450 feet at the height of the glaciation, and whenever this happened a good part of the Florida Plateau was likely to become dry land. When the ice melted, on the other hand, during an interglacial stage, the waves would break again over what are now the Everglades, the Big Cypress Swamp, the flat pinelands, and Lake Okeechobee, as well as over that other half of the peninsula which none of us has ever seen above water. Old sea beaches cutting across Florida have been traced north as far as the Okefenokee Swamp. The flatlands east and west of the northern part of Lake Okeechobee mark the site of old marine terraces, and what is probably a shoreline of the old Pamlico Sea can be seen in the Fairchild Tropical Garden in Miami. Lake Okeechobee, itself, is all that remains of a great inland sea.

Maps of the Florida "that was" show that in the Miocene a long slender finger of land reached through Florida, just touching into Hendry County, and for half of its length it was only the width of a county. In the Pliocene, the next epoch, the shoreline ran south from about Winter Garden (the geologists say "Lake County") to Sebring, then in a gentle curve down to Arcadia and back up to Sarasota. From thence it took off across the Gulf to Tallahassee. During the

Sangamon, the interglacial stage just before the last ice age, Immokalee in Collier County was an island in the middle of the Pamlico Sea, and the mainland was far to the north.

Today our forests, prairies, swamps, and man-made structures rest largely upon sand and limestone, a rock made up of the limy shells and skeletons of marine plants and animals. Such a floor is exactly what one would expect with Florida's history. We can imagine other possibilities. Volcanic action would have given us lava and pumice, but no such material is to be found. Violent underground upheavals or molten rock oozing up through cracks might have produced basalt or granite, but none of this occurs. Extensive mountain-building followed by erosion might have given us many feet of overlying soil. This is missing, too, and all of the evidence points to the facts as we have given them: long periods under water and a fairly recent final emergence (or at least final from our viewpoint—lower Florida may be bound once again for a watery grave in the future).

Some of the surface, or near surface, rock is Miocene, some Pliocene, but most is Pleistocene, and a great part of this was formed during the Sangamon interglacial. The Sangamon limestone takes many forms. During this interglacial stage a living coral reef was built in the area that is now the Florida Keys. In time the coral died, but the remains of the old reef are to be seen in the Key Largo limestone, which runs from Soldier Key in Biscayne Bay to Big Pine Key, and which also underlies Miami Beach. One type of Key Largo limestone, so full of holes that there are more empty spaces than solid rock, has been widely used for decorative purposes. Another solid type when cut and polished looks like creamy marble. This was used for the altar and reredos in the church of St. Christopher's by-the-Sea on Key Biscayne. The corals stand out so clearly one can almost name each species. The upper, more recent part of the Key Largo limestone is thought to be about a hundred thousand years old.

Behind the sheltering reefs of this time another kind of limestone, the Miami oolite, was formed from an infinite rain of calcium carbonate which settled in a fine cloud over tiny calcite crystals, grains of sand, and bits of organic matter on the bottom. Currents kept the sea floor in motion so that little pellets of calcite were built up around each central nucleus and something resembling fish roe was the result. Miami oolite underlies Miami, Florida Bay, most of Dade

County, some of Monroe, and a good part of Broward, and forms the lower Keys from Big Pine to Key West. There are good exposures of it in the ledges and walls along Bayshore Drive approaching Coconut Grove. This limestone may also be pitted with many holes, and was probably the "holey limestone" used in walls and fountains that I knew as a child in western Pennsylvania.

Along the east coast above Miami, and along the southwest coast, a third set of beds appeared—some of them sand, some limestone, some hardened into a brownish-cream or at times a brown sandstone full of shells. This is the Anastasia, and the well-known coquina rock, popular as a building stone, is part of it. Finally there is the Fort Thompson, a slightly older formation dating from the second interglacial stage, the Yarmouth. It, too, can be brown rock dotted over with white shell fragments, many of them of the little venus clam, *Chione cancellata.* Much of the Everglades rests on the Fort Thompson.

The last great sea of the Sangamon was the Pamlico. It rose a mere 25 to 30 feet, but even so was sufficient to cover all of Florida up to the northern shores of Lake Okeechobee. During Pamlico times an offshore current laden with sand swept down the west coast. The current dropped its burden between Naples and Everglades City, forming long barrier islands including Marco. Many other sand dunes that were originally above water are now submerged, but their bases offered a foothold for mangrove seedlings, creating many of the Ten Thousand Islands.

Somewhere between seventy and one hundred thousand years ago, the weather turned colder, the ice advanced once more, and the Wisconsin Ice Age began. As usual, the sea withdrew and great areas of land were exposed. A warm interval brought new flooding, but the waters probably did not exceed their present level. Twelve thousand years ago the ice advanced for the last time, and this cold spell lasted a mere 2,000 years. When it ended, the ice retreated and the oceans rose, and, except for an interval of a thousand years, they have been coming up ever since (the possibility that Florida may be partly covered again is not a wild flight of fancy) but at such a slow pace as not to be easily observed.

During the Miocene, Pliocene, and Pleistocene epochs there was an overwhelming abundance of wildlife, particularly of large game, in

North America. This vast horde reached its peak in Florida during the Wisconsin, surviving all of the ice advances only to die off when the last warming-up spell began. A mere remnant of what was once here is left, and it is quite possible that early man played a part in killing off these original inhabitants of our country.

Many of the familiar plants of the South Florida landscape have only been in their present sites for 10,000 years or less. Saw grass and mangrove appeared as the climate warmed and the seas returned. Cypresses grew up in the swampy lands of Collier County. Currents were still bringing sand and broken shells from the North, and by this means the beaches of the west coast were built, an almost unbroken line of them stretching from a point a little above Tarpon Springs south for nearly 180 miles to Cape Romano. The one at Naples is an almost pure white quartz sand. And the sea wrought other changes. Just south of Miami and extending to Key West, a truly tropical vegetation has sprung up, much of it brought by the waves—frequently during hurricanes.

Man, particularly the white man, has altered the scenery I've sketched, sometimes for the worse—sometimes quite needlessly for the worse. Much of the original character of the Big Cypress region has been changed and more of it is threatened. In the days before timbering, drainage, and the spread of highways and cities, this was an area of cypress swamp, pineland, and wet prairie. Cypresses were so widespread as to give it the name of "Big Cypress Swamp" although they did not cover all of the region by any means. Where the soil was poor there were often wide sweeps of scrub cypress; again there would be intermediate growth, intermingled with frequent stands of big trees. Most of the latter fell to the axe except for that part of the primeval forest that has been preserved for us in the 10,000 acres of Corkscrew Sanctuary. The destruction of the big cypresses was a scenic loss; the extensive drainage that was carried out threatens not only scenery and wildlife but the water supply of the coastal cities as well.

In the Everglades, drainage for truck farming and sugarcane has already taken away a good part of this unique region, and widespread fires have often resulted as the underlying peat and muck dried out. In addition, much of its wildlife has been destroyed: some of it for sport, some for adornment, and some because it was believed to be harmful.

Most recently it has suffered because of commercial sprays, but slowly some protection is being provided. There are many strong voices for conservation in Florida, and it is to be hoped that some, at least, of her rich plant and animal life will be preserved.

And now, before we turn from this wide view of the land, let me fill in some of the details of what is here today—the present plant and animal life and the natural scenery. I have drawn a line from Tampa across to Melbourne as my northern boundary. This division can be justified because it marks the northern limit of much of the subtropical vegetation, while the Caribbean marine province runs from Tampa to the Dry Tortugas and lies below Cape Canaveral on the east coast. South of this line, the central part in the highland ridge is a land of lakes, a most beautiful section of Florida. I well remember a little lake there surrounded by longleaf pines, with the nest of a bald eagle in one of the trees. It's a region also of orange, grapefruit, and lemon groves, countless acres of them interspersed with pine woods and saw palmetto.

Farther south and east of Sebring on Route 98 is the cattle country—immense plains, with the stately Brahman cattle as well as our own Ayrshires, Herefords, and Black Angus. This is the Florida prairie, and driving through it, one has a feeling of having been unaccountably lifted up and then set down bodily in the midst of our western plains. Vultures can be seen in big flocks and occasionally there is a caracara, the great black and white scavenger hawk, the "Mexican buzzard," which properly belongs in the tropics. Sometimes he is to be seen perched on a fence post, often in among the vultures, feeding on carrion. The prairies are home to the little burrowing owl, but my eyes aren't sharp enough to spot him. I know this delightful and rather absurd little bird only from grasslands near Lehigh Acres in Lee County. He is a creature of the daytime, not of the night, and like the caracara, he perches on fence posts as well as on the mound beside his hole.

Below the prairie lies Lake Okeechobee, 700 square miles of lake that, for the most part, is only five or six feet deep, although it reaches fifteen feet in spots. High embankments hide most of it from passersby—alas! I have seen it once from the west shore roiled by high winds, and once from the south, a huge lake full of water hyacinths and lotus beds. Wet prairie lies to the northwest of the lake in the Indian reservation. On the east side, and below the prairie on the west side of the lake, are the flatlands with open pine woods, grasslands, and prairie—a good part of it under cultivation now. To the south are cane fields and truck gardens, again with wide stretches of grassland. Once I came upon a couple of sandhill cranes, beautiful, improbable-looking birds, feeding in the grass by the roadside. They, too, belong properly in the prairies.

Mostly now we have an ever-changing landscape. As we drive south on Route 29, we go through Immokalee, that island of the Pamlico Sea. Today the name is given to a small town that's a center for field workers. There's a labor camp here, bars, packing houses, an orange grove. To the left is the Okaloacoochee Slough, to the right of the cypress swamp. All of this area below Lake Okeechobee is poorly drained, except where it's been ditched, because of the underlying marl, and swamps are everywhere. There are no true rivers or streams here, but the land abounds in shallow pools and depressions. All of the limestone is riddled with sinkholes, some small, some wide and shallow, some deep chimneys in the rock. Most of the ponds lie in the sinkholes. A slough, and there are many in South Florida, is an open marshy channel or depression. That of the Okaloacoochee is about two miles wide and there is a very gradual southward slope, but drainage is hindered by muck, peat, and the heavy vegetation. A scrubby growth characterizes this area. One day, I saw one of the most beautiful birds of all Florida, a swallow-tailed kite, soaring above the slough, and it was of this bird that I was thinking when I referred to a kite's eye-view.

To the right, as we continue south, there are flat grasslands with a rank growth of saw palmetto. Now stands of cypress appear, tall and bleak-looking in the wintertime, shrouded in Spanish moss. Amidst the evergreen foliage of the South, an old tree towers like a dead skeleton, a somber, depressing sight. Its leafless condition is the souvenir of a time when it lived far to the north and became a deciduous tree, just as the larch did, when the climate turned markedly colder. Today, limited as it is to the South, it has no need to shed its needles, but apparently once the adaptation was gained, it couldn't be dropped.

Rarely do the cypresses stand alone. Often swamp growth surrounds them: arrowheads, cattails, and sedges. Willows, elderberry, southern wax myrtle may grow at their feet. Red bay and swamp maple mingle with the young trees, and where the land is a little higher, there is bunch grass, saw palmetto, and slash pine. Every so often a hammock appears, clothed with sabal palmetto (cabbage palm), the state tree of Florida.

Many of the cypresses are adorned with wild pineapples, a bunch of pointed gray-green leaves, clinging to the trunk or perched on a broad limb like a big knob, and, if anything, this adds to the eerie look of the tree. Although their appearance is most unlike, the wild pineapples and Spanish moss belong to the same family (that of the pineapple), and both are epiphytes (living on another plant), but not parasites (feeding on it).

In February, a delicate, feathery, green mantle covers the young cypresses (the older ones turn green later) and the wild pineapple puts up a stalk that varies in color but may be a bright red, standing out conspicuously in the dark cypress swamp. The bird I associate above all with this region is the wood stork. Big flocks of them whirl across the sky above the trees of Corkscrew Swamp.

South of the cypress belt, truck gardens come into view—fields of tomatoes, beans, squash, and strawberries interspersed with fields of gladiolus—and, as we near the coast, we reach the zone of salt marshes and mangrove swamps that stretch from Naples down to Cape Sable, often behind a sandy shore. Islands by the thousand lie along this shoreline (the group called the Ten Thousand Islands is here) and some of them are fair-sized, but many are only a few feet across and support nothing but mangroves. Inlets and lagoons also break the coastline into a watery maze.

On the other side of Naples, pine and palmetto march northward behind the beaches, and in the Gulf a long line of barrier islands reaches from Wiggins Pass up beyond Clearwater and Dunedin, finally ending in the Anclote Keys. An even more impressive line of barrier islands lies along the east coast, forming the Intracoastal Waterway. South of Melbourne, behind the beaches and the waterway, behind the cities and the Sunshine State Parkway, lies another great citrus region mixed with truck gardens. South of that, reaching over to the Okaloacoochee Slough and the Big Cypress Swamp, is the Everglades— an immense expanse of saw grass, broken by hammocks that may bear hardwoods, cabbage palm, pine, and cypress, or at its southernmost end such tropical trees as mahogany and gumbo-limbo. This is a rough outline. The details are infinite: birds in the groves, cypress swamp, Everglades, mangroves, mud flats, park lands; insects in weed-grown lots; and flowers in gardens, streets, and in the wild. Having seen the landscape as a whole, we can now look into its varied and most absorbing parts.

References

Davis, John H., Jr. *The Natural Features of Southern Florida Especially the Vegetation, and the Everglades.* Florida Geological Survey, Geological Bulletin No. 25. Tallahassee, Fla.: Florida Geological Survey, 1943.

Raisz, et al., with text by John R. Dunkle. *Atlas of Florida.* Gainesville: University of Florida Press, 1964.

Part I
The Beach

A marine community. The hermit crab takes over the interior of a tulip shell, while sea anemones are anchored on its outside. The crab gains protection—his shell is concealed by the anemones—and they benefit because their feeding range is extended as the crab moves about.

Previous page:
A small patch of honeycomb rock with coconut palms in the background. Sabellarid worms have built a series of reefs along the eastern shore of Key Biscayne.

1

Morning on Key Biscayne

The first of these more particular parts is the world of the sea beach, and here we have a scene that is almost constantly changing—a never-ending variety in the parade of life. At one time the shore may be littered with seaweeds, sponges, fishes washed in from deep waters. Again it may seem strangely barren. The life of the intertidal zone may be in evidence today, missing tomorrow. Shorebirds appear and disappear. So it goes from dawn to dusk and from day to day.

From north to south it varies, too, and differences may occur even within a few miles. One pattern is more likely on the Gulf shore, another on the Atlantic coast. Here the shoreline is close to a coral reef; there it borders a stretch of turtle grass. In one spot the Gulf Stream approaches land, farther along it veers away. The bottom may slope gradually into the ocean depths or it may fall off sharply. Rocks may occur along the shore. A river may disgorge its contents, turning the water brackish.

Some at least of these variations we shall see if we walk a dozen beaches at different times of the day and under different weather conditions. Many of the beaches of southern Florida are familiar to northerners. Sarasota, Sanibel, Naples, Marco, Miami Beach, Fort Lauderdale all evoke scenes of vacationers: bathing, shelling, playing at the water's edge. But one is less well-known—that of Key Biscayne—and since I mean to come back many times to the life of this island, it would be well to describe it now.

Key Biscayne lies between Biscayne Bay and the Atlantic Ocean just south of Miami. A causeway connects Virginia Key with the mainland and a second causeway runs from that island to Key Biscayne. Until 1947 they could only be reached by boat, but in that year the Rickenbacker Causeway was built, and soon tourists and residents of Miami were flocking to both islets. Virginia Key has the Seaquarium (with the famous "Flipper") as well as the Marine Stadium and the marine laboratory of the University of Miami. Just beyond is Key Biscayne with county and state parks at its northern and southern ends. On the Atlantic, the eastern side of the island, a wide beach stretches from one tip to the other, lying within Crandon Park at the northern end, within the new Cape Florida State Park to the south. In between, hotels and large condominiums front upon the sea, while behind them, smaller apartment houses, private dwellings, and stores fill the rest of the area. My first walks will be along this shore.

Mid-January. 7:30 A.M.

At seven-thirty in the morning on a January day the sea lies before me in all its immensity. Far off on the horizon the reddened half globe of the sun is just showing above the waves and a pink glow fills the eastern sky, while under it the water shimmers with an opalescent light. The sea is quiet now like bumpy glass, and the opalescence plays over its smooth and gleaming surface.

There is an early morning hush in the air and I have a feeling of expectancy. Only the smallest sounds break the stillness: the gentle lapping of waves on the shoreline, the distant crying of a sea gull, a couple of workmen raking sand in front of one of the hotels. No one else is around and nothing stirs behind the hundreds of windows that look down on the beach.

When I come out upon the ocean in the loneliness of daybreak, it seems as if there were no better time to be abroad. This is the hour for a walk on the sands. Turn south with me to Cape Florida and let us see what has been washed in overnight. It's an ebbing tide, and great stretches of wet sand lie between us and the waves that break gently along the beach. Dotting the sands are little shells—red, pink, white, and yellow—with their owners long since gone. Some of the colors are so brilliant that they look like jewels glistening on the beach. I can never quite believe that, if I pick some up, they will turn into very ordinary specimens as soon as they are dry, and in spite of past disappointments, I have to take a few. The brightest are the little red scallops, some looking very lopsided because one ear is so much bigger than the other (the sentis scallop), some (the rough scallop) with equal ears but scaly ribs. Almost as beautiful, though, is the inside of the prickly cockle, glowing with red, salmon, and purple. And then, just as I've decided these are the best, I am stopped by the gleaming pearly whiteness of a lucina and beside it the sculptured loveliness of a star shell. None of the shell collectors are out as yet, and all kinds of rarities may lie ahead. What has been stranded by the tide I shall be the first to see.

One morning as I strolled along the beach I wondered how the shells on Key Biscayne compared with those of other beaches, and the question gave me an excuse for picking up one specimen of every kind. I set a limit on my time—one hour—intending to check it later with other well-known beaches. The final score was a very respectable 44. Looking over the shells, though, I realized that they were far less spectacular than those of the west coast of Florida. Size was one point of difference. Most that I had collected were small, and the large majority were bivalves. One has to admit that the more interesting shell shapes are found among snails or gastropods. Here belong the conchs, whelks, murexes, tritons, and helmet shells, to name but a few of the more conspicuous kinds. The number of different gastropods on Key Biscayne is woefully small, but three—the American and long-spined star shells and the chestnut turban—are characteristic of that beach. If I were set blindfolded upon a seashore, having by some means been whisked from place to place without knowing where I was going, and if the blindfold were removed in a spot free from familiar landmarks, I would know that I was on the east coast and fairly far south by the presence of the star shells. When I saw the many little red scallops and the abundance of seaweed, I would know that at least it could be Key Biscayne.

I shall play this game with other beaches later on, for I found it amusing just as a game. Bird watchers do the same thing when they count the number of birds seen in a specific area on one day or over one season. If you would like to try it, R. Tucker Abbott's *Seashells of North America* in paperback describes most of the common species. For more thorough coverage, I use his *American Seashells* on the Gulf Coast and the somewhat newer *Caribbean Seashells* by Warmke and Abbott for the Keys and the Miami area. To complete my score for the one beach, I noted the additional shells I collected later—22—and also the additional ones for the whole island. The latter figure was 100.

I had paused as I thought of the shells, but now the mewing of sea gulls brings me back to the present. This is not their harsh, more usual cry, but a softer, less insistent note. A long wavering flight is coming up from the south—ring-billed gulls in a single line, returning to their feeding grounds. They used to spend the night on the sands of Key Biscayne, but then, so I'm told, raccoons took to attacking the sleeping gulls, and the sea birds had to find islets that were free from the troublesome mammals.

I like the gulls, even if they are noisy and very much underfoot. The ring-billed is the common large winter gull, the one that parades solemnly up the beach ahead of a human pedestrian and that is always looking for handouts. He and his bigger cousin, the herring gull (more common farther north), are scavengers and have increased enormously because of man's garbage dumps and the refuse thrown from ships.

Behind the gulls the sky is turning blue, and the sea echoes it except where turtle grass makes purple patches. One gull drops from the line because he has spied a stranded fish. In a moment the others are clamoring around him. He flies off with his prize while his fellows dive upon him trying to snatch it away. For a few moments the morning quiet is broken, but they are soon gone, and in their greediness over one fish, they have missed a dead calico crab that was also washed in. I stop to admire his beautiful shell—by rights, a "carapace"—warm yellow or tan, with big reddish-brown spots. When only the shell comes in, the chances are good that the crab has simply moulted. Because many start life together, they moult at the same time and as a result quite a number of carapaces may appear within the space of a few days. Then there may be none for quite awhile. The calico crab and the blue crab are the ones I have commonly found, and no one could mistake the latter because he is the "soft shell crab" of our tables. His color is greenish-gray rather than blue, but no other common crab has that wide shell ending in two long points.

When the sea is rough, seaweed and turtle grass can be seen in the waves as they crest and turn over in long churning rollers. On these days strands of turtle grass are thrown up on the shore, and sponges add their color to the sands. Today, however, the wavelets are talking very quietly, and there is no seaweed at all. Only small bits of coral are rolled over and over as the sea pushes them farther and farther toward shore and finally drops them out of reach of the falling tide. The corals here at Key Biscayne are mostly white and wave-worn with the delicate architecture of their cells nearly obliterated. Some are finger corals with a branching shape and arms the size of a finger. Some are starlet corals in little hemispheres. The star coral also has the shape of a half globe, but its surface is broken by larger and irregular cups. All of these are lying before me on the sands, not in the abundance of the shells, but I can point one out every few minutes as I proceed toward the lighthouse on Cape Florida.

Here is a coral bigger and flatter than any of the others. I was sure we would have a diploria before long because it is probably the most common of all. This is the knobbed brain coral, and it's covered with meandering valleys a little like the convolutions in a human brain.

At this point the hotels are behind me. I have passed the gate into the park and to landward there are sea grapes, big cabbage palms, and masses of feathery casuarina or Australian pine. On the sands ahead is a black-bellied plover, not as big as the gulls and with quite a different shape. Until I became a bird-watcher, I'd have called him a sandpiper, although he would have seemed rather big and stocky. I have to admit that in those days I thought there was only one sandpiper and that a "plover" was something that Britishers shot on their moorlands. Actually the black-belly does occur in Great Britain, but the likely bird of British novels is the golden plover.

The black-bellied plover, like so many of the water birds, has a summer and winter dress. In breeding plumage he has a beautiful and conspicuous black front, but today his coloring is mottled, a kind of nondescript gray. All by himself, and paying very little attention to me, he runs back and forth over the wet sands hunting for crustaceans. Only when I come too close does he fly a little ahead. In flight I have caught the white line down the outer side of his wing, and once when he tilted his body I got a glimpse of the black on the underside of his wing. All of this marks it a black-belly for sure, but I really knew it before from his size—around 12 inches—stocky build, short neck, short bill, mottled gray pattern, and the fact that he was alone.

And now I have come almost two miles. The sun is well above the horizon and it has turned into a beautiful day. Far out to sea small boats, bound for a day of fishing, have been going out steadily. With a freshening breeze from the ocean I can smell the salt air. Behind me people are moving in front of the hotels and it is time I turned back. Before I go, though, let me take a few minutes to rest. Here is a plank tossed up by the waves that will do to sit on. One end of it is resting on the tide wrack, the dried line of seaweed that runs the length of the beach except in front of the hotels. Most people turn up their noses at it as dirty, with too much of a smell, but to me it's an essential part of the seashore, and I should be very unhappy if someone scooped it all up. Besides, it's often full of sea treasures. Small creatures are jumping all over it now, and once I thought they were indeed fleas—their name is "beach flea." In fact, they are crustaceans with a shape something like that of a tiny shrimp and their diet is innocent indeed. They are here because they feed on decaying turtle grass and seaweed.

Most of the tide wrack is turtle grass with long, narrow blades like the familiar eel grass of northern waters. It isn't a seaweed but a true flowering plant that developed on land, found that overcrowded or inhospitable, and went back to the original home of all plants, the ocean. Porpoises and whales have gone through the same cycle.

The name comes from the fact that green turtles feed on it. Surprisingly enough, few other marine animals use turtle grass as a source of food, although it's home to a great many. Loggerhead and green turtles often visit it in search of sea biscuits—those big echinoderms that belong to the sea urchin-starfish family. Loggerheads will also come up where I am sitting later in the year to lay their eggs, and for that reason this is known as "Turtle Beach." In front of me the blue of the ocean is broken again and again by long bands of purple, and wherever I see them I know that turtle grass is growing. In places it forms great forests of waving grass, with strands several feet in length.

If I were to don a diver's mask and go out there I would find a busy small world of its own. Some of the larger snails—whelks and murexes—should be wandering over the bottom, along with the giant starfish, oreaster, which can be 16 inches wide. An octopus might be lying half-hidden under a scrap of iron from a wreck (in the old days Cape Florida was a hangout for pirates and wreckers) and he would be watching for crabs: blue crabs and spider crabs would be common. Sea urchins disguised with bits of shell and turtle grass should be here, together with their relatives the sea cucumbers. In among the grasses, sea horses would drift head up and tail down, their small fins beating like little wings. With them would be pipefish also in a vertical position, mimicking the tall flat blades of grass, while many other fishes would swim in and out of the area. The oddest "regular" would be the sea hare, a four-inch mollusk with no visible shell, greenish in color with scattered violet rings, and two ear-like tentacles. Quite probably he would be nibbling at the sea lettuce (ulva) which often grows on turtle grass. Limpets and snails would be feeding on the grass itself.

The tide wrack beside me is a souvenir of that community, and some of its smaller inhabitants are still here. On this dried piece of grass that I am holding, the worm spirorbis has put his tiny coiled white shell. Just beyond him there is a pinkish patch, a thin sheet of melobesia looking very much like lichen, but actually a coralline seaweed. The fact that 92 different seaweeds can be found living on Florida turtle grass shows how important this plant is to other forms of life.

Once, farther north, we had similar eel grass communities until the eel grass in the Atlantic was wiped out by disease some years ago. Fortunately the Mediterranean eel grass escaped, as did the turtle grass, and our own eel grass is making a recovery.

There is another community even closer to me than the one I have been looking at: the world of the wet sand which lies just a few feet away. Could I roll back the top layer like a rug, I might see living bivalves hidden from sight, but with long tubular siphons stretching up at times to or near the surface for food. There could be lucinas, whose shiny white shells I spotted at the beginning of my walk. There could be cockles like that with the sunset-colored interior. I might see delicate pink tellins, venus clams such as the princess venus and the cross-barred venus. Ponderous arks could be here, too, as well as ghost crabs, other crustaceans, and burrowing marine worms. As I sit watching, a starfish might well come upon one of the venus clams, wrap its arms about it, and pull with all of its tube feet until the clam was exhausted and opened its shell. Then—a most amazing feat—the starfish would extrude its stomach and slide it as a thin wedge through the gaping crack. Once inside, its stomach would absorb the food and then flow back into the starfish.

If we were able to look below the surface this way on the Gulf coast, we would see moon shells, big rounded gastropods, searching out bivalves in the sand. Sometimes their movements leave humped tracks so that one can tell where a moon shell is foraging. When he finds a clam or tellin or lucina, he drills a neat hole and through it sucks up the animal within. Many are the shells with such telltale holes on the Gulf shore, but I have rarely found them at Key Biscayne.

Rachel Carson said when she walked over the sands that she felt as if she "were treading on the thin rooftops of an underground city." Many a time I wonder what is going on in that world underfoot, so near and yet so very invisible. Am I stepping on dosinias, on thin sand dollars just under the surface, on beach hoppers, on sand crabs? Their retreat into the wet sand millions of years ago was intended as protection against gulls, fishes, octopuses, lobsters, and predatory snails, as well as against battering surf and drying winds. But this shelter was never supposed to withstand the constant tread of human feet. How are they getting on? I can only wonder.

Before I go, I have found one last thing in the tide wrack—the brown, horny envelope of a skate's egg. The small fish that was once inside has either escaped or been eaten, and all that is left is this rectangular case with long hooked points at each corner, hooks that probably once caught in the turtle grass and kept the eggcase from being washed ashore. The stillness of the morning, the sense of remoteness, has gone, but I shall take the eggcase as a reminder of this quiet hour when the day's work and the problems of the world seemed of little account and very far away.

For nearly a week the good weather held. Vacationers were all over the beach from mid-morning until late afternoon, and many of them collected shells. Before long the sands looked empty, and while I could always find plenty to examine in the way of bryozoans (moss animals or sea lace) and hydroids—the tiny things that need a magnifying glass—I was in the mood for something bigger and more dramatic.

Then came the storm—a big one that reached its height far out to sea. For a couple of days the wind blew and the waves crashed on shore with a din that could be heard a block away. The tides swept far up the beach, covering all of the normally dry sand and sending fingers of water over the railroad vine that had crept seaward from the jungle of vegetation on land. Spindrift rolled over the wet sand and gulls fought the wind. When the water retreated, it left big ripple marks behind, and I could see its swirling lines all around the chickees of the Beach Club. While the wind blew, it was too uncomfortable to walk very far, but at last it dropped and the hardier vacationers came out in windbreakers with scarves or caps.

Late January, 10:00 A.M.

Let us go up again toward the lighthouse. Today at mid-morning the water is a glittering green and there are whitecaps everywhere. Far out to sea the waves crest and break in long gleaming lines, and gulls are bobbing up and down in the choppy water. Nearing the beach, the waves surge in. They are still great rollers, but they no longer thunder on shore.

Enormous masses of seaweed—turtle grass and sargassum weed—have been washed in, and entangled in it are hundreds of physalia, the Portuguese man-of-war (called locally "blue bottles"), many with their pink and blue floats still expanded like shining balloons. The man-of-war is a kind of jellyfish, though not an orthodox one. Most jellyfish are one animal; the man-of-war is a big colony, with some individuals forming the long stinging tentacles that can reach out 40 to 60 feet, some digesting food, some seeing to it that there shall be new men-of-war to carry on the race.

It's a pity that anything so beautiful should have an end, even though at Key Biscayne the physalia is a frequent danger to swimmers. Cast ashore, the balloon slowly deflates. The deep blue tentacles, which at first coiled around the float like the snaky locks of Medusa, shrink and lose their color. Before long, sand will cover them and the balloon will be just a crumpled, nearly colorless envelope in the tide wrack. But now, while they are fresh, the tentacles can sting, and sting badly, if anyone is careless enough to step on them with bare feet. Almost all coelenterates—jellyfish, alcyonarians, corals, anemones—have poisonous tentacles by which they stun or kill their prey, but only a very few can affect human beings. It's too bad the men-of-war are ever blown out of the Gulf Stream. If they could stay away from shore, it would be healthier both for them and for bathers.

I must walk carefully today. Not only are there men-of-war, but the seaweed is full of tar, most of it unfortunately hidden in the refuse. I am generally made aware of its presence only after my shoes are covered with the horrible sticky stuff, but sometimes one can see a black shining mass covering a shell or sponge. This has come from oil tankers, and it's a pity that so far there is no way to keep them from discharging waste matter out at sea.

A little group of gulls scold harshly now as I pass. For two days the beach has been theirs alone and they seem to object to my return. I am so close that I can see their ringed bills very clearly.

I had hoped for shells, but there is hardly a one on the wet sand. Most of what the tide has left is seaweed—seaweed in many shapes and in many shades of green and brown. Bunches of hypnea lie like patches on the wet sand, and rounded balls of hypnea are being rolled over and over by the waves. Here are torn bits of ulva, the bright green sea lettuce. Next is some olive-green caulerpa with knobby ends, and everywhere there is brown sargassum weed with its distinctive stem and leaves and the conspicuous little round bladders that look like berries. All of this tells a story of churning seas and gale winds. Some of the sargassum weed has been blown in from the Gulf Stream along with the men-of-war. The caulerpa and the sea lettuce have been wrenched from the rocks.

I have passed the hotels now. I have been walking briskly, for the wind is still fairly strong and the hotel clean-up crews have taken most of the debris off the beaches. As I enter the state park, though, the storm's handiwork is spread out in its full extent. What a day for a real beachcomber! Here is a plastic bucket, garishly yellow and so heavy with barnacles that I can hardly lift it. How long has it lain on the bottom? What force was required to heave it ashore? Here is a diver's mask. I try to tell myself that it was discarded, but I still have an uncomfortable feeling. A week ago the sea looked very harmless; today I am afraid of it. Freshly broken planks have been washed up along with children's toys, masses of rope, a broken crate, and dozens of bottles. All of this recalls "flotsam and jetsam," those wonderful old English words: "flotsam"—that which has floated away (presumably from a wreck); "jetsam"—something thrown overboard or jettisoned. I suppose that sums up what I want to know. How much of this was tossed into the water as refuse, and how much has the storm snatched with its hungry waves?

Quantities of sponges have been stranded, ruthlessly torn from their homes: the reefs or hard bottoms where they were anchored. Their colors are beautiful: orange, red, yellow, and purple—some a glistening black. I notice that most of the beachwalkers step around them gingerly, and I suppose that, fresh from the sea and still alive, they look slimy and unpleasant to the touch. Their bright colors, like those of toadstools, appear to be a warning rather than an attraction.

What we know as a sponge is really a skeleton that's been carefully cleaned and dried. Most of our bathroom sponges come from the Mediterranean, but there is a big sponge industry in the Gulf (centered at Tarpon Springs, Florida) and around the Bahamas. The commercial sponges here were hit by a fungus disease in 1938 and were practically wiped out in the early forties. It's again curious that, as with eel grass, the disease was limited to one or a few closely related species. Spongia and hippiospongia suffered; the others, from 60 to 65 common kinds, went unharmed. As with the eel grass, there has been a remarkable recovery.

The shapes of the sponges are as surprising as their colors. Many are vase sponges—cone-shaped, red, and large of size, with a pungent smell of sulphur. Their surface is not what we think of as spongy; rather, it's hard and prickly when dry. Scattered among the vase sponges are orange tube sponges with short hollow tubes coming out of a common base and a much smoother surface. I find brittle stars in many of them, either dead or dying as their home dries out. Somehow the death of the brittle star impresses me more than that of the sponge. The brittle star is a single animal, and its five long, thin arms (it's sometimes called a serpent star) can move around most noticeably, while the sponge is another colony of many individuals and one would probably need a microscope to discover any movement. Early naturalists couldn't decide whether the sponge was a plant or an animal.

Vase sponges and tube sponges are easy to pick out. So are finger sponges with their long red branches that have a way of joining together every so often as they grow. Often the branches are flattened and the openings (or oscules) are always at one side of the tube. But here is a sponge that I am pleased to have found. It's a small loggerhead, and this particular one has the shape and size of an old-fashioned light bulb. It's black and its one oscule is at the end. Full-grown loggerheads can be as big as barrels, and they are conspicuous objects in the undersea world. Some years ago a marine biologist counted the number of animals found living in one of these monstrous sponges and discovered that it was over 17,000, most of them snapping shrimps. My sponge is too small for any such collection, but its base is firmly attached to a lovely red tulip mussel and many other sea creatures are fastened to it.

Earlier I tried to picture what the communities of the turtle grass and below the sand were like. Here I need do no such imagining for the dwarf-like world of the sponge is very evident. Many of them carry living oysters (young ones) and barnacles. Smaller sponges grow on the bigger ones, while threadlike ceramium, a red seaweed, is wound around the tubes and branches. Frequently small crabs live inside of the sponges, and every so often I find a pink, green, or purple sea squirt anchored at the base. At first sight one expects that shapeless blob to be slimy and jellylike. It was long before I could bring myself to touch one, but it was much firmer than I had thought. Pressed hard enough, most will squirt out water.

This is an interesting creature because it verges upon the vertebrate kingdom. Its young have a notochord (that forerunner of the backbone), but as the young ascidian matures, it loses this evidence of the "higher life" and degenerates to an invertebrate that seems almost inanimate. It's odd that such a nondescript, lowly-looking animal should be more advanced, in a sense, than the active and definitely shaped crab. The ascidian I find on the loggerhead sponge is pink, oval, flattened, and about one and a half inches long. I can just barely make out two knobs—one, the mouth; the other, the anal opening.

Wandering from sponge to sponge, I have forgotten to look at the water until a sudden motion catches my eye. Beyond the breakers, a small duck is diving into the choppy sea, swimming below its surface for a time and then popping up again. I know it's a merganser because of the long thin bill and the crest of feathers streaming out behind its head. In the South from November to April the red-breasted merganser is the common duck of the open shoreline, and it's surprisingly fearless. Often I've stood as close as just a few yards and the bird seemed completely unconcerned.

For a few minutes I watch the duck, but then the sponges call me again. It will be many a day before as much as this is washed in again, and what is here will soon be filled with sand and half-buried under the tide wrack. The beautiful, vivid colors will fade to a dingy brown, and the sponges will become dirty objects that everyone avoids. So much destruction! Nature deals with her marine life in a spendthrift fashion, discarding not only the living sponges but all that have made their home in or on them.

At my feet now lies a brilliant orange sponge with a corky feel and warty tubercles or ridges. This is tethya, with finger-like projections on the upper side; the lower side is rounded. More sponges lie all around: lavender and bright blue dysideas that crumble easily, dark red axinellas. But I have dropped them all for a truly exciting find—a three-foot purple sea plume, one of the alcyonarians or horny corals. (Gorgonian is another name for this group.) Sea fans with their lovely latticework of purple or yellow are the best-known of them, and many a time they figure in window displays of sea life. But the sea plume is almost as handsome. Named for an ostrich plume, it's something like a feather except that here, lying on the beach, it feels hard to the touch and when dry it will be quite stiff. Underwater, on the other hand, when still fully alive, it was completely flexible, bending and swaying in all its parts. This piece may have been torn from a reef, or its holdfast may have been lodged in sand and coral debris.

At the base, a tube sponge is growing with an ascidian clinging half to the sponge, half to the sea plume. Barnacles and wing oysters are attached further up, and stinging coral *(millepora)* has spread over sea plumes, barnacles, and wing oysters alike. This is another small world tied to the larger mass upon which it lives and doomed to perish as its home dries out. The Atlantic wing oysters, as a matter of fact, live only on alcyonarians, and one of the barnacles (there were at least two kinds) is found mostly on these horny corals. Stinging coral, finally, builds its encrusting shell on sea whips and sea plumes usually after they have died.

Like a coral, the sea plume is another big colony of individuals, but unlike the true coral, it has a horny inside skeleton and a soft outer layer in which are secreted so many limy spicules that it feels hard. Sea plumes, sea fans, and sea whips are all built the same way, and as they dry the limy layer often splits away like bark.

And now again I am near the lighthouse. In the past this was where the wreckers gathered. A hundred years ago a storm such as we have had might easily have tossed a big ship on the rocks with a loss of passengers and crew. Cargo, ship furnishings, and personal belongings would have been washed ashore. Today it was only sponges, seaweeds, and a scattering of man-made objects. The glittering green sea has a dangerous look, but this time, I must admit, it is mostly its own creatures that have felt its destroying power.

Common and Scientific Names

American star shell: *Astraea americana* (Gmelin)

Atlantic moon snail (moon shell): *Polinices duplicatus* (Say)

Atlantic wing oyster: *Pteria colymbus* Röding

axinella: *Axinella polycapella* de Laubenfels (a reddish hispid sponge with fine, stiff branches)

barnacle: *Balanus galeatus* (L.) (commonly found on alcyonarians)

beach flea: *Orchestia agilis* Smith (probably the one in the tide wrack)

blue crab: *Callinectes sapidus* Rathbun

brittle star (serpent star): *Ophiothrix lineata* Lyman (normally lives in sponges and here is common in the tube sponge)

calico crab (lady crab): *Ovalipes ocellatus* (Herbst)

caulerpa: *Caulerpa racemosa* (Forskal) J. Agardh (there are many caulerpas but this is a common one on this shore)

Ceramium sp. (appears to be *C. rubrum* (Hudson) C. Agardh, although its appearance in Florida has been questioned)

chestnut turban: *Turbo castanea* Gmelin

cross-barred venus: *Chione cancellata* (Linné)

dysidea: *Dysidea fragilis* (Montagu) (lavender sponge, full of sand and shell fragments and quite delicate, as the name suggests); *Dysidea etherea* de Laubenfels (a bright blue, but otherwise like the above)

finger coral: *Porites furcata* Lamarck

finger sponge: *Haliclona rubens* (Duch. & Mich.)

Florida sea cucumber: *Holothuria floridana* Pourtalès

giant starfish: *Oreaster reticulatus* (L.)

hypnea: *Hypnea cervicornis* J. Agardh; *Hypnea musciformis* (Wulfen)

Lamouroux (balls and tufts of these two filamentous, branched
seaweeds are often abundant at low tide)
knobbed brain coral: *Diploria clivosa* (Ellis & Solander)
loggerhead sponge: *Spheciospongia vesparia* (Lamarck)
long-spined star shell: *Astraea phoebia* Röding (flatter and longer-
spined than American star shell; used to be called *A. longispina*)
melobesia: *Melobesia membranacea* Lamouroux (an encrusting seaweed that looks like pink lichen)
Pennsylvania lucina: *Lucina pensylvanica* Linné (note that Linnaeus
didn't know how to spell "Pennsylvania")
pink ascidian: *Pyura* sp.
ponderous ark: *Noetia ponderosa* (Say)
Portuguese man-of-war: *Physalia pelagica* Bosc.
prickly cockle: *Trachycardium egmontianum* (Shuttleworth)
princess venus: *Antigona listeri* (Gray)
rough scallop: *Aequipecten muscosus* (Wood)
sargassum weeds: *Sargassum natans* (L.) J. Meyen; (a floating sargassum
weed); *S. vulgare* C. Agardh (a sargassum weed attached to rocks);
S. hystrix J. Agardh (also attached to rocks); *Turbinaria turbinata*
(L.) (a sargassum weed with greenish-brown cones that are closed
at the top; these look like air bladders but are, in fact, leaves)
sea biscuit: *Clypeaster rosaceus* (L.)
sea lettuce: *Ulva lactuca* L.
sea plume: *Pseudopterogorgia americana* (Gmelin)
sea urchins: *Lytechinus variegatus* (Lamarck); also given as *Lytechinus
variegatus* (Leske) (one of the common often greenish, short-
spined sea urchins of the turtle grass); *Diadema antillarum*
(Philippi) (the sea urchin with long black spines)
sentis scallop: *Chlamys sentis* (Reeve)
smooth tellin: *Tellina laevigata* Linné
spirorbis: *Spirorbis* sp. (coiled worm shell found on turtle grass)
spotted sea hare: *Aplysia dactylomela* (Rang) (the common species of
this area)
star coral: *Montastrea annularis* (Ellis & Solander)
starlet corals: *Siderastrea radians* (Pallas); *S. siderea* (Ellis & Solander)
stinging coral: *Millepora alcicornis* L.
tethya: *Tethya* sp. (orange globular sponges)
tube sponge: *Callyspongia vaginalis* (Lamarck) (this is supposed to be
lavender, but those I have found have been orange)

tulip mussel: *Modiolus americanus* Leach
turtle grass: *Thalassia testudinum* Koenig & Sims
vase sponge: *Ircinia campana* (Lamarck)

References

Abbott, R. Tucker. *American Seashells.* Princeton, N.J.: D. Van Nostrand, 1955. 541 pp.

*Abbott, R. Tucker. *Seashells of North America.* A Golden Field Guide. New York: Golden Press, 1968. 280 pp.

Bayer, Frederick M. *The Shallow-Water Octocoralla of the West Indies Region.* The Hague, Netherlands: Martinus Nijhoff, 1961. 373 pp.

*Carson, Rachel L. *The Edge of the Sea.* Boston: Houghton Mifflin, 1955. 276 pp.

Clark, Hubert Lyman. *A Handbook of the Littoral Echinoderms of Porto Rico and the Other West Indian Islands. Scientific Survey of Porto Rico and the Virgin Islands,* Vol. XVI, Part I. New York: The New York Academy of Sciences, 1933. 147 pp.

*Dawson, E. Yale. *How to Know the Seaweeds.* Dubuque, Iowa: Wm. C. Brown, 1956, 197 pp.

de Laubenfels, M. W. *A Guide to the Sponges of Eastern North America.* Coral Gables, Fla.: University of Miami Press, 1953. 32 pp. O.P.

*Miner, Roy Waldo. *Field Book of Seashore Life.* New York: G. P. Putnam's Sons, 1950. 888 pp.

*Smith, F. G. Walton. *Atlantic Reef Corals.* Rev. ed. Coral Gables, Fla.: University of Miami Press, 1971. xii, 164 pp.

*Stephens, William M. *Southern Seashores.* New York: Holiday House, 1968. 188 pp.

Taylor, William Randolph. *Marine Algae of the Eastern Tropical and Subtropical Coasts of the Americas.* Ann Arbor: University of Michigan Press, 1960. 870 pp.

Warmke, G. L., and Abbott, R. Tucker. *Caribbean Seashells.* Narberth, Pa.: Livingston, 1961. 348 pp.

*Zim, Herbert S., and Ingle, Lester. *Seashores.* A Golden Nature Guide. New York: Simon & Schuster, 1955. 160 pp.

2

Afternoon on Key Biscayne

Late January, Noontime.

It is warm today, Sunday, and the beach is overflowing with bathers, picnickers, young men playing ball, children building castles and digging holes, people lying on the sand, people walking. In the cabanas, politicians and movie stars wear dark glasses so as not to be recognized, but rumors abound. "They say that so-and-so is here." A pet ocelot walks daintily along the tide line and it seems a curious, unreal world. Is this the same beach that I strolled on two or three weeks ago in the early morning? Was it here that I found sponges and seaweed after the storm?

Today a hot sun beats down upon the shoreline and the sand is warm underfoot. A gentle swell flickers over the blue ocean and the waves break lightly, splashing white at the edge of the beach. There is little seaweed, no men-of-war, few shells, and no sponges. Only the gulls are still here, beating in a small cloud around a youngster who is tossing bread into the air. Some are diving for crumbs; some, on the sand, gawk at his feet with open mouths and heads thrust forward in awkward, ungainly poses. All of them are screaming with impatience.

This is no time for a walk on the beach—too many people are ahead of me. I shall go up to the state park as quickly as I can, gather a few pieces of seaweed and broken shells, and find shelter under a coconut palm. Because I knew that the beach would be crowded, I have brought along a jar for seawater and a couple of empty trays from TV dinners.

It doesn't take long to find a spot, spread out a beach towel, collect some seaweed, and fill my jar. Most of the seaweed is put into the trays to float, but some of it I add to the jar after refilling it. This will be a day for the lilliputian world, the tiny inhabitants of a piece of sargassum weed or the broken half of a pen shell.

Let's begin with the sargassum weed. When I was young, the Gulf Stream appeared to be a mysterious and exciting part of the ocean. One might be days from shore on a cross-Atlantic trip and quite suddenly there was seaweed, warmer air, and noctilucent animals at night making ripples and flashes of light as our bow cut the water. Porpoises sometimes broke the surface, somersaulting again and again in sheer exuberant play, or on occasion flying fish skimmed over the quiet sea in incredibly long flights.

I am reminded of all this as I hold the brown bit of seaweed in my hand. In *The Sea Around Us,* Rachel Carson spoke of the then unresolved dispute as to whether all of the sargassum weed was torn from rocks around Florida and the West Indies, or whether some of it had always been a part of the Sargasso Sea. We know now that the latter theory is right, and I have here some of the floating kind as well as some that has been broken from a rock.

Some of the weed is whiter than the rest, and my pocket magnifying glass (5-power) shows me a delicate white network covering the seaweed and its berrylike floats. This is a bryozoan or moss animal, sometimes called sea lace, and this particular kind—one found only on sargassum weed—has very much of a frosty, lacy look. Bryozoans grow in colonies just as do sponges, corals, sea fans, and men-of-war. In life, and under a microscope, a circlet of tentacles, often golden yellow and rather like the rays of a flower, might be seen coming out of some of the cells. Lots of shells have bryozoans on them, sometimes in a delicate tracery, sometimes forming a crust. Thick crusts cover many rocks, and minute as the individuals are, bryozoans have added their bit to coral reefs both in recent times and in the far distant past. I knew them first as fossils, going so far back into prehistory that they must be counted among the early forms of life.

Somewhat idly—for the day is hot—I turn over my shells. Here on the broken pen shell are at least three kinds of bryozoans, some in fan-shaped colonies, some in the form of a disk. The size and the shape of the openings vary, as well as the way the cells are aligned, and before long I've become absorbed in this tiny world.

A beachcomber sauntering toward me calls me back to the present. Without appearing to look, he wants to find out what interests me so keenly. Would he understand? I'm afraid not, although in the past many a shell collector has taken my glass and looked with deep interest at the miniature architecture on the pens. But this young man has already turned away.

Far out to sea a black cormorant is drifting, his head tilted upward, seeming to express all of the laziness, the fullness of the day. I run the sand through my fingers and discover a white land snail, one that used to be called "pupa," I suppose because it has the general shape and size of an insect pupa or cocoon. Now it is "cerion," and there are scores of them under the palms and Australian pines. Originally from Cuba, this cerion was blown here—without doubt—by hurricanes. Many of the plants and animals of the Keys and South Florida arrived in that way, and they have given this island so much the look and feel of the tropics that it's a favorite spot for movie-makers and advertisers when a tropical setting is required.

Overhead I am aware of a red-shouldered hawk, the common buteo of Florida, perched on the top of a dead tree. I wonder if he, too, is peering down at my pieces of sea life.

The sargassum seaweed has other inhabitants: any number of gooseneck barnacles with an orange stalk and two pale blue wedge-shaped shells or scuta covering the lower part of the body. Once I thought that this particular barnacle was found only on sargassum weed—a complete mistake because they attach themselves to many floating objects. Driftwood and coconut husks are often covered with them, and they are common on ships. Some of the sargassum weed has been floating in the jar and I notice movement there, a sudden disturbance that comes and goes. Lying down beside the jar and looking into it with my glass, I can see a gooseneck barnacle kicking out its feet in little bursts of action. All barnacles are crustaceans like the great families of crabs and shrimps, but they have given up wandering (or at least moving from place to place on their own) in favor of a sedentary life.

The more familiar barnacles are acorn barnacles, and I have several of these on my pen shell, some white, some with pink lines. Baby oysters and tiny chama shells are here in numbers, while winding over the back of the shell is a maze of worm tubes, twisting and turning, crossing each other like a writhing mass of serpents—but a stony mass, for the worms have gone and I have only their limy tubes. Some tubes are bigger and shorter; some are made of grains of sand. Sabellid and serpulid worms were the workmen.

On a broken cockle there are more worm tubes, bryozoans, and seashells, but there is something else as well. The entire cockle is riddled with tiny holes and I know that the boring sponge, cliona, has been at work. Looking at this evidence of abundant life, even if in miniature, I realize that a shell can be home to far more creatures than just the mollusk that built it. And this community is obviously no recent invention. Fossil shells very often carry barnacles, worm tubes, and bryozoans. They may have been eaten by boring sponges of some millions of years ago or a telltale hole at the beak may reveal an ancient and untimely end.

Most of the sargassum weed has the familiar white lacework stiffening its fronds, but a few carry a fine white fringe all along the outer edge of the leaf, giving it a positively feathery look. Under the glass this is beautiful indeed. I have quarter-inch hydroids, each the shape of a tiny plume. Hydroids belong to the jellyfish family, and under a microscope I would see tiny cups on the plumes, each of which could produce a minute bell-shaped medusa or jellyfish.

Another sargassum weed has fine hairs springing all over its surface, and this time I can see the elfin cups of the hydroids. A third sargassum weed, turbinaria, whose leaves take the shape of greenish-brown cones, is covered with a veritable forest of hydroids, all of the stiffened little stalks being toothed, or, better, looking as if one wedge-shaped segment were set inside another.

My glass has unlocked for me briefly a fairylike world, one that is rich in beautiful shapes in spite of being so little known. Even when the sands are barren of shells and sponges, the great lilliputian kingdom is almost always at hand. Under the midday sun I have looked at it for a fleeting hour, but it is time to leave my shelter and go back to the world of men.

Early February. 3:00 P.M.

It is February now and the seas are gray-green this afternoon under a lowering sky. Rain has been falling off and on all day and hardly anyone is out on the beach. I can see a man walking his dog, two children ducking and shouting in the shallow water while their mother watches patiently nearby, and, in the distance, a couple strolling over the wet sands, but otherwise the beach is deserted. Today I have turned away from the lighthouse; I will go north past the Royal Biscayne Hotel.

A great expanse of sand lies before me, for the tide has been ebbing and has only just turned. The flood tide marks the busiest time at the shore. At sea, gulls are skimming over the water, plunging downward every so often after a fish. There is a tern with them and I pause to admire his sleek swallowlike form, so infinitely more graceful than that of a gull. He flies with head angled sharply down and when he dives goes into the water like an arrow. It's a beautiful sight.

Everywhere birds are feeding. At the tide line sanderlings run after a retreating wave, then dash shoreward before the incoming one. It's amazing that they never seem to be caught even when an unexpectedly big comber breaks just in front of them. Their little feet race away and the group (there may be seven or eight) swirls back toward dryer land. But a second later they have reversed direction and are following the wave, seizing morsels of food as it ebbs. These are true sandpipers, grayish-white in color, and, from their way of feeding, hard to mistake for anything else.

Heavy masses of seaweed cover the upper part of the sands. A stiff onshore breeze was responsible, and it has carried in hundreds of men-of-war as well. In front of us lies one of them, a lovely flattened balloon, eighteen inches across and light blue at the top of the float, darker blue below. The pink rim is marked by gathers or puckers all along its edge. The tentacles are blue and pink and are still stretched a foot or two over the seaweed. In among them is a dead fish that may have come there quite by accident but may also be nomeus, the fish that commonly lives within the ring of tentacles of the man-of-war. The stinging cells of physalia will kill most fish that come too close—and fish are a normal part of its diet—but nomeus is apparently unaffected and depends upon the man-of-war for protection as well as for uneaten scraps.

I have stepped over the stranded line of seaweed, being careful to avoid tar and men-of-war. I will walk northward now, with the beach litter on one hand and the full extent of the intertidal sands on the other. Just ahead is a sea urchin with a biscuit shape and very short green spines. He sits in a little depression with the water streaming out on either side as a wave pulls back. There are bigger urchins with long spines in deeper water but this is the common one of the beach. Most often I simply find pieces of the shell or test that have been washed clean of spines.

At the water's edge dozens of little holes are appearing as small crustaceans—mole crabs and beach hoppers—put out their legs to sweep in microscopic food. There are more holes ahead, and a willet is working over them along with four black-bellied plovers. The willet is in curious contrast to the plovers. They are so stocky with their short necks and bills, and they run rapidly over the sand, snatching at marine creatures in the water or at a beach hopper above the line of surf. The bigger willet, on the other hand, is unmistakably a sandpiper with his longer neck, long legs and bill, and a much slimmer body. He walks (instead of running) with his head bobbing. Every so often the long bill probes deliberately, carefully down a hole.

From tide line to tide wrack I wander, caught now by movement near the water, again by something half-hidden under the seaweed. Here is velella just ahead. I thought it should be here. Velella is another siphonophore, closely related to physalia although much smaller. It has a flat, rectangular bottom with a flat piece (the sail) set at right angles to the disk and running diagonally across it, the whole looking like an elfin boat. Commonly called "by-the-wind-sailors," these delicate creatures float upon the surface of the ocean far from land in such vast numbers at times that they seem like myriad flecks of deeper blue against the lesser blue-green of the sea. Bright blue tentacles surround these two-inch sailors, but as with physalia, the color of the sail and of the tentacles, the inky-blue of the disk, will soon fade, leaving an apparent scrap of plastic, dried and white in the seaweed, and so light that a breath of wind will spin it away from my reaching fingers.

Velellas come in with the physalias, and following velellas come violet snails, fragile little beauties that ride the ocean waves held aloft by a float that's a hardened mass of bubbles. Violet snails feed upon velellas and here is one now, dining upon a by-the-wind-sailor. Death confronts them both, but even so, janthina, the violet snail, is having one last meal. Shell collectors gather in the violet snails eagerly, but I am likely to throw them back into the waves to give them one more chance at life.

I have come close to the black-bellies now and they bob for a moment, then take off in a little flock. The willet flies, too, but alone, showing the conspicuous black and white pattern of his wing and calling noisily "whee-wee-wee." Following the line of his flight I discover another bird, a black cormorant with outstretched neck, just barely clearing the waves. There is something forbidding about this sea bird. I am reminded that in *Paradise Lost*, Satan sat like a cormorant on the Tree of Life, and gluttons are referred to as cormorants. So it is fitting that the ocean just a few feet beneath him has a somber look with only an occasional whitecap.

In front of the Royal Biscayne Hotel massive boulders have been piled up to make a sea wall and to protect the building from hurricane waves. At high tide one has to go inshore of the rock pile, but when it's low we can walk around it on the seaward side, and this is what I have come for.

As I approach, little black creatures—sea roaches—skitter over the face of the stones and disappear into crannies. One moment there is a flurry of activity; then it's still. The sea roach is another crustacean, not an insect, and it's about an inch long.

I would like to see more of the active inhabitants of the rock. There are sure to be crabs down in the deep cracks, hiding under broken shells, driftwood, and coconuts that have also lodged there, but only the sedentary members of the community are in evidence. There are plenty of these. Periwinkles and nerites are high up, with limpets and barnacles below. The seashells still have their inhabitants, as I know when I try to pull one or two from the rock. I am sorry because I would like one of the pretty little zebra-striped periwinkles. These are zigzag periwinkles and everything about them is delicate and charming, unlike some of their rounded, heavier relatives, but I refuse to kill any live creature just for my pleasure.

Here and there are tufts of mermaid's hair, the green hairlike algae. Sea lettuce lies limply against the rock, but when the tide returns, sea lettuce and mermaid's hair will float again and the lovely green veil of the sea lettuce will wave once more like a delicate scarf.

When the sea comes back it will bring food to the acorn barnacles. These little crustaceans will simply open their doors (the scuta at the top of each cone), kick their feet out, and bring whatever minute particles are entangled in them back to the mouth. But the periwinkles, limpets and nerites go out to feed. Like cattle, they browse on their pastures of lichen and algae—the very small seaweeds on the rock face. When the foragers have had enough, or when the tide ebbs, the community settles down again to a more or less motionless existence. The periwinkle doesn't care what he goes back to as long as it's a part of the rock he can cling to and where he won't dry out, but the limpet has one selected spot to which he must return. Amazingly enough, each finds his peculiar space and settles into it just as he was before he left.

I know that a community such as this should have predators as well as vegetarians, and I have been hunting all over the boulders for at least one. Here he is, at last, a dog whelk lodged securely in a hole! This mollusk feeds on barnacles, limpets, nerites, and periwinkles, drilling a hole into the shell just as the moon shell does, and forcing open the barnacle's "doors." Usually nature provides herds of vegetarians for a few meat eaters (in this way both groups survive) and I'm sure that there aren't many dog whelks around. But I'm also certain there is more than one. The sea roach plays the part of a scavenger in this small world, finishing off the scraps left by the dog whelk.

Straightening up for a moment, I look back at the way I have come. Black-bellies and sanderlings are still busy feeding, although the willet hasn't returned. A gull, though, has landed on the tide wrack and is hunting for violet snails. He finds one and flies away with it,. marking the end of a small food chain. Velella feeds upon microscopic life, which it stings and gathers in with its tentacles. Violet snails feed mostly upon velellas and are finally eaten themselves by gulls.

Now that we have seen the rock community, let us look at the boulders. Key Biscayne is made up of Miami oolite, the rock which underlies Miami and the lower Keys. One of these big masses is full of fossil corals, and many of the other rocks are covered with the molds and shells of ancient clams, lucinas, cockles, and scallops. The cockles could have grown on a reef. Lucinas and clams are sand dwellers but their empty shells may have caught there. Scallops, almost alone of the bivalves, swim after their fashion, but they, too, may have been piled up on one by a storm many thousands of years ago.

No one knows for certain how these particular rocks came into being. We can only guess that shrinking seas and colder water killed the coral animals and that hardening, limy particles filled the openings and bound the shells into the mass. And now what was once a living community is home to a very different one. The picture is an absorbing one but I mustn't linger over it, for I have come to look at another reef that is only above water at extreme low tide.

Reef-building corals have to have warm water—a warmer sea than that which now washes the Miami shores or Key Biscayne, although the true reefs begin just a very short distance south of my island. What I have here is a reef of a very different kind—one built by honeycomb worms or sabellarids—and I have to confess that it puzzled me for quite awhile. I discovered the reef soon after I came to Key Biscayne. It was apparently a long ledge, or series of ledges, paralleling the shore and seeming to run for a mile or more. Parts of the reef have died and here the rock takes on a rough surface that is a source of scratches and discomfort to bathers. Both living and dead parts are generally underwater, but, when exposed, a heavy, slippery mantle of dark green caulerpa, interspersed with sea lettuce and mermaid's hair, can be seen covering much of them. Small depressions on top make rock pools for stranded marine creatures. I was told it was a coral reef, but coral never produced such a shingled, honeycomb effect, and this rock gave slightly when I stepped on it, like the pile of a thick rug.

In time I found its name—honeycomb rock—and knew what had built it. I also learned that many a shipwreck of the past had occurred not because of a coral reef (the official cause), but because of the reef-building efforts of this worm. When I step on the rock, I crush the uppermost layer of tubes, the roof of the house, and it usually takes twenty-four hours to repair the damage. This knowledge makes me feel like a gross, lumbering giant—a Gulliver trampling upon Lilliput.

Today someone has wrought even more destruction, however. Big chunks of the reef have been broken off, probably with a sledge hammer, and the pieces are lying all about on the sand. I could never have done such a thing myself, but it offers a chance to see what the rock is like inside.

The color is astonishing. Outside it was a dull brown; within it is a richer, redder brown with soft pink worms trying to hide from sight. These could be the sabellarids, but they could equally well be other marine worms sharing the rock with its builders. There is also a heavy crust of brick red—stinging coral again—right in the center of the reef, along with various bryozoans. With a microscope and with greater knowledge, I should find much more for I am certain this reef, like that of the coral, is home to many creatures.

Now that I have learned to recognize the honeycomb rock, I see that it is more widespread than I had realized. It covers the base of such boulders as are generally underwater and it spreads over the cement pilings that hold the beach. Wherever rocks provide a foothold, the worm has placed its home. On the ledges that are exposed at low tide, the chief covering is caulerpa. But farther out a slimy red seaweed (gracilaria) takes its place. Marine biologists are very fond of pointing out the constantly changing zones in the ocean world, and this is a perfect example.

Worn fragments of the dead reef, looking like roughly cemented grains of sand, lie on the beach along with fossil shells from the boulder. There are other pieces of stony matter that will also bear investigating. In my hand I have something that resembles a finger sponge that has become filled with sand and solidified into rock. It puzzled me for at least a year and I had to seek out expert help. The answer was astonishing. What I had was fossil mangrove root, known nowhere else but on Key Biscayne. At the northern end is a reef made up of the fossilized roots, and pieces have been carried south along the beach.

Other bits of limy material I assumed were coral until I looked at them with my glass. The cells of coral, unless very much water-worn, can be seen with the naked eye. The cells of bryozoans spring to light only when magnified, but they are abundantly clear under a five-power glass. Bryozoan colonies are usually encrusting, but every so often a species forms its own independent mass, several inches in size, with finger or fanlike projections, and it's one of these that I have picked up.

The tide is inching up now over the honeycomb reef, and the worms, I know are beginning to feed. The intertidal world is sending up siphons, tentacles, or other appendages to pull food out of the incoming waves. Sometimes an animal takes in a whole gulp of water and strains out the particles of food before expelling it. Gulls, terns, and cormorants are fishing; shorebirds are busy on the sand. As I turn homeward I am aware of leaving a scene of bustling activity—not the activity of man that I had seen on Sunday at noon, but the normal activity of the shore—the world that was here long before human beings took over so much of the natural space.

Common and Scientific Names

acorn barnacles: *Chthamalus fragilis* Darwin (a small, grayish-white acorn barnacle); *Balanus amphitrite* Darwin (another acorn barnacle, whitish with pink or red streaks); *Tetraclita squamosa* Bruguière (the common large barnacle on the Key Biscayne rocks)

beach hopper: *Talorchestia longicornis* (Say) (a close relative of the beach flea)

bryozoans: *Holoporella* sp. (a finger-shaped bryozoan); *Membranipora tuberculata* (Bosc) (a bryozoan encrusting *Sargassum vulgare*); *Parasmittina spathulata* (Smitt) and *Steganoporella magnilabris* (Busk) (both commonly found on pen shells)

caulerpa: *Caulerpa* sp. (the short, greenish-brown seaweed growing on the near-shore reefs

cerion: *Cerion incanum* (Binney) (a common land snail)

cliona: *Cliona caribboea* Carter (one of the common boring sponges in the area, although what I had might have been *Cliona vastifica*)

dog whelk (dog winkle, rustic rock-shell): *Thais rustica* (Lamarck)

eastern oyster: *Crassostrea virginica* (Gmelin)

gooseneck barnacle: *Lepas anatifera* L. (a small, common, gooseneck barnacle)

gracilaria: *Gracilaria* sp. (a reddish seaweed covering the honeycomb worm reefs farther out from shore; there are several species of gracilaria here)

honeycomb worm: *Phragmatopoma lapidosa* Kinberg

hydroids: *Pennaria tiarella* McCrady (a feathery hydroid colony that may be found on sargassum weed and also on turtle grass); *Clytia noliformis* (McCrady) (a hydroid colony with hairlike threads running over the leaf, some rising vertically and bearing tiny cups; found on sargassum weeds); *Sertularia cornicina* (McCrady) (the toothed stalks of hydroids, also found on sargassum)

limpet: *Acmaea antillarum* Sowerby (the common limpet)

little corrugated jewel box: *Chama congregata* Conrad

mermaid's hair: *Cladophora* sp.

mole crab (sand bug): *Hippa talpoida* Say

nomeus: *Nomeus gronovii* (Gmelin) (the fish that lives with physalia)

rigid pen shell: *Atrina rigida* (Lightfoot)

sabellid worms: probably *Hypsicomus* sp. (have tubes constructed of sand grains)

sea roach: *Ligia baudiniana* Milne-Edwards

serpulid worms: *Hydroides* sp. (the ones commonly found on pen shells; they build calcareous tubes)

terns: there are two common large terns, the Caspian and the Royal, both with conspicuous red bills. The most common smaller tern is usually Forster's. The Royal is here throughout the year, but the Caspian is present in large numbers only from October to May. Forster's are less frequent during June and July.

tessellate nerite: *Nerita tessellata* Gmel. (the most common nerite)

velella (by-the-wind sailor): *Velella mutica* Bosc (a siphonophore like physalia)

violet snail: *Janthina janthina* (Linné)

zigzag periwinkle: *Littorina ziczac* (Gmel.)

References

*Buchsbaum, Ralph. *Animals Without Backbones: An Introduction to the Invertebrates.* Rev. ed. Chicago: University of Chicago Press, 1948.

*Buchsbaum, Ralph, and Milne, Lorus J. *The Lower Animals: Living Invertebrates of the World.* Garden City, N.Y.: Doubleday, 1960. 303 pp.

Hoffmeister, J. Edward, and Multer, H. Gray. "Fossil Mangrove Reef of Key Biscayne, Fla." New York: Bulletin, Geological Society of America 76 (1965): 845-852.

Hoffmeister, J. Edward, et al. "Living and Fossil Reef Types of South Florida. A Guidebook for Field Trip No. 3." Geological Society of America Convention, November, 1964. 28 pp.

Kirtley, David W. "The Reef Builders." *Natural History* LXXVII (No. 1, 1969).

MacGinitie, G. E., and MacGinitie, Nettie. *Natural History of Marine Animals.* New York: McGraw-Hill, 1949. 473 pp.

Pilsbry, Henry A. *Land Mollusca of North America,* Vol. II, Part 1. Philadelphia: Academy of Natural Sciences, 1946. 520 pp.

Voss, Gilbert L., and Voss, Nancy A. "An Ecological Survey of Soldier Key, Biscayne Bay, Fla." *Bulletin of Marine Science of the Gulf and Caribbean* 5 (No. 3, 1955): 203-229.

*Yonge, C. M. *The Sea Shore.* London: Collins, 1949. Reprint, New York: Atheneum, 1963. 350 pp.

Black skimmers in flight. Large flocks of these striking birds may be seen throughout the year in South Florida.

3

Afternoon and Evening
at Naples

Naples, Mid-March. 4:00 P.M.

The gulls are in full cry today and I hear their harsh plaintive kee-ow long before I can see the Gulf. Wind-tossed, they streak by overhead, and I, too, feel buffeted by the wind. The salty smell of the sea envelops me and the pounding of the surf fills my ears. By touch, smell, and sound, the sea flings out its challenge, and I throw back my shoulders in answer. For a space the water and the shore are hidden until I mount a rise and it is all before me. Once again I look out on angry waves stretching far to the horizon. The sheer size of the sea, whether it be ocean or Gulf, is overwhelming, and when a storm is coming up, this seems to be the ultimate expression of power.

Above me the skies are gray and the sea is a sodden gray as well, broken by an occasional whitecap. I hear the scraping of shell fragments as a wave pulls back, drawn by a mighty force. Then a new big roller crests and breaks in white spray, sending its water racing back over the beach with spindrift blowing far up ahead. Beautiful, dramatic, and a little frightening as well!

Some way out, three dark pelicans are drifting, and there is a brooding quality about these big birds as they rest on the storm-tossed waves. The beach itself is covered with debris, and this is only a beginning. There will be far more before the wind abates, but it promises well for a sea hunt.

Let us put the Naples beach to the same test as that for Key Biscayne. What marks it out from the East Coast or from mid-Atlantic shores? First of all its surf isn't that of, say, Atlantic City. These are not the monstrous waves that sometimes hit the Jersey shore. But during an onshore blow, its breakers seem definitely more impressive than those at Key Biscayne. (Of course I've never seen either beach in a hurricane. The story would be very different then.)

There isn't the seaweed and turtle grass, nor the men-of-war of Key Biscayne, but the line of shells at the high tide mark stands out conspicuously. These are big shells: conchs, whelks, pens, moon shells, and the coiled tubes of vermicularia, the so-called worm shell that belongs to a mollusk. There are great quantities of them, and one sees immediately why the "shellers" come here, for it's an imposing array.

In the tide drift are other things: green cigar-shaped mangrove seedlings, pieces of a horseshoe crab, sponges, and the flabby-looking tubes of parchment worms. If I had come here blindfolded and had to determine where I was by the marine life I could see, I think I would pick two as the touchstone, the certain indicator. One would be the worm shell (vermicularia) and the other, the empty parchment worm tubes. The latter are U-shaped when they are functioning. Built in the sand, the two ends just break the surface. A small crab often lives in the tube along with its rightful owner, and the worm in question has colorful tentacles that can be seen waving in shallow water just above the sandy floor. But all that I've ever found have been empty tubes—hundreds, no, thousands of them—at Naples and on nearby islands.

Among the real casualties of the storm are big nine-armed starfish, brownish on top, orange-yellow below, that have been stranded on the beach. It's seldom that even one of these handsome creatures can be found. Today there are at least a dozen.

With a windbreaker for protection, I walk along the line of crashing surf. One hour is the time for my shell-collecting, and hurriedly—as in a game—I drop the shells into a basket. There is no time to pause over them; the final score is what counts. When I have done, my eyes are smarting from the wind, but I have 57 different kinds. It's a surprising number for one beach in an hour (Key Biscayne you may remember gave me just 44), but the biggest difference is in the size and beauty of the Naples shells. One that I should, perhaps, have included as a marker is the pen shell. The specimens here are nearly a foot long and often quite perfect, while the pens at Key Biscayne were rare and almost always broken. They are alike, though, in carrying a notable burden of lesser shells, bryozoans, barnacles, and seaweeds.

How pleasant it is to see again the big cockles, arks, and clams! Holding up a handful of the lovely things, I think it's little wonder that Naples is famous for its shells. Many can be found only in the Gulf. I look at Van Hyning's cockle, so often used for novelties, and at the southern quahog, the hard shell clam. And there are colorful wedge shells here. I have picked up an olive shell and a moon snail, and pieces, at least, of fig shells, queen conchs, whelks, and a murex. Only in its red and orange scallops, and its star and turban shells, did Key Biscayne rival this assemblage. Only for a true collector was the shell life of the east coast worth the time spent in gathering it in.

What else marks the Naples beach? Since there are moon snails here, many of the tellins and surf clams have round holes in their beaks. The storm has also tossed up a moon snail's egg case, that nondescript sea thing which bears the popular name of "sand collar." It seems more like a piece of discarded wave-soaked cardboard and it's hard to believe that it had an organic origin. It came about, though, as follows: first the mollusk spilled out a gooey mass of eggs, letting them curve around its shell. The collar hardened, incorporating sand grains as it did so, and then the snail slipped away from its mantle of eggs, leaving the fully formed sand collar as the result.

All sorts of astonishing things have come in today. It was worth battling the wind to see them. Just beyond the moon shell's nursery is the egg case of a lightning whelk, still wet from the waves. This has the shape of a snaky coil. Stretched out, it might be three or four feet in length. When I pick it up, I can see that it's a rope of flattened envelopes, each one full of tiny eggs that will come forth as miniature whelks—when they are lucky enough to hatch out.

I have gone quite a way up the beach and I am certain that more treasure lies ahead: a sea fan? (rare in Naples, but sometimes washed in) sponges? sand dollars? a perfect murex? The wind is too much for me, and most regretfully I turn back. As I pass the whelk's egg case, I wonder if it will dry out in the beach litter. Will the moon snail's fragile collar be trampled on and crushed into the sand? I stop to pick up one starfish—such a lovely thing—I shall try to carry it home to Pennsylvania. Here is where I came onto the beach. The pelicans are still drifting offshore, and a little way up, a group of laughing gulls are huddled together, feathers fluffed out, facing the wind. These sea birds are much smaller than the ring-billed gulls, and in their summer dress—black heads contrasting sharply with the white of their underparts—they are very striking. In winter, alas, there is only a gray cap as a souvenir of that black plumage. Laughing gulls are the year-round common gulls of the South, for the ring-bills are here in number only from October to May.

These birds, too, find the wind a challenge, but staring out to sea, they meet it. I feel like a coward turning tail, but the ocean world is rightly theirs, not mine. I shall find warmth and shelter in a human dwelling.

Naples, later in the week. 5:30 P.M.

Many a musical composition has a slow, quiet beginning. There may be the thin thread of a violin, the single note of a flute—piano—adagio. Then the opening theme is embroidered. More violins, cellos, horns enter in; the pace quickens as the sound increases. At the point of fortissimo, perhaps, there is a drum roll, and then quite often comes a decrescendo. The excitement subsides until we are left with the quiet, slow measures of the opening bars. At such a time the music dies away hauntingly with just a lingering breath of sound. In Haydn's Farewell Symphony this dwindling away was given physical embodiment when, at the first performance, the musicians folded up their music, snuffed out their candles, and left the stage one by one as their parts ended, until only the composer was left.

This is the picture that comes to me as I sit on the beach at Naples at the end of the afternoon. The morning began quietly with hushed tones, just as it so often does on Key Biscayne. Then the wind rose and the people poured out from motels and apartment houses: bathers, shellers, walkers, ball-players, children digging in the sand, northerners seeking a suntan. Shouts and laughter could be heard all up and down the beach, with splashing, protesting cries as a swimmer felt the cold water—and then, little by little, the homeward flow. In small groups or singly, they gather up beach towels, pails, canvas bags, balls, picnic baskets, and, like the musicians, quietly leave the scene. The wind drops. Fishing boats pass on the horizon bound for their anchorage. I think of Gray's all-too-familiar lines: "The plowman homeward plods his weary way,/ And leaves the world to darkness and to me."

But it isn't nightfall yet. A couple (possibly honeymooners) are walking hand-in-hand along the water's edge, a child still plays in the sand, and, in the peaceful calm of the late afternoon, I, too, mean to wander along the beach. Come with me and see the ancient world that lies exposed on the Naples shore.

To break the force of the sea and to hold the sands in check, rocks have been piled up in jetties or small groins, reaching from high tide mark into the shallow water. The rock walls are spaced irregularly, but they occur roughly every five or six hundred feet and their boulders, like those near the Royal Biscayne Hotel on Key Biscayne, are many times full of fossils. There is a difference, though. On Key Biscayne, the rocks were almost all the same. Here there is a great variety, and I can only guess that they have come from different places. I know that there is a wide gap in their age.

The day's end is a quiet time on the beach—a time that I love almost as much as I do the early morning hours. Out on the wet sand a single black-bellied plover walks ahead of me. On the rocks beyond, a white heron, the little snowy egret, steps gingerly from stone to stone, eyeing the water for food. With the lull in the wind, the ripples are lapping ever so gently on the shore.

Here at the first line of rocks are massive black boulders, so honeycombed with pits and hollows that they look like lava. For a moment, a very different scene rises before my eyes as I recall the barren desolation of a true lava field. So might the underworld look, the home of demons and the arch-fiend. But this can't be lava, for I know of no volcanic explosions here during the Cenozoic. It has to be sandstone, from which shells and other objects buried in the ancient sandy mud have been washed away. Why is it so dark? Probably from organic material. It may have come from a lagoon or the mouth of a river. Nearby are brown rocks with great ridges and these, too, tell a story. Often, waves will leave sharp ridges, dozens of them, one following another, on a muddy sandy bottom, and here is just such handiwork, thousands of years old, captured for the ages in stone.

Sometimes there are pockets of sand between the rocks; sometimes I have to clamber from one stony surface to another. Surmounting the first line, I come to the second and, with a glow of recognition, stand before a piece of brown sandstone speckled with countless white shell fragments, and occasionally bearing a cross-barred venus clam that can be easily identified. This is the typical Anastasia sand, or limestone, that is so common along the southwest coast. It comes from the Sangamon interglacial, dating somewhere between 275,000 and 100,000 B.C. Prehistoric man was living in European caves when this clam was alive. No human being had yet reached our continent, but here in Florida thousands of grass-eating mammals, predators, rodents, and birds—some of an impressive size—roamed over, or flew above, the dryer sections. Could we step back into that time, we might easily feel that we had entered the Serengeti Plains of Africa.

I wish I could place all of the boulders quite so definitely. If I were a geologist, I could give a name to each and tell just how it was formed and where, but the best I can do is to say that the great number came from the Pleistocene—that is, they had their origin sometime during the last one or two million years. Here is a rock full of brain corals (an ancient reef?), and mixed in with the corals are spiny cockles which may once have had a sunset-hued inside like the one I spotted on my early morning walk. As I mentioned earlier, cockles often grow attached to coral reefs, so the association is "right."

Next there is dark brown sandstone full of scallops and lucinas. This may have come from a beach, while a boulder covered with oysters may well have been originally a rocky point jutting out into the sea. Stories without end—all from rows of rocks!

I have left behind the second rock wall now and have come to the third. Here I find a particularly massive dark stone loaded with whelks and crown conchs (melongenas). The only time I have ever found modern crown conchs in any number was at Sanibel on the muddy shores of Tarpon Bay. It's possible (and even likely) that this rock came from a similar habitat, from a body of reasonably quiet water, protected from the worst fury of oceanic storms, and where mud had settled on the bottom. Mollusks have definite preferences about where they will live, and the assortment of rock brought in here to hold the beach tells us of those differences in very concrete form.

A final boulder—one that I came back to many times—is a light sandstone made up almost entirely of bryozoans, those tiny creatures whose lacy mats are found spread over sargassum weed and sea shells. I said earlier that this delicate architecture, which I looked at with a magnifying glass, could be part of huge colonies in some species, and even add very considerably to the mass of a coral reef. Here is a perfect illustration of the effect of numbers, for this whole boulder is mostly of bryozoans, and their fine, branching network covers the rock like a heavy spider's web. When it was formed, the branches were so fragile I could have crushed them between my fingers, and yet this incredibly delicate structure has survived for hundreds of thousands of years. Is it any wonder that I stand almost spellbound before the miracle of it all?

But this is enough of the Pleistocene. There is another short beach to cross—one last bulkhead to inspect—and as I go over this last stretch of sand, I am stepping backwards in time—not one, or possibly two, but seven or eight million years. Here again I can put a name to the rock; it is Tamiami limestone of the late Miocene or early Pliocene, and its fossil shells are far bigger than anything we have seen so far: monstrous oysters, outsize scallops, a four-inch turret shell that resembles Pacific rather than Atlantic species, jingle shells of a satiny luster that look like flint (the original shell has been replaced by chert), and barnacles that triple the size of their commonly found descendants.

There is another thing that's of interest here. Try to take away this piece of glass. You can't, because it's cemented to the rock and is already being incorporated into the geological record. The same thing has happened to recent shells that have lodged in the crannies. The warm seas that lap southern Florida are heavily laden with calcium carbonate, which, when precipitated down upon dead shells and other objects, binds them to the rock in the very same way it helped to hold the fossil shells of millions of years ago.

Some of these boulders are surrounded by water most of the time. Live oysters cling to them, often holding onto shells that may have belonged to their remote ancestors many million times removed. Modern barnacles cling to Miocene barnacles, and some parts of the rock are riddled with piddock and mussel borings that were made not too long ago. Within these cavities, a recently-inhabited worm tube may be found not too far away from a fossil tube that is now part of the limestone. Side by side, past and present meet the waves. As the tides come in, green sea moss spreads out from the fossil shells, and the black velvety pads of lichen on the gray Miocene boulders glisten as they are wet once again by the flying spray.

The sun has been going down steadily during the short period that

I have walked on the beach and is now just touching a cloud bank on the horizon. Almost within seconds it will disappear with the suddenness that is characteristic of southern sunsets. I sit down on a sun-warmed rock, forgetting, for the moment, all its fossils. No one else is about now; the last child has gone, the couple has sought shelter.

On a piling off to the left, a black cormorant is sitting, his long bill tilted up and sharply outlined against the pink glow of the horizon. Within a very short time, darkness will be at hand, but in the little space that is left, I would like to go back into the past, perhaps to summon it here before us.

With my back to the hotels, looking out to sea, this could be seven million years ago. The scene would be very much the same, with the setting sun and the waters of the Gulf. Even the cormorant would still be there, although now we would have to give him driftwood or a jutting rock for his perch, not man-made piling. But, assuming I have gone back into the distant past, one thing might catch my attention as being different. Broken salmon lights now cover a wide stretch of sea in front of me, and in their midst a huge fin appears—the fin of a seventy-foot shark, a true monster of the ocean. (Once when I was walking along the Naples shore at sunset, I found the two-inch tooth of just such an ancient fish.) In the Miocene setting, a pelican skims above the giant shark and a wavering flight of gulls can be seen against the sky. At my feet, perhaps, are some of the big shells of the rock jetties, but they have color now; their shades of chocolate, white, and tan glisten in the sunset.

And now, with one stroke, wipe out the handiwork of man. Forests rise up behind me—not right at my back, for the southern part of the peninsula was probably under water or a region of shallow lagoons and swamps—but to the north and in the central part. Here grow bald cypresses (they were at their peak in the Miocene), and in among them we can see laurels, magnolias, hollies, and figs—not exactly the same species, but related to the trees that would be found in the undergrowth today. Where the ground is dryer, pine, palmetto and coonties are common, and grass (which first became widespread in the Miocene) covers the plains. The plants seem familiar; the animals are not. In among the pines and on the edge of the cypress swamps are forest-loving horses, bands of peccaries, tapirs, and deer

Some of these last are only a little over a foot in height and very much dwarfed by one of their relatives, a big protoceratid (now extinct) that boasted long horns on its snout. Roaming over the plains are great herds of another kind of horse about the size of a pony. Here and there I can spot groups of rhinoceroses, obviously of different kinds because some are very large and hornless, some quite small. Droves of diminutive camels run across the open spaces, and packs of coyote-sized dogs can be seen, sometimes stalking the little horses, sometimes following the camels. If I am lucky, I will also come upon a huge bearlike dog, amphicyon, as big as a Kodiak bear, but so clumsy and heavy he would have no chance of running down his prey. He might well be found at a water hole, half-hidden in a thicket of willows, lying in wait for some unwary grazer.

What is missing from the picture? What has not yet been developed, or, if living in the Miocene, has not yet come to Florida? Among the larger animals did you notice there were no cats, no antelopes on the plains? Did you realize that we saw no sparrows, no warblers, no swallows? Today, weeds of many kinds—mustards, composites, quantities of small flowering herbs—would have been growing in among the grasses, but most of these familiar plants were missing.

The sun has sunk below the waters now and night is coming quickly. My brief trip back into the past must end, although later, perhaps, I can look at other scenes in the Miocene and in the later Pliocene and Pleistocene.

I have picked up a gray Miocene jingle shell that was lying at my feet and I turn it over in my hand. This mollusk lived, fed, reproduced its kind, in that same world of the rhinoceros, camel, tapir, and amphicyon. Looking at it, I am reminded vividly of Masefield's lines:
"The flying sky is dark with running horses,
And the night is full of the past."

Common and Scientific Names

apple murex: *Murex pomum* Gmel.
common fig shell: *Ficus communis* Röding
Florida coquina: *Donax variabilis* Say
Florida fighting conch: *Strombus alatus* Gmel.

horseshoe crab: *Limulus polyphemus* L.
lettered olive: *Oliva sayana* Ravenel
lightning whelk: *Busycon contrarium* Conrad
mossy ark: *Arca imbricata* Brug.
nine-armed starfish: *Luidia senegalensis* (Lam.)
parchment worm: *Chaetopterus pergamentaceus* Cuvier
parchment worm crab: *Pinnixa chaetopterana* Stimpson
queen conch: *Strombus gigas* Linné
red mangrove: *Rhizophora mangle* L.
southern quahong: *Mercenaria campechiensis* (Gmel.) (a Venus clam)
spiny pen shell: *Atrina seminuda* (Lam.)
turkey wing: *Arca zebra* Swain.
Van Hyning's cockle: *Dinocardium robustum vanhyningi* (Clench & L.
    C. Smith) (the largest cockle)
vermicularia (worm shells): Florida worm shell: *Vermicularia knorri*
    Deshayes; Fargo's worm shell: *V. fargoi* Olsson
yellow cockle: *Trachycardium muricatum* Linné

Prehistoric Fauna

camel: *Nothokemas floridanus* (Simpson)
deer: *Blastomeryx floridanus* (White)
dogs: *Cynodesmus iamonensis* (Sellards) (coyote-sized dogs); *Tomar-
    chus canavus* (Simpson) (coyote-sized dogs); *Amphicyon longi-
    ramus* White (a huge, bearlike dog)
horses: *Merychippus westoni* Simpson (about the size of a pony);
    Anchitherium clarencei Simpson (forest-loving horses)
jingle shell: *Anomia simplex* (d'Orbigny) a gray Miocene shell, the
    same species as found today)
peccary: *Desmathyus olseni* (White)
protoceratid: *Synthetoceras australis* (White) (a protoceratid from a
    family now extinct)
rhinoceroses: *Caenopus* cf. *platycephalus* (Osborn & Wortman);
    Diceratherium sp.
shark: *Carcharodon megalodon* Charlesworth
tapir: *Tapiravus* sp.

References

Andrews, Henry N., Jr. *Ancient Plants and the World They Lived In*
    Ithaca, N.Y.: Comstock, 1947. 279 pp.

*Austin, Oliver L., Jr. *Birds of the World.* New York: Golden Press, 1961. 316 pp.

*Colbert, Edwin H. *Evolution of the Vertebrates.* New York: John Wiley & Sons, 1961. 479 pp.

Darrah, William C. *Principles of Paleobotany.* Leiden, Netherlands: Chronica Botanica, 1939. 239 pp.

*Fisher, James, and Peterson, Roger Tory. *The World of Birds.* Garden City, N.Y.: Doubleday, 1964. 288 pp.

*Olsen, Stanley J. *Fossil Mammals of Florida.* Special Publication No. 6, Florida Geological Survey. Tallahassee, Fla.: Florida Geological Survey, 1959. 75 pp.

The Overseas Highway runs over a stretch of brilliantly colored tropical sea and—midway in this picture—crosses Pigeon Key.

4
Marco Island and the Keys

Marco Island, late February. 10:30 A.M.

Whenever shell collectors meet, the first question is, "Have you been to Sanibel? " and the second is, "Have you done Marco? " Coming out on Marco's well-known beach, it's impossible not to think of the thousands who have dreamed of walking on these sands, who have scraped and saved for it, and perhaps had to coax their less enthusiastic families into just one side trip off the Tamiami Trail.

Behind me in the parking lot are cars with license plates from all over the country: South Dakota, Minnesota, Wisconsin, Michigan, Iowa, Kansas, Illinois, Indiana, Ohio, Louisiana, Georgia, Maine, Rhode Island, Massachusetts, and New Jersey—quite an array of states represented by people drawn by the lure of the subtropics. Before me, New Englanders, midwesterners, southerners search the tide line with baskets, pails, and plastic bags; men and women of many ages and descriptions walk the beach with bent heads and quiet concentration.

There's no question that this is a beautiful spot with an extraordinary expanse of white sand. How much we owe to that southward flowing current that—hundreds of thousands of years ago—carried its heavy burden down along the western coast of Florida, dropping parts of it at Sarasota, Sanibel, Naples, and Marco. At one time, though, the magnificent spectacle of Marco as a developer's dream for future homeowners almost carried with it an end to all the shellers' dreams. Most of the island was bought by the Mackle Brothers for development purposes, and their first act was to fence off that part of the shore to which the shellers came. But the ban couldn't be enforced. People who had traveled thousands of miles, with Marco part of the journey's end, simply ignored the signs and crept under the fence. And before long, there was such an outcry against even trying to restrict access to the beach that it was again opened to the public.

Thinking of this, I walk slowly over the wide sandy stretch to the water's edge. The sea is gray-green today, deepening toward the horizon, with a long swell riding its surface. Its waves crest and break in white foam, their spume at times blown backwards out to sea. This bit of the Gulf of Mexico is today anything but smooth. The big swell is broken into humped wavelets covered with little points like prickles, and as the rollers break on shore, a second line of toppling waves starts to spill over before the first has completed its fall. On quieter days there is only one line of breakers, but as the offshore winds stir up the Gulf, a second and even a third one can be seen.

One of the most beautiful things I know is the curve of a wave rolling inshore over a sandy beach. Sometimes it will crest and break first in three separate places. Then, a second or so later, the intervening spaces will topple. Sometimes the line of cresting runs along the wave, breaking first in front of me, then successively later to the end of the roller, twenty or thirty feet away. I can watch the patterns endlessly—and always, after the wave has broken, the water surges over the sand, ending in a scalloped line with a band of white like the silver lining of a cloud.

A wave comes to a halt now just at my feet and then races back, pulling sand grains with it. The ebbing water is splashed and speckled with foam, and I like these patterns, too. Overhead, massed clouds darken the water at times, breaking fitfully to let the sunlight flood over the sea, the blown spray, and the white sand.

What is it that makes this beach different? How would I know it if I had come here by some magical means? The immediate giveaway would be the number of shellers and the expanse of white sand. But let us suppose that the shellers have disappeared. What else would there be? I check my watch and pick up my basket for a shell count.

Even while I was absorbing the whiteness of the sand, I noted how much color was added by the shiny irridescent light of pen shells, the yellow of jingles and scallops, the brown of broken whelks and cockles. Big shells are lying in profusion all along the low tide line, with another impressive row higher up. Many are very handsome specimens, but it's curious how bivalves dominate the scene. What gastropods I can discover are mostly fragments, with a few very battered fighting conchs among them. It's just this overwhelming abundance of showy pens, cockles, surf and venus clams, scallops, arks, jewel boxes, wedge shells, jingles, and oysters, together with the scarcity of the usual variety of snails, that is a sure indication I am at Marco and nowhere else.

Picking up shells—one of each species—I walk along the water's edge. My fellow beachcombers smile, nod, sometimes ask, "Any luck? " Occasionally one offers me a particularly beautiful scallop or jewel box. They are a friendly lot.

Marco has other distinctive qualities aside from its sand and shells. There is almost no turtle grass, for instance, and very little seaweed (at least today). A few hairlike strands of red ceramium are swirling in the water at my feet, but I can see little else. There are no men-of-war and no violet snails, and all of this distinguishes it from Key Biscayne. I find just two parchment worm tubes that are wet and flabby-looking. Had it been Naples, there would have been scores.

But other kinds of marine life are here in garish colors and in a garish kind of abundance. The great underwater plateau—that drowned half of Florida—is largely responsible, for sea life flourishes in its shallow waters. There is a lavish sweep to Marco that is evident in this huge double-valved pen almost a foot in length. Elsewhere a pen might have a few extra shells, some bryozoans, and worm tubes—one would have to look carefully to see them. This one is literally swamped with oysters. Hardly a spot on the outer shell can be seen, and I wonder how the mollusk ever survived with such a weighty mass of tenants.

Here is another pen carrying a three-inch pink ascidian (the sea squirt) on its outside, while a bright yellow spiny mass sticks out of the interior. The yellow stuff looks soft and slimy and it's another ascidian—a colonial one. Let me continue with the catalog of one shell's boarders: oysters, of course—scores of them—a slipper shell, a mass of solitary coral (astrangia), bryozoans, and tufts of red coralline (a calcareous seaweed that's stiffened with calcium). A limpet is fastened to the pink ascidian, and on the slipper shell I find a smaller slipper carrying minute shrimp-like animals. What an abundance of living things jostled together, of living thing upon living thing! Nature seems to have spewed out her creatures here with a carelessness that was truly prodigal.

And they are ugly as well as beautiful. Near the pens is a spotted sea hare, even more unpleasant looking than the ascidians. The sea hare, in spite of his name, is a mollusk without any apparent shell, much like the land slug that gardeners know only too well. This one is five inches long, a sickly olive-green with purple spots. It feeds entirely upon seaweed, mostly sea lettuce, and lives in the turtle grass, on patch reefs, or wherever else its food is to be found, but females come inshore to lay eggs and commonly die in the process. I have found quite a few of them on Key Biscayne. When stranded on the beach, however, they are shapeless blobs and one can't see the tentacles that look something like a rabbit's ears and that give them their name.

Look at this queer specimen of marine life—the "chimney" of a plumed worm. I hesitate to pick it up because it, too, looks like a disagreeable piece of refuse, dull black, with bits of shell, seaweed, and turtle grass stuck all over it. It's only another worm tube though, and this is the part that normally sticks above the sea bottom. For that reason it's thoroughly camouflaged, while the rest of the tube, buried in sand or mud, is not so dressed up. The chimney is usually two or three inches long and often breaks off. The hidden section is of parchment texture and may be three feet long. Its owner is one of the most beautiful worms along this shore with an irridescent body and plumed scarlet gills on the upper segments near the head.

Now there are more ascidians: some pink, some brown, some red, and one that's cream-colored, with brown lines converging on the mouth, giving it a striped effect. This is indeed proving a day for the oddities of the sea world. Under my feet is the purplish shell of a mole crab, a small humped affair that reminds one of a mole's body. The animal is also called a sand bug because it lives in the sand, sometimes in great colonies.

My hour has come to an end and I have gathered most of the shells to be found at this particular time on Marco. Surprisingly, there are only thirty kinds—much fewer than at Key Biscayne and only about half of what I found at Naples. Is it the intensive shelling that makes the difference? Or is it because there are hardly any snails? I think the latter, since I have been picking up broken pieces when I couldn't find whole shells, and few collectors will bother with imperfect specimens. And I have observed at other times that Marco is a beach mostly of bivalves.

I turn away somewhat regretfully. This is a strangely memorable spot, with its army of shellers from so many parts of our country, its farflung beach, and its array of oddities. I should like some time to stay long enough to learn more about these curious and absorbingly interesting creatures of the sea.

Lower Matecumbe on the Keys, early February. 11:00 A.M.

The scenery, ever since I came onto the Keys today, has been one of intense beauty. Part of this is because of the clouds. Most cumulus formations never seem to be anything but what they are—masses of wispy, insubstantial vapor. But in Florida and in the Caribbean something else, on occasion, rises up in the sky. This morning the towering white cumulus head is sharply etched against its blue background with innumerable delicate scallops. Other scalloped lines soar into the white bosom of the cloud and these are set off by shadows so that the whole seems to have body and substance. Surely one could step from hump to hump without falling. Yet this semblance of terra firma is a white mountain of cloud drifting a few hundred feet above earth. Along its flattened base there is a thin veil of purple, and lavender scarves are flung like bridges from one billowing mass to another. Cloud castles—cloud wonderlands—are spread out before me.

And the water, with its ever-changing color, is almost equally beautiful. Driving along the Overseas Highway connecting the Keys, I look down now on a patch of ethereal pale yellow. This slides into a rich deep brown. Adjoining is a stretch of heavy purple and then turquoise of a depth and brilliance that is breathtaking.

I can explain the changing look of the sea. Some of it is cloud shadows. Here, only a few inches of water cover the sandy marl; farther along, there is turtle grass; beyond that, the bottom sinks down and the sea reaches a greater depth. The richness of color is due to the fact that this is a tropical ocean—unlike that at Miami which is only subtropical and too cold for coral reefs. Everywhere there is heavy sediment that often gives the water a milky look or makes the color more opaque. But sometimes I prefer to forget the geology and the biology responsible and simply enjoy its overwhelming beauty.

Lower Matecumbe is another of the beaches known to shellers. Although it's a small one—quite unlike Marco—campers, station wagons full of camping equipment, and cars are parked in the little space beside the road, crowded against the piles of marl. Along the water's edge, working over the sandy marl, are the collectors—again drawn from all parts of our country.

As I look at the scene, my eye is caught by a big white bird a little apart from the shellers. It's the great white heron, standing with one leg drawn up under his body in a pensive pose. I am pleased to have found him, for this is Ardea, the central figure of M. B. Sanger's *The World of the Great White Heron.* The common big white heron of the mainland is the American egret, but on the tip of the peninsula below Miami, and here in the Keys, we have a larger white bird, even bigger than his cousin, the great blue heron. From his size and his yellow legs, he is easily recognized.

A short while ago the great white heron wasn't at all easy to find. I can remember hunting everywhere for one in 1962, but today I have passed at least half a dozen. It's a good comeback. Early in the century the great white heron suffered from plume hunters, and when Hurricane Donna hit the Keys in 1960, many of these beautiful birds were again destroyed. But now there is a definite upturn and it's good to see.

There are no really satisfactory beaches on the Keys proper. Most of the shoreline is either rocky or given over to mangroves, and the shelling isn't very good either. Lower Matecumbe is about the best there is and the shells here have lost their color. Those on the beach above the tide line are a chalky white; in the water they look brown.

Taking off shoes and stockings, I step gingerly over the great banks of broken coral and small shells (one has to admit their tremendous quantity) and work my way over the sun-warmed marl to the water. Bigger bivalves are clearly visible below the light ripples but, as I wade in, the slippery clay oozes around my feet, and when I lift the shells out, they are obviously discolored. It's too bad, for these might have been nice lucinas: tiger, thick, and Pennsylvania.

Returning to a shell bank, I sit down in the middle of it and begin to drop specimens into my basket. The old question recurs. What is distinctive? There are more snails here than at Marco, but they are small. I find great numbers of ceriths, cones, and the little coiled fellow that's called Atlantic modulus. Finger corals are everywhere—a reminder that coral reefs parallel this shore and are not too far away.

The water is still beautiful with its near-shore yellows deepening to olive, the purple of turtle grass lying in patches, and farther out the sunlit, glowing turquoise of the more distant sea. Just beyond are the reefs with their incredible multitude of shapes and colors. Of the three kinds of scenery—cloud castles, tropical seas, and coral reefs—the last are the most extraordinary. They are best seen with a snorkel or with scuba equipment. A glass-bottomed boat can be good, but in winter it can also be a disappointment. Before coming on to Lower Matecumbe today, I made the trip into the John Pennekamp Coral Reef State Park, just off Key Largo. This is the first section of a coral reef to be set aside as a wildlife preserve and it covers 75 square miles. Visibility was so poor on this day that only dim shapes could be seen, and almost no color. I spotted one porkfish and one little school of fingerlings. Since I could see no markings, they were quite unidentifiable. Winter trips, I believe, are quite often unsuccessful because of sediment and the frequent disturbance of the water, but in summer this can be a breathtaking experience. In the Bahamas, and in the Virgin Islands, I have seen a similar wonderland many times in all its beauty.

Hundreds of brilliantly colored fishes should be in evidence, among them angelfish, butterflyfish, sergeant majors, beau gregories, grunts, snappers, spadefish, parrotfish, wrasses, rock beauties, filefish, and porkfish. A long string of reefs stretches from Fowey Rocks Light (near Soldier Key) to the Dry Tortugas, a distance of 220 miles. The one nearest to Lower Matecumbe is Alligator Reef, where close to 400 different species of fishes have been identified. This number included only those whose home was in the coral reef. When outsiders were added—wanderers from the deep sea who came in to prey on the reef animals—the total was a surprising 517.

These creatures, with their bizarre stripes, spots, and contrasting blues, yellows, greens, and reds, swim through a forest of elkhorn coral and the five- to six-foot branches of gorgonians. Beneath them are mounds of brain and star corals, while purple and yellow sea fans wave sinuously in the currents. Color is everywhere. Most of us know the branched elkhorn coral only as a chalky-white skeleton, but when it's alive it has an orange-brown hue, while the brain coral looks red, and the star coral, green. This is due to microscopic algae that live within the coral animals, feeding on their waste matter and in turn providing oxygen for the corals. At night, when the corals feed, the great antlered, domed, and pillared shapes take on a feathery look and are even more brightly colored, but since this spectacle is known only to divers with lights, I shall limit myself to the coral world that I have seen.

Viewed through the glass bottom of a boat, the reef looks like a miniature mountain range, with jagged peaks and sharp gorges. Rifts and caverns dot the sides of the precipices, and fishes dart in and out of them, appearing and disappearing from sight. Brilliant red, yellow, black, and purple sponges cling to the coral or grow from the sandy bottom. Small armies of long-spined sea urchins may also be visible, conspicuously black against the white sand, and occasionally one can see a big queen conch lumbering over the sea floor.

The setting changes constantly. Sometimes coral is most in evidence; sometimes gorgonians take over. In the John Pennekamp park it was the gorgonians that impressed me with their inch-wide rounded stems that must have been three or four feet in length. Like snakes standing on end, they undulated back and forth, and we seemed to be floating over long ranks of them. These were purple sea whips—closely related to sea fans and sea plumes, more distantly to corals. In among the sea whips were lower gorgonians—possibly eunicea—and I could barely make out the smaller sea fans and sea plumes at their feet. Here and there I spotted finger corals such as those I am sitting on at the moment, but the great mass of finger corals are to be found in the shallow water between the reef and the shore.

Occasionally one can see even stranger creatures. Once when I was wearing a snorkel I looked, rather uncomfortably, into the staring eyes of a moray eel. Below me at another time, a big ray, possibly three feet wide, glided over the sea bottom, and I have also seen feather-duster worms waving their tentacles from the midst of a star coral.

William M. Stephens says in *Southern Seashores* that something like 3,000 different species of plants and animals may be found on one reef. It's a staggering number—quite as surprising as the 517 kinds of fishes—but students of marine biology all stress the abundance of life in this kind of environment, and its complex interrelationships: small fish cleaning larger ones, a fish that makes its home in the sea cucumber, shrimps that live within the stinging tentacles of an anemone. Almost everything that I've referred to earlier can be found on the reef: shrimps, crabs, spiny lobsters, barnacles, sea urchins, starfish, brittle stars, ascidians, sea slugs, sea hares, mollusks of many kinds, bryozoans, worms, anemones, jellyfish, and hydroids, not to mention a multitude of seaweeds. Stony corallines—the calcareous algae I found on a pen shell—are important for they encrust large parts of the reef, cementing it, and often, in fact, forming a large proportion of the stony mass. Something else that we looked at earlier in a very small and unimpressive form—the coating that a stinging coral forms over a dead sea whip—here takes on a dominant role. In leafy folds the stinging coral, or millepore, spreads over wide areas, offering a serious threat to the unwary diver.

All of this lies four or five miles away. While I pictured the reef scene, I have been busily dropping shells into my basket, occasionally getting up and finding another seat on the windrow a few feet away. Stopping to count them, I find I have a very respectable number—50 in all—but I am surprised that I had already collected most of these species at Key Biscayne. The exceptions are a couple of tellin shells, a tiny lucina and a star arene. In coming to the Keys proper, I knew that I had entered the tropics, and many mollusks are supposed to occur here and nowhere else in Florida. The greatest rarities, however, are to be found on the lower islets, those nearest Key West.

Natural history books are often full of zones and boundaries, but the northward limits are not always the same. One zone is fairly definite: there is general agreement that the Keys, while slightly north of the Tropic of Cancer, have a tropical flora and fauna because of the nearness of the Gulf Stream. One can make another line a little farther north at Soldier Key, where the true coral reefs begin. North of this, the waters are too cold for reef-building corals. On land, this line comes close to marking the northward limit of many plants. Yet there are a great number of mollusks whose habitat extends from Miami south through the Keys. Clarence J. Hylander in *Wildlife Communities* used the Tamiami Trail as a northern boundary for tropical vegetation. Tampa provides another line; some of the Caribbean fauna is not limited to the extreme south, but generally manages to survive up to this point, though not beyond it. The different life zones bring changes in the characteristic plants and animals, and following them north through the United States is an absorbing study. Some mollusks are widespread—the common species of moon snail, for instance, extends to Massachusetts, while, at the other extreme, some species may be limited to a single key.

As I check the beach I note that today, at least, little has been washed in except shells and corals. There are dried shreds of turtle grass and some manatee grass. The latter also grows off Key Biscayne. One little shell is different from all the others, and it carries my thoughts back into prehistoric ages. *Spirula spirula*—the fragile, white, ram's horn—has the shape of a flat spiral and it once belonged to a squidlike animal. Its relatives back in the days of the dinosaurs were legion. In the Cretaceous and Jurassic periods these ammonites filled the ancient seas. Now we have only the chambered nautilus of Pacific waters, the paper nautilus, squids, octopuses, and spirula with its delicate chambered shell. The ram's horn lives in the depths of the ocean, but empty shells are often cast up on beaches. This one has a necklace of baby gooseneck barnacles all around its edge.

My allotted hour has come to an end; but before I go, there is one last thing to be done. To the left, the beach curves out in a point, and beyond that, unseen by most shellers, is a stretch of sandy mud where water birds and shorebirds gather. I round the point cautiously, to avoid disturbing them, and raise my field glasses. Most are in winter dress, but ahead I can see hundreds of Forster's terns, easily identified by their conspicuous black eye patches. Black skimmers are lined up in rows, their bright red bills an extravagant note of color, and everywhere are plovers with dovelike heads, stubby bodies, and short bills. The familiar black-bellied plover I spot at once. Next in size is the semi-palmated plover with a single ring across his chest, while the smallest is the piping plover darting in and out with a sweet piping call. Turnstones are here with a heavy mottling of black, chestnut, and white, a kind of harlequin pattern that is particularly noticeable in flight. For years these were included with the plovers—for they, too, have a rather stocky build—but of late some authorities are grouping them with the sandpipers. Finally there is a conspicuous sandpiper—a little one, much smaller than the willet or sanderling. This fellow, one of the "peeps," also has the name "semi-palmated." (The word means "half-webbed" and refers to the feet.) It's confusing to have both a semi-palmated plover and a semi-palmated sandpiper, particularly since the two are common Florida shorebirds and are often found together running back and forth at the water's edge. But, as I've said, they can easily be distinguished by the chunkier shape and shorter bill of the plover.

Why do seabirds and shorebirds congregate in particular areas? The answer is often hard to find, but I do know that Lower Matecumbe is one of the best spots for them on the Keys and that they can be found here during many months of the year. The makeup of the group will vary, of course. In May, the larger Wilson's plover replaces most of the semi-palmated plovers. Piping plovers would probably be gone by then, although black-bellies and turnstones would be here. There would be fewer black skimmers, but Forster's tern could still be seen. Other terns would probably be in evidence: sandwich, least (robin-sized), and (possibly) gull-billed. Overhead, a magnificent frigate or man-o'-war bird would be soaring with a wingspread of seven and a half feet, providing another of the spectacular sights in the Florida sky. Its long scissorlike tail—often folded to a point— and the long thin wings, with their conspicuous crook, stand out against the billowing clouds. Males are all black as seen at a distance, females black with a white breast; immatures have a white head and white underparts. June and July are the low point in the year for many sea- and shorebirds, but the sandpipers and plovers begin to flock in again late in July and in August.

Four beaches were chosen for my walks, and in doing so I have omitted the most famous one—that of Sanibel on the west coast. Over 300 different kinds of mollusks have been identified on this island, and a few years ago it would certainly have produced the largest count of all during an hour's collecting.

I first set foot on Sanibel one November in the early thirties—long before the causeway was built and before thousands of shellers had combed its beaches. The main part of my collection of Florida seashells was made here and at Sarasota, for shells were abundant at both places. Indeed, in the first third of the century there was good shelling from Longboat Key all the way down to Marco. Sanibel provided me with horse conchs (the biggest of all Florida snails), great quantities of lightning whelks (one of the handsomest), tulip band shells, pens, jewel boxes, and the lovely sunray venus shells. I found angel wings (often broken, but still beautiful), calico clams, buttercup lucinas, alphabet cones, and many more. From a beach on Siesta Key, near Sarasota, I amassed not only shells, but sponges, purple sea whips, and a shrubby gorgonian with rounded branches whose identity escaped me for years. I know now that it was a plexaurid and closely related to the eunicea whose waving stems I saw in the John Pennekamp Coral Reef State Park.

When I returned to Sanibel twenty years later, there was still a profusion of shells but little that I had not already gathered, and I was very much more interested in the birds on the island. It has always seemed to me one of the very best places for birding in southern Florida. I did collect a junonia at this time, though, and for many collectors this is the prize shell of all.

By 1964 a causeway was built to Sanibel, and the shoreline at Sarasota was no longer empty and wild. Shellers were everywhere, and interesting shells seemed at a minimum; I had too clear a memory of what had been there in days gone by. The newcomer to Sanibel nonetheless finds it a fabulous beach with—generally—an abundance of the big gastropods that are missing at Marco. One of the conspicuous sights is the egg case of the horse conch, looking a little like the cone-shaped leaf of turbinaria, the sargassum seaweed. Since the cases are attached at the tip of the cone, the whole mass has a more or less flaring shape. Large egg cases belong to the horse conch; smaller ones to its near relative, the tulip shell. Since 1964, there has apparently been a real decrease in the seashells, with the cause uncertain. It probably came about through a combination of over-collecting and the burial of near-shore sands by silt, brought in with hurricane-forced waves. Possibly the causeway, with its interruption of normal currents, also played a part. In time, however, there should be some recovery.

It's always been true at Sanibel, as on all South Florida beaches, that the quality of the shelling can vary remarkably. Some years there is a marked shortage of seasonal storms and, in consequence, little is washed in. Perhaps the best time of all is after hurricanes, but few tourists are likely to be around (or want to be in the area) at that season. In May, the spring tides can also reveal many sea things: black spiny urchins, sea biscuits, sea anemones, and jellyfish that are usually hidden. Even the normal tides of March sometimes bring in to Key Biscayne great numbers of the moon jelly, aurelia—the males adorned with four beautiful pink loops (the reproductive organs or gonads) standing out noticeably in the otherwise colorless body. Some southern beaches have had little to show when I was there, though it's always possible one has come at the wrong time. Fort Lauderdale for a naturalist was particularly empty, and this is undoubtedly due to the fact that the shoreline on the east coast drops off abruptly into deep water. Duck Key also offered little, aside from corals, although these were exceptionally good.

In these four chapters on the life of the seashore, I have had no thought of covering all the beaches of southern Florida. Rather, I have hoped to bring an awareness of their quality and the fact that this is an ever-changing world—one closely interrelated, and, in its natural state, a living, busy community, despite the fact that what we see on the sands is mostly the dead or dying remnants of the marine realm. It is my hope that with a growing understanding of the living world of the sea, we shall do more to assure its continuance, for it would be an inestimable loss if over-collecting of shells and corals, together with man-made disturbances of the sea bottom, should do away with much more of this entrancing community.

Common and Scientific Names

alphabet cone: *Conus spurius* Gmelin
angel wing: *Cyrtopleura costata* (Linné)
antillean limpet: *Acmaea antillarum* Sow.
ascidians: *Styela partita* (Stimpson) (ascidian with converging lines at apertures); *Microcasmus claudicans exasperatus* Heller (large pink ascidian)
Atlantic jingle: *Anomia simplex* Orb.
Atlantic modulus: *Modulus modulus* (Linné)
Atlantic surf clam: *Spisula solidissima raveneli* Conrad
banded tulip: *Fasciolaria hunteria* (Perry)
buttercup lucina: *Anodontia alba* Link

calico scallop: *Aequipecten gibbus* (Linné)
clubbed finger coral: *Porites porites* (Pallas)
common spirula (ram's horn shell): *Spirula spirula* (Linné)
coralline algae: *Lithothamnium* sp.
dwarf cerith: *Cerithium variabile* C. B. Adams
dwarf cup coral: *Astrangia solitaria* (Lesueur)
eastern oyster: *Crassostrea virginica* (Gmelin)
elkhorn coral: *Acropora palmata* (Lamarck)
finger coral: *Porites furcata* Lamarck
Florida cerith: *Cerithium floridanum* Mörch
Florida horse conch: *Pleuroploca gigantea* (Kiener)
Florida spiny jewel box: *Arcinella cornuta* (Conrad) (formerly *Echinochama arcinella*)
fly-specked cerith: *Cerithium muscarum* Say
jasper cone: *Conus jaspideus* Gmelin
junonia: *Scaphella junonia* (Shaw)
kitten's paw: *Plicatula gibbosa* (Linné)
knobbed brain coral: *Diploria clivosa* (Ellis & Sol.)
long-spined sea urchin: *Diadema antillarum* Philippi
manatee grass: *Syringodium filiforme* Kützing
mera tellin: *Tellina mera* Say
mole shrimp (sand bug): *Hippa talpoidea* Say
moon jelly: *Aurelia aurita* Lamarck
Morton's egg cockle: *Laevicardium mortoni* (Conrad)
plexaurid: *Pseudoplexaura wagenaari* (Stiasny) (the common plexaurid of the southwest coast)
plumed worm: *Diopatra cupraea* Claparède (builds "chimneys")
purple sea whip: *Pterogorgia anceps* (Pallas)
red coralline algae: *Jania* sp. (possibly *Jania rubens* L.)
saw-toothed pen shell: *Atrina serrata* (Sow.)
sea fan: *Gorgonia ventalina* L. (the sea fan found at Key Largo)
sea hare: *Aplysia willcoxi* (Heilprin)
sea plumes: *Pseudopterogorgia americana* Gmelin: *P. acerosa* (Pallas)
sea whip: *Lophogorgia hebes* (Verrill) (the sea whip of the southwest coast)
speckled tellin: *Tellina listeri* Röding
spinose lucina: *Phacoides muricatus* Spengler
spotted slipper shell: *Crepidula maculosa* Conrad
star arene: *Arene cruentata* (Mühl.) (it looks like a small star shell)
stocky cerith: *Cerithium litteratum* (Born)
sunray venus: *Macrocallista nimbosa* (Lightfoot)

Tampa tellin: *Tellina tampaensis* Conrad
thick lucina: *Phacoides pectinata* (Gmelin)
tiger lucina: *Codakia orbicularis* (Linné)
true tulip: *Fasciolaria tulipa* (Linné)
white-bearded ark: *Barbatia candida* (Helbling)

References

Brookfield, Charles N. "Key Largo Coral Reef: America's First Undersea Park." *National Geographic* 121 (No. 1, 1962).

Galtsoff, P. S., coordinator. *The Gulf of Mexico, Its Origin, Waters and Marine Life.* Washington, D.C.: U.S. Dept. of the Interior, Fish and Wildlife Service, Fishery Bulletin 89, 1954. 604 pp. O.P.

Starck, Walter A. "Marvels of a Coral Realm." *National Geographic* 130 (No. 5, 1966).

Van Name, Willard G. *The Ascidians of Porto Rico and the Virgin Islands. Scientific Survey of Porto Rico and the Virgin Islands,* Vol. X, Part 4. New York: The New York Academy of Sciences, 1930. 145 pp.

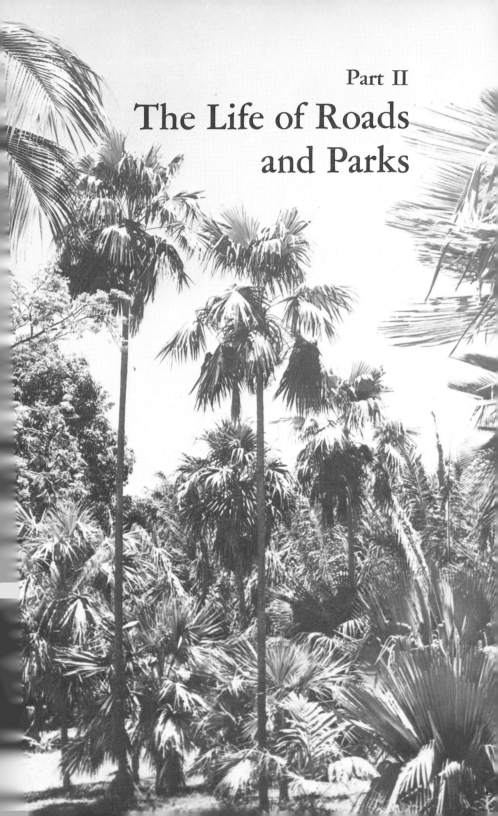

Part II
The Life of Roads
and Parks

The silk spider nephila

Previous page:
Part of the impressive palm section at the Fairchild Tropical Garden in Miami.

5

The Sea Lane

Patches of wild tangle—"unimproved lots"—can be found even in the cities of Florida. They abound wherever the land is less heavily populated, and they provide areas of wildlife over which the naturalist rejoices. Some are open stretches of weeds, palms, and palmettos; or, nearer the sea, of palms and sea grapes; some are heavy tangles of tropical growth—but all are deserving of a second look.

One of my favorite places is a small overgrown lot on Key Biscayne that is bordered on one side by a paved walk, which I call my sea lane, running down to the ocean. Rarely do I go down the sea lane at anything faster than a snail's crawl, and I am as likely to backtrack as to go forward.

Walk with me along it on a Sunday morning early in January. The air is warm and peculiarly soft, but the heat of the sun has not yet silenced the birds. Two anis, exotic creatures with parrotlike beaks, fly into the tangle ahead of us, and a red-bellied woodpecker gives his scolding chuck from a perch high on a coconut palm. I can see his red head bobbing just under the coconuts. A pity that he was ever named "red-belly," for the real red is on top and at the back of his head. The red-headed woodpecker, with which he is sometimes confused, has a completely red head. Red-bellies are the most common of the southern Florida woodpeckers.

The ani really belongs to the West Indies and South America but has ventured into the southernmost part of the state and seems to be increasing in numbers. In Grand Bahama, where I first encountered this black, gracklelike bird, a number of them laid claim to a certain thicket, and anyone approaching it was bombarded with noisy calls which continued for some time after the intruder had gone his way. One or two never break into such raucous clatter. It takes a group—at least in my experience—to produce that rather pleasant bombardment. The two or three I have found together in Florida have never been quite so vocal.

For years, birders used to make special trips to Clewiston as a sure place for an ani. I have seen them there, but I have also found them in the area south of Miami near Homestead, on Virginia Key, and now on Key Biscayne.

The overgrown lot looks as if it would provide shelter for many a bird, for it's a wonderful tangle, dominated, as are most waste lots, by the ever-present coconut palms. Below these are pithecellobium trees, sea grapes, date palms, palmettos, and castor beans, many of them almost engulfed by the twining morning glory. As I've said, it should be wonderful for land birds, but very few are here in January, just as there seem to be surprisingly few on the key generally. The villain is probably the DDT used for mosquitoes. DDT has certainly routed the land birds that once were so plentiful on Marco Island. It must have taken its toll in many other places. Occasionally I pick up the plaintive chip of a palm warbler. A yellowthroat called once, and I have heard the squeaky note of a gnatcatcher. Sometimes mourning doves fly in and out, but these—with the woodpecker and the ani—are about all.

There are other beauties, however. The lane's entrance is bordered by a riot of flowers: the deep violet and rose of a southern morning glory, the pearly white of periwinkles, the splashy yellow and brown of beach sunflower. This is supposed to be the off-season—officially spring hasn't arrived—but to a northerner, fresh from a snowy landscape, it presents a welcome sight. Morning glory everyone knows; the beach sunflower is very much like a black-eyed Susan; and the periwinkle—the periwinkle fooled me at first because it looks like phlox with an evergreen leaf. Some even have the pink heart of a phlox, and some are a magenta pink with a deeper center. Like the ani, the periwinkle is a foreigner, hailing from far-distant Madagascar.

I have often wondered how it got here—through early seamen,

adventurous botanists, or how? Whatever the means, it has become widespread throughout the tropics and subtropics. I have encountered it in Brazil and in many of the West Indies. For the most part it is a cultivated plant, but so well does it like its new habitat in Florida that it has gone wild in many places.

This population explosion of intruding plants and animals is always a fascinating subject. One thinks of how the descendants of a similarly small island (Britain) have come to dominate so much of the world. Politically, Madagascar may be of little account, but its periwinkle plays an important role in the subtropical garden.

In among these showy blossoms of my wild flower patch are less conspicuous ones. Here is a small dainty cousin of the familiar poinsettia. It is native to Florida and quite unmistakable. Here also is Spanish needles, a scrubby-looking little composite, daisy-like, but with a small ragged flower that soon turns to a bur. Nearby is a melanthera, another insignificant little off-white flower—looking to me like a small country relative of our garden scabiosa. Oddly enough, the bees and butterflies, of which there are a goodly number, are all on the melantheras and Spanish needles, not on the much handsomer morning glories, beach sunflowers, and periwinkles. What a moral lesson a Victorian writer might have drawn from this fact!

I must admit that at this point my erratic steps take me up and down the pavement, but progress is nil, for I can hardly bear to leave the butterflies. Most common are the dozens of little Miami blues (so very similar to our spring azures), but my attention is caught by the white peacock, a butterfly of the subtropics, unknown to northern eyes. What a lovely pattern—creamy pearl base with a yellow edging, and a smattering of black spots. More dramatic, perhaps, is the zebra—black, crossed by yellow bars—another southerner whom I never fail to admire. And finally in this quartet of subtropical beauties, the long-tailed skipper, with green body and dusky wings trailing off into absurdly long tails. The fore wings have a few pale yellow markings on the outer portion. All are sipping honey from the melantheras. They are joined by sulphur butterflies bearing a general resemblance to our own common sulphurs, and could easily be dismissed as such, but these are larger and without any black markings. They are a pure yellow-orange, and are undoubtedly cloudless sulphurs, or orange sulphurs. One viceroy, a smaller edition of the monarch, sails briefly into view. The butterfly concentration is mostly at two spots—here, and farther along where there is another explosion of wild flowers.

From the flowers, my gaze turns upward. Not one familiar northern bush or tree is in sight. This is a truly southern landscape and it's pleasant to have been transplanted into such a very different world. Far behind me in a snow-covered land are the leafless sycamores, maples, oaks, and willows of Pennsylvania. No spruce, hemlock, or yew can be seen. Instead there are sea grapes—a long line of small trees edging one side of the path. With its rose-veined, big, round, leathery leaves, the sea grape is one of the commonest shrubs, or small trees, of the seacoast. I welcome it, together with the coconut palm, as perhaps the two most characteristic plants of the shore. The sea grape is a native and the coconut palm has been here for so long it's often referred to as such, even though it almost certainly originated elsewhere. Both are jostled for space by a definite foreigner, the castor bean or castor oil plant, a most striking shrub, with red stems and a huge conspicuously cut leaf having seven or nine fingers. The oil of this plant—responsible for the castor oil of medicine closets—comes from the seed, and that seed is contained in big burlike containers a cluster of which is grouped now at the top of many of the stalks. Often the plants grow in clumps or thickets, like bamboo.

The castor bean is from India and Africa where it is grown both for its commercial value and as a decorative plant. It is said to have been one of the earliest plants in cultivation. (What a sad commentary on man's digestive problems!) So well does it like South Florida's soil and climate that it, too, has become naturalized and symbolizes very well the lush growth of the tropics; the twelve-foot shrub before me may well have achieved this height and size in just one year. As an annual, it frequently dies in its second year, even though it doesn't have the frost to contend with which cuts down our northern annuals. Many of the castor beans, particularly in the area between South Miami and Homestead, were planted during World War I to provide a lubricating oil for airplanes rather than people.

Absence of frost accounts for the jungle-like look of the whole area to the left of the walk. Vines have grown rampantly over the palms, pithecellobiums, and sea grapes. Some of it is morning glory, some of it balsam apple, looking quite out of place so far above the ground. But the whole effect is of an impenetrable tangle.

As my eye roams over the middle ground, the area of the shrubs and the heaviest growth of vines, I catch sight of a dwarf palmetto. Palmettos appear here only sparingly, which is curious because they are so common elsewhere; the newcomer to Florida should pin down at the start this distinctive palmate or fan-shaped leaf. The common shrubby palmetto found so abundantly in the pinelands is the saw palmetto. It appears to be stemless because the stem creeps along the ground and is hidden by the leaves. What is growing here is the dwarf palmetto, which is indeed stemless, but has up to four-foot leaf stalks. The most magnificant common palmetto is the sabal, often called "cabbage palm." Its trunk is most obvious and some trees reach a height of eighty feet. The trunk of this palm often has a basketlike weave because of old leaf bases.

Julia F. Morton of the University of Miami gives an interesting account of it in *Some Useful and Ornamental Plants of the Caribbean Gardens*: "The cabbage palmetto was a staff of life to the Indians and early white settlers. The fruits, small and black, were eaten fresh or made into syrup and were an important feed for domestic animals. The terminal bud was, and still is, cut out and eaten as 'palm cabbage,' although its removal kills the tree. The trunks of the palms were commonly employed for stockades, fences, barns, troughs and crude aqueducts, and also as a source of tannin. Found resistant to marine borers, they were also used for wharf pilings. The leaves, formerly used for thatching, are now made into baskets, hats, mats and brushes and the young, unopened leaves are used as religious symbols on Palm Sunday." I might add that the leaves are still used for thatching Indian chickees.

Turning again to the area a few feet from the ground, I note with interest a perfect big orb web. There are any number of them—now that I stop to look—strung between the plants. Up north, such perfect orbs would very likely be the work of the handsome big black and orange garden spider, miranda. I am curious as to whether miranda is found down here and check the center point of the web because that is where its owner should be found. Sure enough, a spider is poised there, waiting for an insect to blunder into its trap, but it is much smaller and not nearly as conspicuous as our common northern orb-spinner. This spider has to be looked at closely, but the inspection is most rewarding, for what I see is a very curious creature, pale yellow above, with a few small but decorative black markings, and three bright red spikes on either side. The underside of its abdomen is black with a center red spike pressed against the web. I am looking for the first time on a gasterocantha. Almost all the webs, today, and there are at least a dozen, have been made by this same spider.

More flowers are appearing now, though not in the profusion of the entrance path. As a matter of fact, morning glory, Spanish needles, and melanthera have been in evidence, and I have been aware of small cuckoo bees and syrphid flies on them, as well as the Miami blues.

One more palm should be noted—a palm that tells us something of the past history of this lot, for it is definitely an ornamental, very specially planted, and no wildling at all. This is the Senegal date palm, with the feathery frond that we usually associate with palms, but with a very short trunk. In a well-established clump the trunk is often invisible, and we see only the leaf stalks with their very distinctive big spines. The presence of such an exotic is a reminder that some years ago this lot was part of the Key Biscayne Coconut Plantation, the biggest of the early plantations in this country. This date palm came from Africa, and the man responsible was Dr. William J. Matheson, who bought a large tract on the island back in 1909. As a boy, he had spent a couple of years in Brazil and developed a great love for tropical vegetation. Key Biscayne attracted him as a place in which many of these plants could be grown, and he set himself to build what he thought of as a "tropical paradise."

Dr. Matheson was also responsible for the coconut plantation here and is said to have brought in some 4,000 coconut palms from Malaya. This, in part, accounts for the great number on this key. Like the Senegal date, the coconut palm has a feathery frond. Its original home has never been determined, but it seems likely that it came from lands around the Indian Ocean. It was widely distributed even in prehistoric times, which explains the difficulty in pinpointing its place of origin. There is no question, however, that it is thoroughly naturalized in South Florida, the seeds still being carried by the waves and sprouting on many a sandy shore where they come to rest. I've noted often the number of green coconuts washed up in the tide wrack, and thought them out of place on the beach. But the fact is that the ocean constitutes one of their means of distribution. In its seedling state, this palm is most deceptive, for the ribbed leaf is whole and swordlike, giving little evidence of the feathery frond that will start to appear in about a year's time.

It's curious, since this tree is not indigenous to Florida, that it was apparently established on the island as early as the sixteenth century, the Spanish priest, Father Francisco Villareal, having referred to it in a letter dated January 1568—some 400 years ago. This may mean that it had already been brought here by men or that a wave-tossed seed was responsible for its presence.

There is one last tree to be mentioned—another foreigner, *Pithecellobium dulce,* or Manila tamarind, from the Philippines, Mexico, and Central America, related to two Florida plants—the black bead and cat's claw, both of which, however, are much smaller. Pithecellobium abounds in this small lot and, as a matter of fact, is all over Key Biscayne, introduced here also by Dr. Matheson, no doubt. With its small oval leaf, it seems at first sight very similar to many of the southern trees. It belongs, however, to the pea family and has one most characteristic feature. The leaves grow in groups of four, with two distinct opposite pairs; or sometimes there is a single pair and one extra leaf. The rather inconspicuous white flowers seem to be mostly stamens growing in little clusters on six-inch terminal twigs at the end of the branches. The whole tree, with its highly conservative leaves and flowers, provides an effective contrast to the more flamboyant foliage of palms, sea grapes, and castor beans.

I have noted the characteristic interrelationship of most sea life. This close relationship occurs on land, too, although it's less noticeable here. It's of interest that the little Miami blue butterfly is quite normally associated with Spanish needles and that its caterpillar feeds on pithecellobium.

Now, even though our progress has been slow, we are finally coming to the beach. With sandier soil, the plants are changing. Here is yellow burnut, with a flower like that of a primrose, but with cassialike leaves. Actually it's not a legume, but a member of the caltrop family to which lignum vitae belongs. The reddish stem creeps over wide areas of sand, and its round fruit bears several sharp spines—hence the name. This is an annual from tropical America that has become naturalized as far up as Georgia. Balsam apple is now carpeting much of the ground with an occasional pale yellow, rather unimpressive flower. Later on these will be replaced by the familiar yellow-and-orange pods. Even without flowers or pods, balsam apple is easily recognized by its yellow-green, five-parted leaves.

Still farther along, railroad vine sprawls over the sand, bearing an occasional morning glorylike flower, for this is its family. Its botanical name is *Ipomaea pes-caprae*—literally, "goat's foot." The morning glory climbing through the trees is *Ipomaea cathartica* and has a heart-shaped leaf, while the leaf of the railroad vine is round and leathery. Beside it is one of my favorite plants, the seaside or beach croton, with gray-green velvety leaves and a very pungent spicy smell, a little like skunk cabbage. You can tell it for sure by looking at its leaves with a magnifying glass. The hairs form a pattern of little stars all over the leaf that is most delightful, and a certain identifying mark. As it grows here, it's almost a small shrub—and it marks the end of the walk.

On the beach itself, I look down on sandspurs, so miserable to step on with bare feet, and more of the railroad vine, with its long tendrils stretching out to conquer the sands. Now there is a familiar crackle, the sound of grasshopper wings brushing together as the insect makes a sudden takeoff. I have come too close to a gay-winged locust, a creature of this particular area, with yellow wings showing in flight.

With the grasshopper and the beach, this particular walk has ended. I have tried to play fair by describing only what I have actually seen on one particular day. Too often, all that might have been seen is gathered together into one tale, and the naturalist (new or old) winds up feeling frustrated because only a fraction of what is described can actually be found. The scene varies, of course. Time of day, weather, all play a part. Insects are less abundant at 9:00 A.M. or at 4:00 P.M. than at ten in the morning, and a cold wave will definitely send them into hiding. A windy day will also discourage the birds.

I should be surprised if I came out with the same notes from any two strolls along my sea lane, but this variety is part of its charm. As a matter of fact, I was to find later that January had been the high point during the winter for insects, and that birds would be most plentiful toward the end of March, when a big wave of migrants came in. On the other hand, to my surprise I found no such increase in the number of flowering plants during the spring as I'd expected to see.

In January, the greatest difference from day to day was in the insect and spider life. Having decided that the only orb spinner was she of the six red spikes, I was very shortly proved wrong by the discovery of a two-inch nephila with conspicuous outsized legs banded in red, yellow, and black, and a black abdomen crossed by a yellow band at the top. With the exception of some of the fish of the coral reefs, there are few living animals that have such striking markings as spiders. I was pleased to have found nephila, although there was only one, because so much has been written about her. She comes into the pages of Charles Torrey Simpson's *Florida Wild Life* as the common spider of his own hammock, and she is described by W. E. Safford in *The Natural History of Paradise Key* (now Royal Palm Hammock in the Everglades National Park). There is, in fact, much to be said of her, beginning with the facts that she is our only silk spider and the quality of her silk is better than that of the silk worm. Her tropical relatives snare small birds in their webs because those webs are so remarkably large and strong, and, finally, nephila (though now known only in the South) has been found as a fossil in Colorado as far back as the Oligocene.

It seems likely that most of the common butterflies of this area can be spotted along the sea lane at one time or another. Monarchs and red admirals (both northern) come here. So does the lovely gulf fritillary, largely red above, with very light markings underneath—the usual fritillary contrast of brown or red above and whitish spots below. There are any number of skippers which I won't attempt to describe. The beautiful utetheisa, a day-flying moth with deep salmon-pink hind wings and pale yellow fore wings, lightly spotted with black, is quite common, and I have also seen the striking blue-black melanchroia moth, with white-tipped fore wings and a red, somewhat pointed head.

Most remarkable of all, though, is *Composia fidelissima*, a big moth with black fore wings heavily spotted with white, and a bright bar of red on the front margin. The hind wings are blue, the brilliant blue of the morpho butterfly, and it was a long time before I could be convinced that I had a moth and not an exotic West Indian butterfly that had been blown northward during a winter storm.

This lovely creature is by rights tropical. It enters our country only in the extreme southern part of Florida and is a good example of the many truly tropical insects, birds, and other animals that have come from the West Indies, perhaps carried by hurricane waves and winds, as so many seeds have been, and thus established here.

Black and yellow syrphid flies can generally be seen, and so can a cuckoo bee, so-called because the female lays her eggs in the nests of other bees. This small insect has a shining green thorax (its fore part), and an abdomen banded in black and yellow. Once I noted among all the honey-seekers a rather fearsome assassin bug, a predator, motionless on a leaf, waiting for an unwary insect to come in for the kill.

As January marches on, an occasional orange balsam apple appears on the vines. Such improbable looking fruits they are! They look more like discarded plastic toys or other man-made articles. I discover also a clump of heliotrope, one of the common, though lowly, members of that family, with long drooping spikes of tiny white flowers, as inconspicuous as the balsam apple is showy. Sea rocket (a white mustard) comes into bloom and I finally find a name for the abundant yellow five-parted flower that reminds me of St. Johns-wort, but obviously isn't. It turns out to be poor man's patches, with barbed stinging hairs that also make it a very formidable sticktight.

February is unusually cold, and there is a surprising decrease in the number of butterflies. At times I can find only a single zebra butterfly floating in the background, in and out among the leaves of sea grape. White peacock butterflies disappear completely, and only the little Miami blues sip the honey of Spanish needles. Is it the ending of one brood and the lag before another? Spiders are fewer, too, and there is less bloom on many of the plants.

But, as if in compensation, mourning doves begin to coo, that "voice of the turtle" to which the Bible refers, meaning, we now think, "turtle doves." In the South, they tell us that spring and nest building have begun, even though it's only February. Cardinals are singing, too, and by the middle of the month, a dozen or so parula warblers can be found on the sea lane, flitting in and out of the pithecellobiums. What is true of the butterflies is also true of the birds. One can dash through the sea lane and see hardly anything of interest. But stop and watch for awhile, and a quite astounding number of things may appear.

The first of March has come, and I spend a half hour on my pathway. The parulas are still here and they have been joined by a catbird and a chat—migrants, in all likelihood. Yellowthroats and gnatcatchers are around. The red-belly is scolding high up on a palm, and I hear cardinals, mourning doves, and mockingbirds. Only the ani is missing, the few birds here having taken off when their nesting site in a nearby lot was laid low by a bulldozer. New building cannot be stayed for anis, but I am sorry their lot, with its thicket of bamboo, had to be the one taken.

Late in March, the lane is overwhelmed by a wave of migrating warblers. Never in my life have I seen so many parulas—easily a hundred—in such a small space. With them are twenty-five or thirty prairie warblers, those handsome black and yellow birds—not uncommon in Florida, but in my northern home so rare that we are pleased to see one bird during the entire spring migration. I stand thoroughly bemused by such wealth. This is the high point of all my walks along the sea lane.

Much of what can be found on the sea lane appears in other "vacant" lots, although not in such abundance. One that I stop to look at is dominated, as always on this key, by coconut palms. Beneath them are the familiar sea grapes and saw palmettos, a pithecellobium tree, and some young Australian pines, or *Casuarina equisetifolia*. This lovely feathery evergreen, that looks so much like a long-needled pine, isn't one at all—another instance of Nature's deceptive trickery. Its botanical name is most descriptive. "Casuarina" comes from cassowary—an allusion to the flowing plumes of that bird, while "equisetifolia" is translated "horsetaillike leaves." These trees are common throughout southern Florida, appearing often as a line of windbreakers. All have been introduced, and most of the original casuarinas on Key Biscayne were planted by Dr. Matheson. Another foreigner I see, which he may also have introduced, is the tropical almond from the East Indies. While these are all seedlings only a couple of feet high, the mature tree is handsomely tall, with big, leathery, oval leaves, which turn reddish in winter and drop.

Heavy grasses and weedy Spanish needles are everywhere. For the most part one's impression is of weeds, not of a wild flower garden as along the sea lane, but there is one exception. Over all the homely little flowers of this lot sprawls moon vine. It climbs over the sea grapes and mounts to the very top of the casuarinas. By day, the big white flowers hang limp, their petals curled inward, but at night, the huge morning glorylike white blossoms dominate the area, gleaming ghostily in the moonlight. I love to walk by them then and listen to all the night sounds: the trill of tree crickets, the buzzy sound of cone-headed grasshoppers, the broken call of a meadow grasshopper, the long-drawn-out sound of some of the ground crickets. The chorus isn't what I heard last August at home. This is a much thinner rendition of the song and I wouldn't dare put specific names to the various performers, but I can spot the different groups, and it's extremely pleasant to hear them again after the silence of the winter months in Pennsylvania. When the insect chorus rises once again, one has indeed come back to summer.

Common and Scientific Names

ambush bug: *Phymata guerini* Leth. & Sev.
Australian pine: *Casuarina equisetifolia* Forst.
beach sunflower: *Helianthus debilis* Nutt.
black bead: *Pithecellobium guadalupense* Chapm.
burnut (puncture weed): *Tribulus cistoides* L.
cabbage palm: *Sabal palmetto* (Walt.) Lodd.
castor bean: *Ricinus communis* L.
cat's claw: *Pithecellobium unguis-cati* (L.) Benth.
coconut palm: *Cocos nucifera* L.
composia: *Composia fidelissima* Herrich-Schaefer
cuckoo bee: *Agapostemon radiatus* (Say) (one of several cuckoo bees)
dwarf palmetto: *Sabal minor* (Jacq.) Pers.
garden spider: *Miranda aurantia* Lucas
gasterocantha: *Gasterocantha elipsoides* (Walck.)
heliotrope: *Heliotropium parviflorum* L.
Madagascar periwinkle: *Lochnera rosea* (L.) Reichenb. (formerly *Vinca rosea* L.)
Malabar almond: *Terminalia catappa* L.
melanchroia: *Melanchroia cephise* Cramer
melanthera: *Melanthera hastata* Michx.
moon flower: *Calonyction aculeatum* (L.) House
morning glory: *Ipomea cathartica* Poir.

pithecellobium: *Pithecellobium dulce* Benth. (pithecolobium was the old spelling, but the other form is now preferred)
poor man's patches: *Mentzelia floridana* Nutt.
railroad vine (goat's foot): *Ipomoea pes-caprae* (L.) Sweet
saw palmetto: *Serenoa repens* (Bartr.) Small
sea grape: *Coccoloba uvifera* (L.) Jacq.
sea rocket: *Cakile lanceolata* (Willd.) O. E. Schultz
seaside croton: *Croton punctatus* Jacq.
Senegal date palm: *Phoenix reclinata* Jacq.
silk spider: *Nephila clavipes* L.
southern sandbur (cockspur): *Cenchrus tribuloides* L.
Spanish needles: *Bidens pilosa* L.
wild balsam apple: *Momardica charantia* L. (this is not the wild balsam apple of the North, which is *Echinocystes lobata* Michx., although both belong to the cucumber family; *Momardica charantia* is a tropical vine, introduced as an ornamental, which has become naturalized in South Florida)
wild poinsettia: *Poinsettia pinetorum* Small

References

Baker, Mary Francis. *Florida Wild Flowers.* New York: Macmillan, 1938. 233 pp. O.P.
Comstock, John Henry (revised by W. J. Gertsch). *The Spider Book.* Ithaca, N.Y.: Comstock Press, 1940. 729 pp.
*Greene, W. F., and Blomquist, H. L. *Flowers of the South.* Durham: University of North Carolina Press, 1953.
Holland, W. J. *Moths* (The Nature Library). New York, Dover, 1968. 479 pp.
*Klots, Alexander B. *A Field Guide to the Butterflies.* Boston: Houghton Mifflin, 1951. 349 pp.
Lakela, Olga, and Craighead, Frank C. *Annotated Checklist of the Vascular Plants of Collier, Dade, and Monroe Counties, Florida.* Coral Gables, Fla.: Fairchild Tropical Garden and University of Miami Press, 1965. 95 pp. O.P.
*Lutz, Frank E. *The Field Book of Insects.* Rev. ed. New York: G. P. Putnam's Sons, 1948. 510 pp.
*McGeachy, Beth. *Handbook of Florida Palms.* St. Petersburg, Fla.: Great Outdoors, 1960. 62 pp.

Morton, Julia F. *Some Useful and Ornamental Plants of the Caribbean Gardens*. Naples, Fla.: Caribbean Gardens, 1955. 55 pp.

*Peterson, Roger Tory. *A Field Guide to the Birds*. Rev. ed., Boston: Houghton Mifflin, 1947. 290 pp.

*Sargent, Charles Sprague. *Manual of the Trees of North America*. New York: Dover, 1965. 2 vols. 934 pp.

Small, John Kunkel. *Manual of the Southeastern Flora*. Chapel Hill: University of North Carolina Press, 1933. O:P.

*Zim, Herbert S. *The American Southeast*. A Golden Regional Guide. New York: Golden Press, 1959. 160 pp.

6
Lawns Behind the Sea

The beach is still in its essence wild. Man may strew it with tar and beer cans. He may tear away the railroad vines and rake the offending seaweed, but the ocean is still dominant. The same is true of the sea lane. Even though some of its plants came originally from distant lands, they have become thoroughly acclimated. They blend into the native vegetation and are accepted by our insects and birds. Essentially it is a wild area.

But a hundred feet from the sea lane, the story is very different. Exotic trees and shrubs are massed against the buildings. Ground plants from other countries fill the carefully manicured beds with few North American plants allowed in this artificial world of hotels, apartment houses, and dwellings. When I walk the streets of Key Biscayne, I am surrounded by foreigners. Here is oleander from the Mediterranean, bougainvillea from Brazil, bottlebrush from Australia, and figs from tropical Africa. At my feet I look down on crown of thorns from Madagascar. It's clustered around a century plant from Mexico, while in the background there is Chinese hibiscus.

Insects are hard to find, for our native bugs depend largely on native plants. Insecticides also discourage plant visitors, and with the exception of scale insects, and aphids, I have found few on the lawns and patios. Birds are correspondingly scarce. Only five might be called common: the red-bellied woodpecker—at home wherever there are coconut palms; the brownish little palm warbler, here from mid-September to June, always wagging his tail, hopping over sidewalks, grass, low shrubs (he finds insects, obviously, where I think they are nonexistent); mourning doves and their smaller cousins, the pretty little ground doves; and finally the ubiquitous gray mockingbird, with white patches in his wings, white streaks on the side of his tail.

Whenever northerners first encounter the mockingbird, they are charmed. What a song! For beauty, variety, the notes of no other North American bird seem comparable. But wait until he pours out all that melody, hour after incredible hour, throughout the night, just under your window! Wait until he drives all other birds (as some "mockers" do) from your bird-feeding stands. Wait until he invades the nests of other birds. I have a kindly feeling for the mockingbird only when he stays with me in the man-made world of foreign plantings.

A few of our other native birds come in occasionally—mostly cardinals and boat-tailed grackles. Older residents and visitors who have been coming here for years always ask, "Where have our birds gone? Why are there so few around? We used to have many more! " And the simple reason is: spraying, and disappearing vacant lots. The solution isn't easy. People want more housing in the South; without spraying, mosquitoes are unbearable (I'm told) in the summer. All we can do is realize we can't have full development of the land, along with complete protection from all insects—and have birds.

There is one very conspicuous new bird in this island landscape—an exotic, blending in with the exotic vegetation. The cattle egret came originally from Africa and India where this little white heron followed close upon the heels of water buffaloes and Brahman cattle, perching at times on their backs to feed upon flies and other parasites. Somehow the African cattle egret flew from the western bulge on the African continent across to Brazil. From thence it worked its way northward into the Caribbean and finally into Florida and up along the eastern coast of the United States as far as Massachusetts. The first to be identified in our country appeared in 1952. When I saw a little band of them at Cape May in 1953, they were still a rarity. But today cattle egrets are widespread. A freshly cutover lot here on the island may bring in a good three dozen of the birds to feast on the insects that have been disturbed. They pose like statuary on lawns and golf courses, as artifical looking as the landscape which surrounds them.

One of my favorite books on Florida wildlife is Olive Bown Goin's

World Outside my Door, an account of reptiles and amphibians found in one backyard. Mrs. Goin's yard was in northern, not southern, Florida, but I was convinced that if the grounds about one house in Florida could shelter so many, there would certainly be toads, frogs, lizards, and snakes in South Florida as well. And again I was disappointed. The principal toad on the lawns and patios of Key Biscayne appeared to be an intruder from tropical America, one of the largest and ugliest of its kind I've ever seen. The marine toad is not exactly a pleasant addition to our fauna, for cats and dogs attacking him, have, on occasion, been poisoned as the result of a secretion from glands at the neck. Once or twice I have seen our native southern toad here; I found one small, pink, rat snake curled up in a tree; and the Carolina anole (the American "chameleon") is often common, although in the Fairchild Tropical Garden the Bahama anole is now more in evidence than our native lizard.

Elsewhere in the Miami area, catfish from Thailand have been seen walking across lawns during rainy spells. Red-whiskered bulbuls (an Old World bird) are abundant in parts of South Miami; the spotted-breasted oriole (from Central America) now breeds from Florida City to Palm Beach County, and the scarlet ibis has been brought in from Trinidad. In this influx of foreign plants and animals, some of the natural world of South Florida has been displaced.

Perhaps what symbolizes best this curiously artificial scene is the overnight creation of what appears to be an established lawn planting. Time and again I've watched bulldozers sweep into an "unimproved lot." Every last piece of vegetation falls before them, from the coconut palms, sea grapes, palmettos, pithecellobiums, tropical almonds, and their covering sheets of moon vine, to the lowly Spanish needles. Not a green blade is left.

On this barren waste, the new building arises. One day the area fronting it is a scene of desolation. Broken boards, pails, chunks of cement, cardboard wrappings, beer cans, rubble, stretch from one end of the lot to the other. Then an order is given—the wreckage left from the job of erecting a modern apartment house is somehow swept away. The sandy ground is bare again, but nothing else is done to make it acceptable to plants.

Perhaps a day later, trucks arrive with fully grown coconut palms—trees that may be twenty-five to thirty feet high. They are planted singly down the front of the lot, perhaps three or four of them in all, and some have decorative curves in their trunks, while others are intentionally set in on a slant. A few small boards prop them up, but even so they have the look of having been there for many years. I rub my eyes as Cinderella must have done over her coach-and-four. Was I dreaming when I looked at that earlier scene of total destruction? Were these trees miraculously spared? I know they were not, but it is still hard to believe.

Sometimes the landscaper adds some sabal palmettos for a change of leaf form and a tighter crown. These are usually in groups—maybe three here, possibly five in another spot—all lower and smaller than the coconut palms. Next, for a complete change in form and texture, he puts in three umbrella trees (scheffleras) that are eight or nine feet in height, and planted as single specimens right against the wall of the building. The umbrella tree comes from Australia and is an easy one to spot, even though it has the big oval leathery green leaves that I find so bewildering. These leaves are in whorls of nine to thirteen, and they do have the look of an umbrella. The trees can be quite large—some as high as thirty feet—but those used for foundation plantings are obviously young ones. I wonder what will happen when they grow up.

The scheffleras make solid masses against the wall, and are most effective at this stage of their growth. But clearly, something airy and light is needed to offset them. A great favorite is the bottlebrush (callistemon), another Australian, which fortunately won't grow out of bounds since it is really a shrub and rarely goes over ten feet. "Callistemon" comes from the Greek "kallos"—beauty, and "stemon"—stamen. The so-called brush is a four or five-inch spike of bright red stamens which hide the green petals of the flower. The brushes are very decorative, and I have found them blooming as early as January. The shrub, itself, looks like a weeping willow (the weeping form is the one generally used), and its fruits resemble small gray buttons. A most delightful little thing!

In the past twelve weeks I have watched plantings go in before four apartment houses. All four had coconut palms—this is a must; all four had umbrella trees—another necessity, it would seem; and three added the bottlebrush. Three also had Spanish bayonet or yucca, a plant I welcomed as one familiar note, although in Pennsylvania our yucca never grows much above a low clump. Here it is a different species that is often a six- or eight-foot plant and may reach twenty-five feet when full grown. I like it much better as a tall pillar than as a clump.

In the planting we are watching (the last of the four), a couple of bottlebrushes have gone in, one six feet tall, one, eight. Yuccas have been planted at either end of the lot, and now a walk of polished coral limestone (Key Largo) is laid, with two lampposts on either side of it, close to the sidewalk. Shrubs are needed beside the lampposts, and the designer has chosen oleanders, about ten feet tall.

When I was very young I mastered the names of three flowering tropical shrubs: oleander from the Mediterranean, hibiscus from China, and bougainvillea from South America. All three were growing in a Jamaican garden, and I first saw them dripping with wet from the rainy season, but lifting their blossoms to the sudden bursts of sunlight. I didn't know then that I was looking on three of the most widespread of tropical flowering shrubs, and that their sure identification would stand by me for the rest of my life. I did know that they were beautiful and that I would always be happy to see them again. With them were two vines I also came to love—the yellow allamanda from Brazil and the blue thunbergia of India—but these are much less common.

How shall I describe oleander? I can spot it now, even without its distinctive flowers. The leaves are long, lance-shaped, and pointed, dark green above, paler beneath. They grow in whorls of three, and the shrub makes a bushy clump. Later there will be big blossoms of white, pink, rose, or yellow that may be either single or double.

Our earliest flowering plants came from the Cretaceous and had their beginning some hundred million years ago. It was in the Cretaceous that the oleander first bloomed, along with magnolias, laurel, and tulip trees. They were among the forerunners of our present flowering world, and because of this, as I watch the planting today, I am pleased to see oleander—oleander of my youth, oleander of the Cretaceous—going into the two holes by the lampposts.

At this stage, the biggest plants have been set out and it is time for ground detail. Swiftly a carpet of grass is laid—heavy sod going down in squares or rectangles, unstacked, fitted in, in a matter of hours. Empty spaces are left for a long low planting against the building, for big sweeping arcs near the sidewalk, for a circle around each of the palmetto clumps. The circles are filled with white pebbles, and a big chunk of coral rock is set close to one of the coconut palms.

All this, perhaps, is the work of one day. On the next, new truckloads are brought in, and the work proceeds with an equal and quite astounding speed. Wedelia, that coarse-looking ground cover from tropical America, with its yellow composite flowers, fills up the curving arcs. Crown of thorns and an agave, or century plant, go into one pebbly circle; in the other we have a second agave and a clump of oyster plants. All four of these plants are so common that it would be an unusual lawn that boasted none of them. Much of the landscaping in South Florida includes all four.

Wedelia should be easily recognized by its coarse, rank growth. It looks very much like a weed, or even like our northern pachysandra, but properly trimmed, it provides a close, green cover. In today's planting, it's the only thing that doesn't immediately appear well-established. Hundreds of little spikes have been poked into the sandy soil, but, well-watered, they will spread out very shortly. The crown of thorns from Madagascar I know as a northern house or conservatory plant. With its spiny stems and double coral bracts, it has the look of a cactus (though it isn't) and it seems to fit perfectly against the white stones. So does the agave, with its long, pointed, stiff leaves growing in a rosette. This particular one is a lovely gray or bluish-green and its leaves are armed with sharp teeth or spines. Some are more of a yellowish-green, and some are banded with cream. There is no sign now, of course, of the immense flowering stalk that will reach between twenty and forty feet and will be produced when the plant is mature at ten years. According to legend, it requires one hundred years—hence the name "century plant." After blooming the plant will die, but new shoots will come up from its roots. The century plant comes from more tropical lands, but has become naturalized here. We do have two native agaves, and there are a number of Mexican species, from some of which come the potent alcoholic drinks, pulque and mescal. One produces sisal.

The last of this quartet is also familiar as a northern pot plant. I have always known it as the oyster plant, but here it has the more colorful name of Moses-in-the-bulrushes. This, too, has swordlike leaves and grows in a rosette, although it's much smaller than the century plant; its leaves are unarmed and are green above, purple underneath. The small white flowers nestle in the axils of the leaves, hence the picturesque name. This is another Mexican.

The final touch in this landscaping project is a two-foot hedge. Natal plum, or carissa, is set right against the cream wall of the apartment house where its glossy evergreen leaves stand out most effectively. In its hedge form, this shrub is another plant commonly found. It has small leaves, spiny stems, and a waxy white flower that looks very much like a star. From time to time, it bears red plumlike fruits an inch and a half in diameter. Every little while, Japanese yews, four feet high and looking more like oleander than yew, break the line of Natal plums.

Near the sidewalk, now, we have a few specimens of a second hedge plant with somewhat larger evergreen leaves. This is an ixora or flame-of-the-woods from the East Indies. It bears brilliant scarlet (or occasionally pink) flowers with four petals that grow in a small cluster. Some bloom can generally be found on ixora throughout the winter, although there is more in spring and summer.

At this point the work of plant decoration is complete. In two or three days, the scene has been changed from one of wasteland to an apparently old and established planting. It would take some five or ten years to achieve such an effect in Pennsylvania, and then it could only be done if the large trees on the lot were preserved during the process of building. I marvel at this instant landscaping every time it occurs.

In its natural state, Florida is a land of flowers. Its name comes from the Spanish words for Easter—*"Pascua florida"*—bestowed by Ponce de León when he first landed on the Florida coast on Easter Sunday; "Florida" by itself means "flowery," or "full of flowers," and has always been a most appropriate term for the state. The changes wrought by man have not altered this fact. The blooms that have been introduced are showier and more exotic than most of our wild flowers and, without question, they are very beautiful. In dwelling upon the artificial look of landscape plantings, I do not mean to decry the industry and skill of those who have drawn upon the floral wealth of the tropics and brought it here to southern Florida for our benefit. Let us recognize the planting as artificial and generally unsuited to our birds and insects; let us make certain that some really natural areas are retained; and then let us find pleasure in this tropical bounty, for living in the southern part of the state is very much like living in a botanical garden.

It would be a great pity to pass by all the foreign plants, just because they are foreign, or to dismiss the tropical vegetation as something too bewildering to recognize by name. In the course of learning the plants used by a few landscape gardeners, my pleasure in the Florida scene was enormously increased and my memory was burdened with only thirteen names. In fact I could hardly say that I had to learn thirteen, for I already knew the coconut palm, the sabal palmetto, oleander, and yucca. And for two more, crown of thorns and oyster plant, it was mostly a case of recognizing house plants I had seen in the North, even though I hadn't quite pinned down their names. The century plant I knew from pictures.

I was surprised at how far I could go with just my baker's dozen. It gave me the same feeling of achievement that I had when I'd mastered a few pages in a Spanish phrase book and was suddenly able to order meals, ask directions, and make such small polite remarks as, "How are you," "Thank you very much," and "I'm sorry."

I checked out my thirteen on Marco Island, walking up and down before a line of model homes. The block was beautifully landscaped, and I was pleased to see coconut palms, sabal palmettos, and umbrella trees dominating the lawns. Here again was weeping bottlebrush for lightness; ixora and Natal plum, those small distinctive evergreens; the desert plants, agave and yucca; and crown of thorns that seems as if it ought to belong to that barren landscape. Finally, there was oleander, everywhere. Only wedelia and oyster plant were absent. I could see the landscaper dismissing both as "too commonplace."

Instead, as ground planting, there was a purple trailing lantana and a feathery asparagus fern. In our northern climate, I have known lantana as a yellow or orange annual. This is another species, but one that appeals to me very much. *Asparagus sprengeri,* the emerald fern, is a common ground cover in Florida.

Going over the planting, I realize that another twelve, added to those I already know, will take care of everything used on an entire block, and I am pleased to find that my second group comes almost as easily as the first. Two I have already mentioned: lantana and asparagus fern. Sea grapes and periwinkle were familiar from the sea lane, while hibiscus I had known for years. It calls to mind Hawaiian beauties with hibiscus blossoms in their lustrous dark hair. The plant is of the mallow family—and a hollyhock, or mallow, is what the flowers are like, with a long, protruding staminal column, arching out of the five- or sometimes even nine-inch flower. This shrub from China has become enormously popular. It is the state flower of Hawaii, and there is a large American Hibiscus Society. More than 5,000 varieties are in existence, with a wide range of shades in yellow, pink, rose, and salmon, in addition to white and the original luxuriant red.

Next come crotons from the South Pacific, for Marco offers a plant tour of the world, just as had the landscaping on Key Biscayne. This is another house or conservatory plant that I had often seen and never quite learned to recognize, although the swordlike leathery leaves in variegated patterns of red, burgundy, orange, yellow, green, and white are most distinctive. In my childhood they were enormously popular, but I can't say I ever liked them, which is why, probably, I've never been sure of their name. Quite obviously they were a favorite with the landscaper at Marco since they seemed to appear in front of every house.

The second half-dozen of my twelve I shall skim over lightly. There is pittosporum, looking to me very much like bayberry with similar two-inch dark green leaves curling at the margin, and twisted light-gray branches. It has the same general size and shape as the bayberry, and comes from China and Japan. Wax-leaf ligustrum from Japan is an evergreen form of privet, easily recognized by anyone familiar with our northern shrub. The very small white flowers are in a panicle. With spider lilies we come, surprisingly, to another native. Like the century plant, the spider lily has big swordlike leaves growing out of a rosette, but its white flower has long narrow petals, reminding me of a woman's wet hair.

One little palm is common—the pygmy date palm from China. In the North we find it as a potted plant in hotels, and it has one of the most feathery and graceful fronds of any palm. The trunk, when visible, is often short, although along South Miami Avenue, where a handsome line of pygmy dates can be seen, the trunks treach fifteen feet. Another potted house plant in the North is philodendron, and this, too, is grown out-of-doors in this area. Originally from Central and South America, most philodendrons are either heart-shaped or deeply lobed, with cuts almost to the midrib. The leaves are often huge, and the plant is a great favorite with those who can grow house plants (I never could), but it reminds me too much of dentists' offices. The cut-leaved form does have an exotic look—I admit that—and it's definitely used to produce a tropical effect. I like philodendrons best when I find them growing as luxuriant vines in one of the man-made jungles or rain forests of southern Florida. This is their natural habitat and here they no longer seem artificial. Here, for me, they seem to belong.

The last of my dozen is from Brazil, the Brazilian pepper, which can take the shape of tree, bush, or hedge. It, too, leads a double life, appearing on lawns as an exotic and also along highways, where it has been extensively planted, and in hammocks, where it certainly has gone wild. The heavy clusters of red berries are very conspicuous during December and January and are responsible for its name "Florida holly."

The names of thirteen plants seen on Key Biscayne carried me very far: these plus twelve more (a total of twenty-five) served to place almost everything at Marco, and later enabled me to name practically everything I saw in Naples. They have gone a good way toward covering the plantings on the Keys, and when I walked up Sunrise Drive on Key Biscayne, I found myself nodding with satisfaction at every lawn. Of course, here and there, I have to confront a maverick landscaper who has rung in an orange tree, a gardenia, a poinsettia, a hedge of Spanish jasmine (white starlike flowers), shore juniper, hedge cactus (unmistakable), or something else not on my list, but for the most part I am well prepared.

As I walk, a little green anole darts over a white wall. This species at least is native, and his green color is due to the leaves on which he has been resting. From overhead sounds the piercing shriek of a boat-tailed grackle, bigger than our northern bird, and with quite an extraordinary collection of calls. But where are the butterflies, wasps, and bees? Does the lovely red ixora hold no honey? Is jasmine with its waxy starlike flowers of no account? Can oleander and hibiscus provide nothing to draw our insects? I have found tree crickets on the oleander, but never a butterfly.

Before me, bougainvillea and allamanda tumble over a balcony. Bougainvillea I have known ever since my visit to Jamaica, but when I think of it now, I recall a most extraordinary sight—purple masses of the flower cascading over a wall and down an embankment in Saint Thomas in the Virgin Islands. It was breathtaking then in its tropical exuberance and brilliance, and I welcome even a small vine here for the memory it brings. "Paper flower" is one of its names, and this is just what the magenta bracts look like. The actual flower petals are small and yellow—rarely seen. Bougainvillea comes from South America and is really a woody vine, though it can be pruned for use as a tree or hedge. In southern Florida there are sheets of bloom at the Hialeah Race Track and at the Parrot Jungle, and there are also red, salmon, orange, yellow, and white forms.

Allamanda is a vine from Brazil of which I've spoken earlier. I first discovered it in Jamaica, forming a heavy screen at one side of our second-story porch. Tropical hummingbirds darted in and out of its big yellow trumpetlike flowers, and lizards climbed over its branches. It is a lovely sight with its waxy, tubular blooms, a soft yellow in color.

One more vine creates a brilliant splash of color wherever it occurs. The flame vine, like allamanda, has a tubular flower, although its tube is long and narrow and of a startling reddish-orange. I have seen it falling over a high white wall, adding a dramatic note to the landscape.

Obviously these three have to be added to my list, and I have three more that I would like to include. Melaleuca (the cajeput or punk tree) can hardly be ignored, even though it wasn't used at Marco or in front of the apartment buildings. It's generally grown as a small tree, planted in little clumps, and this fact, together with its peeling white bark and narrow leaves, makes it look very much like our northern paper birch. Actually, it's a tropical evergreen from Australia, and is closely related to the bottlebrush. It even has the same flowerlike brush, composed of conspicuous stamens (although melaleuca's is white), and the same buttonlike seeds.

Melaleucas are everywhere. They are still enormously popular as lawn trees although their roots are far-spreading and likely to be destructive. They line Alton Road on Miami Beach, as well as many other streets, and they have become thoroughly naturalized outside the city—almost, although not quite, to the extent of the casuarina. I noted a veritable forest of them on Route 27 north of Miami; and in parts of the Everglades National Park, melaleucas have taken the place of native pines. This may well turn out to be another foreigner whose introduction will in time be regretted. But in residential areas it is not yet out of bounds, and it is a lovely small tree.

A second very interesting addition to our lawns is a diminutive royal palm, with the same upper green column as can be seen on the royal palm, but with brilliant red fruit, borne here at Christmas time. This is the Manila or Christmas palm. And finally, there is dracaena, the "monkey palm"—an odd little tree often planted near doorways. I find this, too, as I wander up and down the streets of Key Biscayne. It has a long woody stem, an inch or two in width, with a diamond pattern, and a tuft of dark green swordlike leaves at the top. The leaves are something like those of a yucca, so it comes as no surprise they are related, both being members of the lily family. From a distance, dracaena looks like a toy palm, and people who know much more about conservatory plants than I do find the monkey palm an old friend.

As I bring to a close this account of lawn plantings in South Florida, I am well aware of many interesting flowers, shrubs, and trees that I have omitted. The *Florida Plant Selector,* published by Lewis S. Maxwell, describes more than a hundred common landscape plants and is a most useful small guide to their identification. Standard gardening books give many more. I have proceeded here, as in the chapters on the beach, on the theory that if we know what is most likely to be found, the problem of identification becomes that much easier.

For tropical plants, the Miami area is probably one of the richest in the world. Some of this can be attributed to the Fairchild Tropical Garden, for not only has it introduced many exotics to landscape gardeners and homeowners, but it has also, in its yearly sales, distributed seedlings and cuttings of many such plants. I hope that some, at least, of my readers will be enticed, as I was, to go on and on learning the names of the tropical lawn and garden plants of the world.

Common and Scientific Names

allamanda: *Allamanda cathartica* L.
Bahama anole: *Anole distichus distichus* Cope
bougainvillea: *Bougainvillea glabra* Choisy

Brazilian pepper (Florida holly): *Schinus terebinthifolius* Raddi
Carolina anole: *Anolis carolinensis carolinensis* Voigt
century plant: *Agave americana* L.
croton: *Codiaeum variegatum* (L.) Blume
crown of thorns: *Euphorbia milii* des Moulin
dracaena (monkey palm): *Dracaena marginata* Lam.
fiddleleaf fig: *Ficus pandurata* Sanders (*Ficus lyrata* Warb.)
flame of the woods: *Ixora coccinea* L.
flame vine: *Pyrostegia ignea* Presl. (*Bignonia venustra* Ker.)
gardenia: *Gardenia jasminoides* Ellis
hedge cactus: *Cereus peruvianus* (L.) Mill.
hibiscus: *Hibiscus rosa-chinensis* L.
Japanese pittosporum: *Pittosporum tobira* (Thunb.) Ait.
Japanese yew: *Taxus cuspidata* Sieb. & Zucc.
lace tree philodendron: *Philodendron selloum* C. Koch (a well-known
    cut-leafed species)
Manila palm: *Adonidia merrilli* Becc. (*Veitchia merrillii* Becc.)
marine toad: *Bufo marinus* L.
melaleuca (cajeput, punk tree): *Melaleuca leucadendron* L.
Natal plum: *Carissa grandiflora* A. DC.
oleander: *Nerium oleander* L.
orange: *Citrus sinensis* (L.) Osbeck
oyster plant (Moses-in-the-bulrushes): *Rhoeo spathacea* (Sw.) Stearn
    (formerly *R. discolor* Hance)
pink rat snake: *Elaphe guttata rosacea* (Cope)
poinsettia: *Euphorbia pulcherrima* Willd.
pygmy date palm: *Phoenix roebelinii* O'Brien
shore juniper: *Juniperus conferta* Parl.
sky flower: *Thunbergia grandiflora* Roxb.
southern toad: *Bufo terrestris terrestris* (Bonn.)
Spanish bayonet: *Yucca aloifolia* L.
Spanish jasmine: *Jasminum grandiflorum* L.
spider lily: *Hymenocallis palmeri* S. Wats. (there are several species,
    but this is probably what I had on Marco and Key Biscayne)
Sprenger's asparagus fern (emerald feather): *Asparagus sprengeri* Regal
trailing lantana: *Lantana montevidensis* (Spreng.) Briq. (*L. sellowiana*
    Link & Otto)
umbrella tree: *Brassaia actinophylla* Endl. (formerly *Schefflera actino-
    phylla* Harms)
wax leaf ligustrum: *Ligustrum japonicum* Thunb.
wedelia: *Wedelia trilobata trilobata* (L.) Hitchc.
weeping bottlebrush: *Callistemon viminalis* Cheel.

References

*Allyn, Rube. *Dictionary of Reptiles.* St. Petersburg, Fla.: Great Outdoors, 1952. 86 pp.

Bailey, Liberty Hyde. *Manual of Cultivated Plants.* New York: Macmillan, 1924. 851 pp.

*Carr, Archie F., and Goin, Coleman J. *Guide to the Reptiles, Amphibians, and Freshwater Fishes of Florida.* Gainesville: University of Florida Press, 1955. 341 pp.

Catalog of Plants of the Fairchild Tropical Garden. Coral Gables, Fla.: Dade County Division of Parks and the Fairchild Tropical Garden Association, 1970. 102 pp.

Dickey, R. D., West, Erdman, and Mowry, Harold. "Native and Exotic Palms of Florida." Gainesville, Fla.: Florida Cooperative Extension Bulletin 152-A, 1966.

*Maxwell, Lewis S. *Florida Plant Selector.* Tampa, Fla.: Lewis S. Maxwell, 1961. 113 pp.

Mowry, Harold, and Dickey, R. D. "Ornamental Hedges for Florida." Gainesville, Fla.: Florida Cooperative Extension Bulletin 162, 1955. 35 pp.

*Truitt, John O. *A Guide to the Snakes of Southern Florida.* Miami: Hurricane House, 1962. 46 pp.

7

Street and Highway Plantings

This chapter is a story of trees—the beautiful, often exotic trees, which, more than anything else, give to South Florida its characteristic quality. When I think of Florida, pictures of trees rise up before me: long avenues of royal palms outside of Fort Myers; royal palms in Palm Beach; live oaks in Coconut Grove; casuarinas at Sanibel; coconut palms and sea grapes at Naples near the shore, and inland, tall imposing slash pines. I see the moss-hung cypresses of wetlands; the beautiful reddish gumbo-limbos of the Keys.

Most of this scenery I know well only from traveling by car (for no one could cover all of South Florida on foot), and as a result, much of the detail was lost. But I mean here to provide some knowledge of the landscape for others who travel by this means, whether they are driving through the streets of Miami or other cities, or speeding along the turnpikes, U.S. 1, the Tamiami Trail, or Alligator Alley. If undue emphasis seems to be laid on Miami plantings, it is because this is the richest area of all. If we know the conspicuous trees of Miami and the area below it, we should be able to identify many of the trees of southern Florida. The wealth of tropical vegetation thins out rapidly as one goes north. Many varieties can't take the cold, and the number of individual plants of any non-native species dwindles noticeably. Then, too, in the extreme South, coconut palms and many other tropical plants look as if they had gone native, as many have, whereas in Naples and above Fort Lauderdale, they seem to owe their existence solely to man.

In the Introduction I sketched some of the changes in the South Florida landscape. It's time now to fill in some details and to explain more of the reasons for these changes.

As I noted earlier, the Keys, because of the Gulf Stream, are held to be part of the tropics. The rest of southern Florida has a subtropical climate, which isn't just a matter of temperature but depends, also, upon the heavy rainfall. (The state as a whole has an average of 50 to 60 inches a year.) Definite zones further subdivide the area. One such climate zone runs from Charlotte Harbor on the west coast up to Palm Beach on the east with a big center dip, showing more likelihood of a freeze in the interior. Charles T. Simpson pointed out in *In Lower Florida Wilds* that just a hundred rods inland may produce temperate rather than tropical vegetation. Different trees, of course, will tolerate varying amounts of cold, and many will grow for a number of years in the northern part of their range, only to be cut down by the first severe frost.

Soil also plays an important part in the matter of what can grow where. There are zones of greater and less acidity, and one of the latter runs south from Hollywood, on the east coast. Here the earth overlying the Miami oolite is non-acid and quite unsatisfactory for acid-loving plants.

In much of the southern area the soil is sand, marl, peat, or muck. Often only a thin crust rests upon the limestone rock, too little to support hardwood trees of any size except where sinkholes allow the tap roots to go deeper. Palms, pines, cypresses, and the Australian casuarina are shallow-rooted and these are the preeminent big trees of southern Florida. It's just because of these shallow roots that coconut palms of a surprising size can be used in landscape work.

Some trees put out great bastions at their feet to help support their weight. The cypress is the common example, but I was also pleased to find a massive kapok with flaring buttresses and snaky roots on Key Biscayne. Some have roots that run over the surface of the ground. Besides the kapok, the gumbo-limbo and strangler fig have this habit. Some—like the banyans—send down aerial roots which in time become additional trunks. Many of these devices are intended to offset either a watery habitat or the inability to develop deep roots.

Where there are sinkholes, however, roots can go down, and it's interesting to note the immediate response of plant vegetation. From

Fort Lauderdale south, there is a conspicuous limestone ridge, created by that same southward-flowing current that produced the islets along the west coast. Some 100,000 years ago, this current piled the oolitic mud into a long curving ridge that today is the eastern rim of the Everglades. The Miami oolite, said to be among the most porous limestones in the world, is riddled with sinkholes. Pineland and hammocks follow the ridge and it is in this area that we find some of the most splendid trees. The Brickell and Matheson Hammocks, with their wonderful native growth, came into being because of it. We couldn't have Fairchild Garden, the Parrot Jungle, the Monkey Jungle, and the Orchid Jungle, with their magnificent display of native and exotic trees, without the sinkholes and the reservoir of water just below the limestone surface. From Perrine south, the ridge is broken by transverse glades which used to be flooded during wet seasons, the higher land being left as islands. Some of the earlier writers called these "keys," so that we still have such names as "Paradise Key" and "Long Pine Key" in the Everglades National Park.

Another element in the picture I have touched on briefly before—the influx of tropical plants due to hurricanes. Because the extreme tip of the eastern United States reaches into the Caribbean, it has received over the centuries thousands upon thousands of wave- and wind-borne seeds from the West Indies, particularly from Cuba. Some have even come up from South America and a few have been traced to Africa. Since the climate was generally suitable, many seeds were able to sprout and produce plants that could survive. Much of our "native" southern flora had such an origin, and there may be as many as 130 kinds of tropical trees which came to us in this way, among them mahogany, gumbo-limbo, lignum vitae, and our two wild figs. Most of these are to be found only around Biscayne Bay, in the southern hammocks of the Everglades, and on the Keys.

Aside from its southern tip, the natural vegetation of Florida belongs mostly to the warm temperate zone, the region south of the mid-Atlantic states. A small part is cool temperate, left behind, no doubt, when northern plants crept south during the last ice age. I have found forests of red maple along Alligator Alley, for instance.

Man has been influencing the picture since the Spaniards first set foot on Key Biscayne back in 1497. It's likely that these early adventurers were responsible for coconut palms and that they started planting them as far back as the early 1500s. Oranges came from China; lemons from India; figs, bananas, and mangoes from southern Asia; and these highly useful trees were followed by many others whose chief value lay in their decorative appearance.

When wealthy northerners discovered Florida as a winter haven, they were eager to create tropical settings on their new estates. With the means to secure exotic trees and to provide proper conditions for their growth, the newcomers put their mark on such early resorts as the Tampa-Saint Petersburg area, Fort Myers, and Palm Beach. It was no accident that Beth McGeachy could illustrate her *Handbook of Florida Palms* with many photographs of well-established trees growing in Clearwater.

Within the cities, and particularly within the coastal cities of South Florida, palms, live oaks, and exotic trees dominate the streets. Outside the city limits, or even pressing hard upon those limits, is the natural landscape: cypress, bay, pond apple in the wetter areas; long-needled pines, saw palmetto, and cabbage palm where it's dry; mangroves by the shore.

Let me describe one main route—the Sunshine State Parkway from Miami to West Palm Beach—to indicate the character of many highways in this region. Casuarinas line the turnpike, having been planted as windbreaks. Melaleucas are used the same way, sometimes along the highway, often around nurseries and truck gardens visible from the pike. Canals run by the roadside—canals choked with water hyacinths and bordered by scrub willow, coco plum, and elderberry.

For a time as we go north, coconut palms are common; then more and more slash pines appear, tall, beautiful trees, bearing a ruggedly patterned crown of needles at the top of a long straight trunk. In Collier, Monroe, Dade, and Broward counties, the slash pine is the common one. Farther north, the long-leaf pine takes over, while along the sandy shore we have sand pine, with shorter needles and lower branches.

The prospect changes almost constantly: first a flat plain, nearly treeless, with an immense herd of Brahman cattle and a flock of cattle egrets scattered among them; later, a grove of live oaks; next, truck gardens and citrus groves. Most of the coconut palms are left behind at Fort Lauderdale, and sabal palmettos take their place. Stands of cypress appear, and some treeless wet prairies. In Palm Beach County, saw palmetto becomes conspicuous, and we have the typical pine-saw palmetto forests, interspersed with scattered stands of cabbage palm. These are the piney flatlands, and could we see them close at hand, we might pick out the low growth: dwarf oaks, sumac, cat's claw, wax myrtle, and the coontie that was once the source of the Seminoles' and early settlers' flour. Saw palmetto is often full of rustlings. Many a time I've listened to the cracklings and stirrings, and wondered whether a rattler was at hand. Quail are in the pinelands, though hunters have taken their toll, and there are still wild cats and Florida deer.

On later trips we will follow trails through the mangroves, the cypress swamps, and the hammocks of the Everglades, but let us return now to the city.

Some trees have been used again and again in avenue plantings and the result is often quite spectacular. This is the only adjective to be applied to a double line of royal palms, stately and beautiful, the upper part of each column a clear, strong green. Such a line borders the avenue leading south from Fort Myers. There is a similar row in the Caribbean Gardens at Naples, and a triple row along Biscayne Boulevard in Miami. I always feel as if they called for a triumphal march blown by trumpets. This is the way royal palms should be planted—great monarchs, marching in ranks, side by side, along an avenue. Like the coconut palm, the royal can be grown as far as south central Florida. It's a native tree and was once common in the Big Cypress Swamp, on the Ten Thousand Islands, at Cape Sable, and at Royal Palm Hammock in the Everglades. Fire and man's axe have taken a heavy toll, however, and it wasn't until the Everglades National Park was created that the trees had any real chance of recovery. They are growing wild in the Park today and also in Collier Seminole State Park off the Tamiami Trail.

None of the magnificence of the royal palm can be found in the Manila palm, which seems like a dwarf edition of the bigger tree. It's a charming little palm, though, with its bright Christmastime fruit. I mentioned it in the last chapter as a lawn tree, but it, too, often appears as an ornament to city boulevards.

Another tree much used in street plantings is the coconut palm. One of its most distinctive features is a bending trunk, topped by an array of curving fronds—a combination much in demand by landscape architects. Some bends came from battering winds which caused the young tree to lean at an angle. New growth resumed on a vertical line, but the curve remained. Other palms, growing in dense vegetation, lean to one side to obtain light. Whatever the origin, a gracefully bending coconut with its drooping lower fronds has come to symbolize the tropics more than any other single plant.

Palms are a confusing lot. There are something like 1,200 of them in the world, with between two and three dozen common in Florida. Most are used as individual specimens, not for avenue planting. We have already seen Senegal dates (the sea lane) and pygmy dates. Canary Island dates have a massive trunk, shaped something like a pineapple. Areca, or butterfly palms, normally grow in clumps, and have yellow trunks, ringed like bamboo. The queen palm has extremely feathery drooping fronds, while the fishtail palm is distinct from others of its kind by having a wedge-shaped leaflet that bears notches, or deep cuts, and does indeed resemble a fish's tail.

The above are all "feather" palms. The second group is that of palms with fan-shaped leaves. The sabal palmetto—used in some street plantings—saw, and dwarf palmettos have been mentioned earlier. The Washington palm has a conspicuous "petticoat skirt" of dried fronds and can be seen in Bayfront Park and along the MacArthur Causeway. European and Chinese fan palms (the latter is the common potted palm of hotel lobbies) have graceful and very wide fans. Lincoln Road Mall on Miami Beach has quite a good collection of palms—I wish more of them were identified—and one can see many of the other fan palms on the streets of Miami Beach. The Florida thatch palm, native to the Keys and to the southwest tip of the mainland, can be recognized by its very slender trunk with the crown of leaves high in the air. There is a fine display of these in front of the Seaquarium. Both palms and live oaks have a particular value in Florida because of their ability to withstand hurricanes.

Most important after the palms are the figs, and there are a goodly number of these, 800 in all. In the ficus group are the so-called rubber plants (the rubber tree of Brazil belongs to another genus) and banyans. Actually, "banyan" is a habit of growth which almost all members of the family display to some extent. Very simply, banyans produce aerial roots from their upper branches which grow downward until, on reaching the soil, they develop into extra trunks. A really large banyan may extend 2,000 feet and reach 100 feet in height. Alexander is supposed to have camped his whole army under one, but I am afraid this is stretching the truth.

Several species produce latex, and all of these have a pronounced banyan habit. Two well-known ones are from India: *benghalensis,* a graceful weeping fig which is actually the true banyan and is frequently shown in books on tropical trees, but appears to be rare around Miami; and *elastica,* the rubber plant of greenhouses. This last is the source of India rubber, and in a tropical climate it grows into a large tree. It's easily recognized by the long red pointed sheath which covers the new leaf. The most common banyan fig in the Miami area is *altissima*; it appears as a magnificently spreading tree in the Parrot Jungle and at Bayfront Park, and is also planted extensively, along with *benjamina,* on many streets. Both are from India, and they, too, have glossy evergreen leaves—those of *altissima* are broader than *benjamina*'s, which are long and narrow—with smooth, gray bark, and spreading branches. Whenever I see oval leaves of this type on a broadheaded tree, my first thought is always *ficus.* Avenues lined with these handsome shade trees are common in the Miami area—parts of Coral Way in Miami, Main Highway in Coconut Grove, and Old Cutler Road in Coral Gables come to mind in particular—and like the palms, they play a significant role not only in creating the tropical atmosphere, but in making the subtropics livable.

For the most part I make little attempt to separate the figs, but three kinds are distinctive. The fiddle leaf, from Africa, is generally a small tree with an enormous (ten- to fifteen-inch) leaf in a fiddle shape. The edible fig, from the Mediterranean, is also small and has a three- to five-lobed leaf. And one of our two native figs, the Florida strangler, has an oval leaf that is much smaller than those of the Indian trees. This plant begins life, usually, as a seed dropped by a bird in some other tree. High up in the branches, it develops into a vine, winding around its host. Soon it becomes a heavy twining rope-like plant which, in time, smothers the tree upon which it started growth. It has taken root in the soil at this point and the typical aerial roots are in evidence. Eventually the host rots and dies and the strangler fig assumes the look of a perfectly ordinary and quite respectable tree, with little hint of its murderous past.

Another impressive and well-known avenue tree is the live oak, with its widespread, almost horizontal branches. The evergreen leaf is oval and rather small, and the brownish-gray trunk of the tree is conspicuously ridged. Because of its rough bark, live oaks are particularly favored by epiphytes—in fact, that's how I often identify it. Look for a horizontal limb arching over the road along Brickell Avenue, South Bayshore Drive, or west of Miracle Mile as it again becomes Coral Way. Resurrection ferns, wild pineapples, orchids, and other air plants may crowd its upper surface—as Charles T. Simpson puts it in *Florida Wild Life,* like "chickens on a roost." With their burden of smaller plants and their spreading limbs, live oaks are among my favorite trees.

The mahogany, reminiscent of the great shade trees of more northern climes, has a somewhat similar look but its limbs are more upright and the leaves are compound, with small leaflets that are brownish-green in color while those of the live oak are a glossy dark green. The fruit of the mahogany is a woody capsule, ripening in the fall. The tree is primarily West Indian, but is native to the Keys and the shores of Biscayne Bay. Because of its valuable timber (it's considered the best cabinet wood in the world), and because it grew on land that man wanted for other purposes, the original growth has been largely exterminated in our country. It is, however, extensively used for avenue planting in the Miami region, and there are fine rows of it along Le Jeune Road as it extends south of the crossing at U.S. Highway 1.

Many of the big trees with glossy, evergreen, oval to lance-shaped leaves seem impossible to identify during the winter months. Later on, flowers or fruit will provide an answer, but one of this group can be given a name during the early part of the year. When in bloom, the mango has tiny pinkish flowers, growing in panicles, a sort of candelabra effect, at the very tips of the branches. They remind me of the wands of horse chestnuts, although the latter are bigger. The leaves are narrow, about half an inch wide and six inches or more in length, while the fruit, which is borne during the summer, is egg-shaped and from three to eight inches in length. Considered one of the most delectable tropical fruits, mangoes have been cultivated for the past 4,000 years. While not purposely planted as a street border, these handsome trees may be seen in some areas where subdivisions were created in former groves.

Another tree with similar long narrow leaves is the black olive (bucida) also widely grown on Miami streets. It can be recognized by the dense whorls of leaves at the very tip of the twigs and by the orange-brown inner bark, revealed where the scaly outer layer has peeled off. The broad rounded head of the tree is made up of horizontal branches.

The sapodilla has this long leaf and is a big tree, too. While it produces chicle for chewing gum, the brown, three-inch fruit drops and has an unpleasant smell, and hence the tree is unsuitable for street planting. The prospect of unwanted, even though edible, fruit explains the fact that many fruit-bearing tropical trees appear mostly in backyards, or in commercial groves. This is true of the mammee apple, a big tree with broad leathery leaves, white fragrant flowers, and spherical brown fruits; of the soursop, a handsome conical tree with green prickly fruit; sweetsop, having a fruit with conspicuous knobs; avocados, with green pear-shaped fruit; and guavas, with yellow or white rounded fruit. While nuisances as street adornments, all these are held dear by homeowners who have learned to prepare them for the table.

One small tree that does appear along streets is the tropical almond with rounded leathery leaves that turn red in winter. I know this from the sea lane, and there is a center line of them on S.W. 26th Street in Miami. Black olive and tropical almond are favorite trees of the yellow-bellied sapsucker—another misnamed woodpecker that is mostly black and white, with a small red cap and a red chin. Often tropical almonds are riddled with holes (woodpecker work) for the entire length of the trunk.

Many of the avenue trees have beautiful flowers, and one of the loveliest is the orchid tree or bauhinia. The big orchidlike blossoms (lavender-pink or white) borne throughout the winter and spring make identification easy, but should there be any doubt, look at the leaves. That cloven hoof is a dead giveaway. No other leaf that I know is like it—heart-shaped at its base, it looks as if it had been split in two at the tip. Reddish pods, as much as fifteen inches long, follow the bloom. The Hong Kong orchid, more recently introduced, has deep purple, cattleya-like flowers, and no pods. While less springlike in its general effect, its lack of pods, which clutter a lawn, has made it popular. It also has a long period of bloom—from November to May.

The most spectacular of all flowering trees, though, is probably the royal poinciana with its brilliant display of scarlet blossoms. "Flamboyant tree" is another name for it, and flamboyant it is! In the West Indies (Jamaica, Martinique, and Trinidad come to mind in particular), there are long avenue plantings and the tree can be seen in all its splendor during the winter months. In Florida, we must wait until June for one of the finest shows of the South. Palm Beach, Fort Myers, Miami, and the Keys—particularly Key West—all have lavish bloom; but even without its flowers, the flamboyant tree is easily recognized by its fernlike feathery leaves (it's a senna) and umbrella top. The seed pods that often persist throughout the year are sometimes two feet long and surprisingly heavy.

There are so many poincianas in and near Kingston, Jamaica, that I had assumed it was native to that island, and so I was surprised to find that here was yet another plant from Madagascar. How much that country has given us: rose periwinkle, crown of thorns, the traveler's tree, tropical almond (also from Malaya), the common screw pine, cane or areca palms, and, now, the royal poinciana. Many of the trees in this chapter, as I have noted, have a foreign origin, and quite a few are from India. This is true of a number of the figs, of mangoes, and of orchid trees. Sapodilla, mammee apple, soursop, sweetsop, avocado, and guava are from tropical America, while my next tree, the woman's tongue, comes from Africa.

Like the poinciana, woman's tongue has feathery compound leaves, but it is easily distinguished by its very different type of growth. Where the poinciana is almost flat-topped, the woman's tongue is upright, and its flowers, looking like yellow puffballs, are far less showy. The thin, twisted pods are smaller, reaching twelve inches at the most. The tree loses its leaves in late winter, but the dry pods persist, and their rattling in the wind has given it the name of "woman's tongue."

There is never a time when some flowering trees and shrubs are not in evidence in the South, but spring here, as elsewhere, is the season of greatest bloom. This is when the Brazilian jacaranda, with leaves much like those of the poinciana, is covered with violet-blue flowers. In Naples and the Saint Petersburg-Tampa area, some of the streets are lined with jacarandas. The golden shower tree (a cassia from India) provides another of the Miami spectacles when it's covered with yellow blossoms borne in foot-long drooping clusters that carpet the streets and sidewalks with their fallen petals. The pink-and-white shower (a Javanese cassia) also puts on a show, and springtime evenings are often filled with the fragrance of night-blooming jessamine (popularly known as jasmine), a West Indian shrub that bears small cream-colored flowers.

But now, lest we seem to slight our native growth, let us look at three unusual and interesting trees that can hold their own in any company. The seaside hibiscus or mahoe never gets much more than fifteen feet high. Its five- to eight-inch leaves are orbicular in general outline, but, looked at more closely, one can see a heart-shaped base and a pointed tip. The big flowers are yellow or orange, with a purple center, when they first open, becoming coppery red by evening. Simpson, in *Florida Wild Life,* devotes a full chapter to the mahoe as "A Tree that Walks." His description is a vivid one.

The tree he planted "began as a little seedling forming a single upright stem but after reaching a height of ten feet it became top-heavy and leaned over as if it was tired. Later the end of it lay on the mud and in a very short time it had become firmly rooted. Then the growing tip started on, forming a tolerably erect trunk, only to lop over again and root, something after the manner of a walking fern or strawberry plant." Later he says: "Let us look under the tree if we can get in, for it is so dense in places that a rabbit could hardly crawl through. ... It is a maze of overhanging limbs, crooked, twisted, coiling and writhing about each other like so many colossal serpents. ... This tree not only covers the land but it is a destroyer of anything which happens to grow in its way."

Just once I saw a mahoe behaving like this in a hammock on Key Biscayne. Not having read Simpson at the time, I looked at it in astonishment, wondering what it thought it was doing. Simpson believes that the seed of this odd plant, which is now considered native to the Keys and the Everglades, may have been carried by currents from the Indian Ocean around the southern tip of Africa, into the Atlantic, and thence to Florida. If so, this may be the tree that has come to us by natural means from the greatest distance of all.

The geiger tree grows naturally only on the Keys. It, too, has striking blooms, carrying big flame-colored, trumpetlike flowers throughout most of the year. I have spotted geiger trees here and there in Miami, and even as far north as Naples.

Gumbo-limbo, another of my great favorites among tropical trees, has reddish-brown or coppery peeling bark, and the big limbs have the appearance of smooth muscular arms. Often they grow horizontally and have dips or bends which look as if they were designed as seats. Anyone who has ever climbed trees when young knows what a wonderful perch such a rounded dip can provide. Gumbo-limbo is another native, and one of the few deciduous trees in South Florida. Its resin was once widely used for medicinal purposes and the name apparently came from Jamaicans as a mispronounciation of *"gumma elemba."*

Three birds occur so commonly along the highways of southern Florida and seem so closely associated with the plants I have just mentioned that they deserve a few words here. All three sit on the electric and telephone wires and poles and are an integral part of the picture during much of the year. Mockingbirds I spoke of in the last chapter. The boat-tailed grackle, much bigger than our common grackle of the North, has a longer tail that widens out at the end. The male is an irridescent steely-blue; the female a warm brown. These two are year-round residents. The little hawk on the wires—and there are bound to be scores of them between September and mid-March—is the sparrow hawk or kestrel. His markings are rusty-red, black, white, and slate-blue.

This chapter has provided a large sampling of exotic and native plants, but, as with southern lawn landscaping in the last chapter, I also found that the trees described here do in fact include the great majority seen on the roadways and in the parks of South Florida, and I hope that my list will serve others as well as it has served me.

Common and Scientific Names

areca palm (yellow butterfly palm): *Chrysalidocarpus lutescens* Wendl. (formerly *Areca lutescens* Bory.)
avocado (alligator pear): *Persea americana* Mill.
bald cypress: *Taxodium distichum* (L.) Rich.
banyan figs: *Ficus benghalensis* L. (the true banyan), *F. altissima* Blume
benjamin fig: *Ficus benjamina* L.
black olive (oxhorn bucida): *Bucida buceras* L.

Canary Island date palm: *Phoenix canariensis* Chaub.

Chinese fan palm: *Livistona chinensis* R. Br. (a large fan palm reaching thirty feet)

coco plum: *Chrysobalanus icaco* L.

common fig: *Ficus carica* L.

coontie (Florida arrowroot): *Zamia integrifolia* Ait.

dwarf live oak: *Quercus minima* (Sarg.) Small

European fan palm: *Chamaerops humilis* L. (a dwarf palm with usually a two- to three-foot trunk)

fiddleleaf fig: *Ficus lyrata* Warb.

fishtail palm: *Caryota urens* L. (the common large fishtail palm)

Florida elderberry: *Sambucus simpsonii* Rehder

Florida strangler fig: *Ficus aurea* Nutt.

Florida thatch palm (Jamaica thatch palm): *Thrinax parviflora* Sw.

geiger tree: *Cordia sebestena* L.

golden shower: *Cassia fistula* L.

guava: *Psidium guajava* L.

gumbo-limbo: *Bursera simaruba* (L.) Sarg.

jacaranda: *Jacaranda acutifolia* Humb. & Bonpl.

lignum vitae: *Guaiacum sanctum* L.

live oak: *Quercus virginiana* Mill.

longleaf pine: *Pinus palustris* Mill.

mahogany: *Swietenia mahogani* Jacq.

mammee apple: *Mammea americana* L.

mango: *Mangifera indica* L.

Mexican Washington palm: *Washingtonia robusta* Parish

needle-leaved air plant: *Tillandsia setacea* Sw. (a wild pine commonly found on live oaks)

night-blooming jessamine: *Cestrum nocturnum* L.

orchid tree: *Bauhinia purpurea* L.

papaya: *Carica papaya* L.

pink and white shower: *Cassia javanica* L.

pond apple (custard apple) *Annona glabra* L.

queen palm: *Arecastrum romanzoffianum* Becc. (*Cocos plumosa* Hook.)

red bay: *Persea borbonia* L.

red maple: *Acer rubrum* L. var *trilobum* K. Koch

resurrection fern: *Polypodium polypodioides* (L.) Watt.

royal palm: *Roystonea elata* (Batr.) Harper

royal poinciana (flamboyant tree):*Poinciana regia* Bojer)

rubber plant: *Ficus elastica* Roxb.

sand pine: *Pinus clausa* (Engelm.) Sarg.

sapodilla: *Manilkara zapota* (L.) Van Royen (*Achras zapota* L.)

screw pine: *Pandanus utilis* Bory

scrub willow: *Salix caroliniana* Michx.

seaside hibiscus (mahoe): *Hibiscus tiliaceus* L.

shortleaf fig (wild banyan tree): *Ficus brevifolia* Nutt.

silk cotton tree (kapok): *Ceiba pentandra* Gaertn.

slash pine: *Pinus elliottii* Engelm.(often called *Pinus caribaea* Morelet but not currently recognized by authorities.)

soursop: *Annona muricata* L. (a tropical American tree of the custard apple family)

southern sumac: *Rhus copallina* L. var. *leucantha* (Jacq.) DC

Spanish moss: *Tillandsia usneoides* L.

sweet bay (swamp bay): *Magnolia virginiana* L. (the bay after which bay heads were named)

sweetsop (sugar apple): *Annona squamosa* L.

traveler's tree: *Ravenala madagascariensis* Gmel.

tufted fishtail palm: *Caryota mitis* Lour. (smaller than fishtail, but better for lawn use)

water hyacinth: *Eichhornia crassipes* (Mart.) Solms

wax myrtle: *Myrica cerifera* (L.)

woman's tongue tree: *Albizzia lebbeck* (L.) Benth.

References

*Craighead, Frank C. *Orchids and Other Air Plants of the Everglades National Park.* Coral Gables, Fla.: University of Miami Press, 1963. 125 pp.

Simpson, Charles Torrey. *Florida Wild Life.* New York: Macmillan 1932. 199 pp. O.P.

Simpson, Charles Torrey. *In Lower Florida Wilds.* New York: G. P Putnam's Sons, 1920. 404 pp. O.P.

West, E., and Arnold, L. E. *The Native Trees of Florida.* Gainesville University of Florida Press, 1948. 212 pp. O.P.

8

Parks and Public Gardens

The public parks and gardens of South Florida must easily number a hundred, with an extraordinary range of settings and some remarkably beautiful scenery. Since it would be impossible to cover them all, I have chosen a half dozen or so that I hope are fairly representative.

Cypress Gardens

One of the most famous is the Cypress Gardens near Winter Haven. When I wander along its stone walks, past the incredible amount of bloom, this garden never seems quite real. Vista after vista seems to have come from a picture postcard. The lovely woman in a pale blue gown with crinoline skirt drifting across the greensward, the southern belle sitting on the lawn, with her voluminous pink skirts spread out in a great circle, are as fanciful as the beds of azaleas, gardenias, roses, and camellias, all so exactly edged and curved. The beautiful lawn with its winding walks seems to have come straight out of the Old South—but not the real Old South; this is the imagined one of romanticism. Here are moss-hung cypresses, rising out of Lake Eloise, and beside them a gracefully arched Japanese bridge. A woman in a yellow dress that might easily have come from *Gone with the Wind* awaits me on the bridge and greets me in honeyed accents.

Now masses of crimson bougainvillea arch above the pathway, while beyond are many kinds of palms, as well as crotons with their richly variegated leaves; and heavy vines: some the deeply-cut-leaved philodendron, some philodendron with a massive heart-shaped leaf, and some monstera—looking like the lacy-leaved philodendron, but easily distinguished by holes near the midrib. Poinsettias are here, too, for there is an emphasis on red flowers. And always in the background are the cypresses. Azaleas, camellias, roses, cypresses, even gardenias, in a sense, belong here as part of an antebellum garden, and as suited to the climate. But the tropical exotics—croton, philodendron, monstera, poinsettia, and bougainvillea—seem definitely out of place, and hundreds of smudge pots, half-hidden in the shrubbery, bear witness to this fact.

Water is everywhere, for the garden was built around a number of lakes or lagoons, and the natural waterways have made possible the development of a national center for water-skiing. The water displays draw more visitors, probably, than the gardens: there are four shows a day, with aquamaids performing a so-called ballet on water skis, and champions demonstrating their skill. The gardens are beautiful but my pleasure in them is broken by an insistent loudspeaker announcing another show, the blare of music, and the noise of speedboats. It makes it hard to believe that I have really stepped back into the gracious antebellum world of the "Old South."

The Mountain Lake Sanctuary

Most of the time the Mountain Lake Sanctuary at Lake Wales is very quiet. It's unpretentious, too, with its largely native pines, hardwoods, cabbage palms, and ferns. Live oaks dominate the fifty-nine acres of the park, and while there are flower beds and plantings of azaleas and magnolias, the effect is of a natural setting. What I remember best are the dirt paths through the woods, the occasional quotation from a naturalist or philosopher, and the feeling of peacefulness. The term "sanctuary" was no light choice. This was designed not only as a sanctuary for wildlife, but for people, too, and Edward Bok's original intention has been well carried out. A friend told me once that this was her favorite place in Florida and I can appreciate her feeling.

As I walked through the park, birds were singing from the

shrubbery and flying about among the live oaks. (I hadn't been aware of any birds at the Cypress Gardens.) A bamboo screen had peepholes looking out on a feeding ground, and I stood for some little time watching cardinals, blue jays, titmice, and a towhee. Wood ducks, brilliantly beautiful in their green, blue, brown, black, and white plumage, swam in the moat surrounding the tower—for this is the Sanctuary of the Bok Singing Tower. More could be seen in a nearby lagoon and I wondered if any other ducks could equal them in color.

Rising above everything was the tower itself, a Gothic structure of coquina rock and pink and gray marble, with a frieze of pelicans, herons, and other wildlife visible from the ground. The tower stands on top of Iron Mountain, one of the highest points of land in the whole state, and reading this, any northerner would picture a lofty eminence. But not in Florida! Iron Mountain is only a gentle rise—something some would hardly dignify as a hill.

Most people come to the Sanctuary for the carillon concerts; the carillon of the Singing Tower is one of the finest in the country. The music is on the popular side, but it is pleasant, and what I heard didn't break the overall feeling of peace and quiet.

Lehigh Acres - Community Park

When I ventured upon a hundred as the number of parks in South Florida, I was including the many unostentatious plots of land set aside for public use. One such small area is at Lehigh Acres in Lee County. It hasn't been "improved" except for the addition of cooking pits and is probably used only by local people. There is a pond at one side, and the place is quiet. As a naturalist, I like it particularly because I find here more birds per acre than in any of the well-known parks.

Greater and lesser yellowlegs stalk in the shallows of the pond, hunting for crustaceans and minnows. These are inland sandpipers, comparatively large, with long bills and yellow legs. Both are well known to me from their spring and autumn visits to Pennsylvania ponds and lakes. A flock of warblers—parula, black and white, and magnolia—flit among the live oaks and pines. I hear the distinctive "chick-a-per-weoo-chick" of the white-eyed vireo (to me it sounds like an adulterated "whip-poor-will"), and a red-headed woodpecker chops at a big tree. The true red-headed woodpecker has a completely red head and is far less common, particularly in southern Florida, than the red-bellied with which he is often confused.

Robins surround me—robins en route north—for the time is early March. A month ago they were in Naples, and a big flock also spent a few days, but only that, in Miami. Now they are headed for the northern states and some, I'm sure, have already reached Pennsylvania. This particular flock may stop short of the mid-Atlantic states, or it may continue on to New England, arriving there as a late wave.

The Caribbean Gardens

Many of the well-known parks have had to include side attractions to provide for their upkeep. This is true of the Caribbean Gardens in Naples where, until recently, trained ducks and other animals performed several times a day. Now it has become Jungle Larry's Safari at the Caribbean Gardens and the show features a chimpanzee, a young elephant, and a boa constrictor, with a lion act in preparation. Until the garden changed hands, exotic waterfowl also roamed freely throughout the area; they blended into the scenery, however, seeming to be a part of the setting. With the addition of mammals and reptiles, this exotic element has assumed a bigger role, and it seems better to consider this aspect of the Caribbean Gardens in a later chapter—one devoted largely to "jungles," and to speak here only of the botanical part and of native wildlife.

The original plant collection was made many years ago by Dr. Henry Nehrling, whose "Tropical Garden" in Naples contained one of the earliest such collections in Florida. At one time 3,000 different species could be seen in the garden's thirty acres, but after Dr. Nehrling's death, some of this was lost through sale, theft, and removal. Fortunately, enough was left to form the basis for a fine, modern, tropical garden. It hasn't the sweeping lines of the Cypress Gardens or the uncluttered peace of the Mountain Lake Sanctuary. Rather there is a feeling of tropical exuberance as the paths wind through heavy vegetation, but in this setting, in the subtropical climate of Naples, the exotics no longer seem out of place.

I pause in the parking lot because of the tremendous rustling of bamboo, and my eye lights on masses of crimson bougainvillea, a clump of pentas, and a beautiful display of orchids. I am pleased that tropical vegetation is no longer a wholly bewildering mass of trees, shrubs, and flowers. There is still much that is unknown, but the known far outweighs that which I fail to recognize.

One proceeds now counterclockwise, instead of clockwise as formerly, and seen from the opposite direction, the planting takes on a fresh and different look. I am impressed again with its charm. The entrance now takes me through huge clumps of bamboo, and within a few yards I come upon two handsome powder puff bushes, one red and one white. These are tropical American shrubs and have been added to signal the beginning of the Amazon jungle. As with the bottlebrush, the conspicuous "flowers" are really long stamens in a rounded mass. Powder puffs are occasionally found on the lawns of South Florida, and beautiful plants they are!

The new management intends to fit flora to fauna, but it will take time to create this proper background since the present planting mixes trees and shrubs from the worldwide tropics and most of them are fine specimens, too well established to be moved. Only where there is space or where a plant needs to be replaced, can the "right" vegetation be put in.

As I wander along the wood-chip path, the trees are almost all familiar. Here is a young cabbage palm, its trunk adorned with ferns that have lodged in the old leaf bases—the so-called boot jacks. Here, too, are fishtail, fan, and royal palms, figs, an umbrella tree, and melaleucas. Skirting the old Spoonbill Lagoon, I am amused to see Florida water birds swimming beside the South American tapirs. Coots, gallinules, and wood ducks have come in on their own and I should be surprised to find either our North American coots or wood ducks in the true Amazon basin. The coots are funny little water birds, black, with white bills. Their relatives, the gallinules, have much the same shape but can be distinguished by a white stripe on each side and a bright red bill with a red frontal plate above it.

Near the end of the lagoon, a tawny fulvous tree duck flies whistling by overhead. He, too, is becoming a native, although he came originally from the Gulf states and Texas. I have grown fond of his distinctive call from earlier visits to the gardens and am pleased to hear it again.

In the Asiatic section, a Chinese litchi (responsible for litchi nuts) has been added, and bamboo (typically Asiatic) should go in before long. A baobab has been acquired for the African Safari, and nothing could better represent that continent than this strange tree with its broad base rapidly tapering to a small tip, and its dwarfed, often bare branches. And now, having touched on the possibilities for true habitat planting, let us enter the other part of the garden—the part that is still devoted primarily to plants.

Here the settings undergo constant change. A short distance from the pavilion lies the "orchid cathedral," a cypress head in which have been established orchids from South America and Asia. Later in the year there will be heavy blooms of cattleyas, waxy-white flowers of phalaenopsis, and the colorful airy blossoms of vandas. The growth is luxuriant, for epiphytes are everywhere, from the curtains of Spanish moss draped over pond cypresses, to other bromeliads, ferns, and orchids. The favorite hosts of all these tree dwellers are cypresses, pond apples, live oaks, and buttonwoods, all four having conspicuous rough bark. Philodendrons also wind around the trunks, and on the ground are clumps of anthuriums with big heart-shaped leaves, varicolored crotons, and ginger, with long narrow blades. Ferns on the trees are echoed by terrestrial ferns of many varieties, and a graceful tree fern bends over a bench in the orchid cathedral glade.

From the cypress head, I enter a small swamp crossed by a boardwalk. Standing on the wooden planks, I look down on a patch of open water, glistening above its dark brown bottom, hemmed in by leather ferns. A small alligator lies half-submerged, watching me with unblinking eyes. Surrounding the swamp are cypresses, heavily hung with moss, some carrying other air plants as well. Buttonbush, leather ferns, and red bay press upon the boardwalk, and I could very well be in the midst of a true swamp, such as that at Corkscrew, instead of in the small part of the garden devoted to such plant and animal life.

The tropical leather ferns interest me. With their heavy, rank growth, they sometimes reach twelve feet and are the biggest ferns in North America, a reminder of the giant ferns of the Coal Age. I would see them many times later in the Everglades, at Corkscrew, and in swamps on Key Biscayne, and I often stopped to wonder at them.

For a short distance now, the path runs through an avenue of royal palms, and then we are again in the swamp. At two places along the way, a cypress and a cabbage palm lean over the walk and their bromeliads and orchids are practically at eye level. One has a red spike coming out of a rosette of blue-green leaves. It's a stiff-leaved or cardinal wild pine (or pineapple), the most common of all air plants (with the exception of Spanish moss), and the one usually found on cypresses. I have been hearing the white-eyed vireo's "chick-a-per-weoo-chick" as I paused on the boardwalk, and now a sharp scolding chip draws my attention to a yellowthroat with black eye mask, darting in and out of the bushes, almost at water level. This little warbler belongs in the wetlands, and one is almost as sure of finding him there as of finding stiff-leaved wild pines on at least some of the cypresses.

Emerging from the swamp, I pass a stand of sabal palmettos (cabbage palms), many bearing orchids and ferns, and enter a grove of live oaks, moss-hung and reminiscent of avenues and plantations. From thence the path leads me under spreading banyans with their tropical junglelike atmosphere. A beautiful shell ginger is in bloom with flowers in long drooping clusters, the outer petals a pearly white, the inner petal yellow speckled with red. I never fail to stop and admire it.

Just before the exit lies the African section with, as yet, few of the typical African plants to give it the character it should have. A brilliant orange flame vine behind the lion's cage is from Brazil, while bauhinia is Asiatic. Only Senegal date palms can be said to belong, but in time this will undoubtedly be changed.

Native wildlife has not been conspicuous, although I know that raccoons are plentiful, and otters and bobcats can be found here (they are seldom out except at night). There is a resident barred owl and a pileated woodpecker, but neither has been visible today. Cardinals are generally about, while in winter, ducks such as mallards, lesser scaup, and shovelers are quite common. The last of this trio is often seen at the Hialeah racetrack and is one of our truly decorative ducks, with a wide black bill and a colorful pattern of green, brown, and white. During migration, warblers sometimes come in in numbers (they like the bottlebrush trees particularly), but in general, as I've said, a big public garden full of visitors is seldom a good spot for native birds.

Bayfront Park

Bayfront Park in Miami is as far removed from the Caribbean

Gardens as it is from the Cypress Gardens, the Mountain Lake Sanctuary, and the park at Lehigh Acres. Most of it is a conventional city park, although a very handsome one. Covering thirty-nine acres, it has many standard features: handsome old shade trees, paved walks intersecting well-kept lawns, formal beds filled with flowering annuals and perennials (changed frequently to preserve constant bloom), statuary, and benches. It has, in addition, an excellent view of Biscayne Bay, a wide range of trees, and a rock garden, the last deserving special comment.

A city park is intended to provide restful shade and a place of retreat from the noise of the city. To do this, many of the trees must be planted along bench-lined walks, but within these limits, effective groupings have been made at Bayfront Park: a line of fishtail palms in one place, farther along, one of queen palms, rows of Manila palms interplanted with ixora, a hedge of dwarf poinciana. There are beautiful groves of mahogany, and again, groves of live oak. Traveler's trees surround a statue of Columbus, which overlooks an avenue lined with royal and thatch palms. Down the center runs a long rectangular bed full of rose periwinkle, double marigolds, scarlet sage, blue salvia, and blue ageratum. A big circular bed with petunias, roses, and scarlet sage interrupts the avenue planting, but then the trees continue in a double line to the band shell at the end. In another formal planting, yellow marigolds edge a rectangular stretch of lawn, are backed by a clipped evergreen hedge, and end before another piece of statuary with the bay in the background.

Pigeons (those traditional birds of every city park) are abundant and most of the time someone is giving them food. Boat-tailed grackles strut on the sidewalks and blue jays fly noisily from tree to tree. Once I came upon some older men who had tamed the jays and trained them to eat from their hands. I held out peanuts, too, and for a short space had a blue jay perching on the edge of my palm. But when I tried it later, without the men whom they knew, not a jay would come near. One more bird belongs to Bayfront Park. Whenever I visit the park, I almost always glimpse, at least once, a brilliant flash of black and orange—the beautiful spotted-breasted oriole from Central America.

Most of the trees are familiar and the less common ones are often labeled. (I wish all park superintendents would do the same.) Poinciana is here, bauhinia, and the geiger tree. There is a spreading, dramatic banyan, as well as other figs, mahoe, tropical almond, melaleuca, pygmy dates, a cluster of Senegal dates, and a Washington palm. Two kapoks draw my attention. I spoke earlier of their thin, far-flung buttresses, but they have another feature that's of interest— the cottonlike fiber from their seed pods is used in mattresses and life belts. One of the two here has a spiny trunk, one a smooth one, but they are the same species. The presence or absence of spines can be due to age or simply be an idiosyncracy of the particular tree.

Black-throated blue warblers are passing through Miami now (March 21), and I hear their "trees, trees, trees, trees" as they skim over the scarlet flowers of a coral tree—erythrina. No leaves have appeared as yet on the tree and the flowers are very striking against the big bare limbs. A label tells me that another leafless tree is frangipani or plumeria. In May this will be lovely with its rosy-hued flowers. The blossoms (there are rose, white, and yellow varieties) are used in Hawaii for leis, and beautiful leis they make!

By the time the frangipani blooms there will also be other birds here—summer residents that go farther south in the winter. Among them will be black-whiskered vireos (small birds slightly bigger than most warblers) and gray kingbirds (easily recognized by their big bills). Both are limited, in our country, to the Keys and the extreme southern end of the Florida mainland; and birders, intent on rarities, come down here in the spring and summer with these two high on their lists of birds to be seen.

Many colorful plantings catch my eye today: blue salvia in front of red crotons and dwarf poincianas with their red and orange flowers; more blue salvia backed by scarlet ixora and hibiscus. But I mustn't linger over them, for I have reached the small quiet corner, the fenced-in area of the Rock Garden that is one of my favorite spots. As much as anything, this is a miniature jungle planting, refreshingly wet and seemingly remote from city life. At the entrance, a small upsurge of water splashes down over three levels of a fountain, and the sound of its cascade fills the air. A dark rectangular pool below it is full of water lilies. Ferns and mosses grow in rock crevices near the waterfall, and the pool is edged with blue ajuga and pink sedumlike kalanchoe, backed by a dark neat hedge of Natal plum. There is an almost immediate feeling of enchantment in the place. No matter how often I enter the garden, I sense once again its particular charm.

From this central point, paths wind away in both directions, some paved in coral limestone, some edged with chunks of the rock. Palms are all about: coconut, areca, fishtail, Washington, and the native thatch palm, looking like a taller, slimmer version of the cabbage palm. Everywhere there is a prevailing atmosphere of exotic tropical growth.

Being curious as to how the effect was produced, I had noted the ingredients in several places: the Caribbean Gardens, the Sunken Garden at Fairchild, the Parrot and Monkey Jungles, as well as here. Palms are standard, of course, particularly the fishtail palm. Bamboo is likely—it is here—along with the four distinctive members of the banana family: bananas themselves, traveler's tree, heliconias (with striking bananalike leaves), and the showy bird-of-paradise. Near them is a cordyline, related to the monkey palm, with red swordlike leaves. It's often used, I find, and so are those two most exotic of all tropical vines, the philodendron and monstera. The latter is also called "ceriman," but I prefer "monstera," for a monster is what it seems, looking as if it would smother whatever it climbed upon. Here it is sprawled over the side and top of a grotto, and I can hear a waterfall inside, echoing within its stony chamber.

Flowers appear only occasionally, although some, particularly the hybrid hibiscus, are quite. astonishingly beautiful, but for the most part they stand out as single blossoms in the overwhelming mass of green, and I am more aware of leaf color and shape than of bloom. What dominates is red of croton leaf, purple of oyster plant, yellow green of feathery asparagus, and deeper green of fern. In one small area there is a desert planting, and here are added blue-green of aloe and agave, the rounded prickly shape of opuntia, and the cactuslike growth of night-blooming cereus.

My last look at the garden is from a bridge of coral rock. Now I can see the fountain in the grotto with a pool at its feet, full of pink and blue water lilies. Out of the shadows flutters a black and yellow zebra butterfly—a fittingly exotic insect for an exotic tropical garden.

Fairchild Tropical Garden

The Fairchild Tropical Garden with its eighty-five acres of tropical plants (the largest such garden in the United States) is understandably the most impressive and to me the most beautiful of the parks and gardens of this chapter. Much of the effectiveness of the planting is due to its arrangement, with big groups of trees or shrubbery separated by wide and rolling vistas of lawn. I stood in front of the main pavilion one day looking down at the two lagoons, one behind the other. Just in front was a wide grassy area with the towering wands of various agaves at one side, and a group of cycads nearby, backed by two beautiful palms. In the distance, skillful planting had achieved the effect of a forest. It was a beautiful piece of landscaping, unmarred by any suggestion of artificiality, or undue edging, trimming, or exact geometrical placement.

The scientific aspect of the garden is ever-present in the background. Much of the grouping is based on families, so that one can compare the different trees of the pea family, for instance, with all the specimens right at hand. I have done this, myself, to be sure that I had poinciana, woman's tongue, wild tamarind, and Indian tamarind properly separated. Viewed together, in spite of a general similarity, I could see the flat-topped shape of the royal poinciana, the extreme laciness of wild tamarind (quite common on the Keys), the coarser look of woman's tongue with its long, twisted seedpods, and the shorter leaves and very much smaller pods of Indian tamarind. The stubby pod of this last tree is marked by two or three constrictions, as if it had swelled around the seeds.

Because of the size of the garden, the conducted tour on a motorized tram train is an invaluable introduction. After that, one can seek out areas of particular interest.

The main specialities at Fairchild are palms and cycads, and the 500 kinds of palms that have been gathered here make it the largest collection on the United States mainland. For the most part, though, as in the Caribbean Gardens, I make little effort to remember names. There are some interesting trees which the guide points out, calling attention particularly to the bottle palms, but I am likely to come back only to those commonly planted. One of my favorite spots in this section is the Bailey Glade with a long rectangular pool, lined for its entire length with the extremely graceful Chinese fan palm. The Bailey Glade was named for Liberty Hyde Bailey, one of our leading American botanists. Among many other things, Mr. Bailey wrote the *Manual of Cultivated Plants,* and without this work, my task of sorting out the exotic plants of Florida would have been far greater than it was.

Cycads are a very interesting group, standing halfway between ferns and flowering plants. In the Mesozoic, the era of the dinosaurs, they were widely scattered all over the globe. Today, only a fraction of their original number is left and these are confined to the warmer parts of the earth. Again, as with palms, Fairchild has assembled an impressive number, only one genus, however, having native species in Florida. This one is zamia or, as it is popularly called, coontie. Many cycads are of tremendous size and look like trunkless or nearly trunkless palms, with long feathery fronds. Compared to these, the coontie is unimpressive, resembling a fern more than a palm, and with an odd brown cone in the center of the tuft. The coontie was enormously important to the Florida Indians and even to some of the early white settlers, since the starchy flour obtained from its root was the basis for their bread.

I will mention some of the other outstanding collections briefly. That of bignonacea is considered the best in the world. Here belong the familiar trumpet vine, a plant of the temperate zone, and the tropical jacaranda, a tree with beautiful lavender flowers. The vines, for the most part trained to grow over a pergola, are often spectacular, and include a rare purple allamanda as well as the yellow, blue thunbergia, pink pandorea, and masses of bougainvillea. Later on, herald's trumpet will add its fragrant white flowers to this section.

Many of the smaller flowering trees are grouped along a bank. Here are bauhinia, the golden shower tree, double hibiscus, and the Chinese hat plant—all familiar to southern gardeners. The larger trees with conspicuous blossoms: the African tulip tree, the kapok or silk cotton tree, the geiger tree, the coral tree, and others are with their respective families. There is usually a generous amount of bloom in the garden throughout the year, with some of the showy legumes coming into flower later in the season. I think particularly of the rich buttercup flowers, veined in dark red, of the yellow shower tree (May to October) and of the lovely Ceylon senna or red cassia that blooms in October. Glory colvillea, another legume from Madagascar, has orange-red flowers in the fall.

Other good collections are of philodendrons, figs, ground covers, Bahamian and native Florida plants, bromeliads, and orchids. The latter two are now housed in a new building and beautifully displayed, but since I am writing of the out-of-doors, I must slight them.

Although I haven't made use of the word, there are definite ecological zones on land as well as in or by the sea. Ecology means simply the study of the whole environment—soil, climate, and plant and animal life—and their effect upon each other. In the chapters on marine life I stressed these small worlds and how closely their life was intermeshed. In a sense, we were looking at different ecological units in the Caribbean Gardens, and some of these exist at Fairchild.

The Sunken Garden, like the Rock Garden at Bayfront Park, is full of lush tropical jungle plants. Characteristic of an even damper junglelike area is the live oak rain forest, kept moist with water sprayed from the ground and from the trees. Here again are huge philodendrons of many kinds, monstera, heliconias, tree ferns, other ground ferns, and the curious staghorn ferns growing on the trunks of trees. Epiphytes crowd upon the limbs, there are sprays of a lavender dendrobium, and another lovely pink orchid hangs down directly in front of me.

In the desert planting, strangely-shaped rocks and sandy mounds form a background for aloes, agaves, yuccas, opuntias, and other cacti, and for crown of thorns and cathedral bells. Poinsettia, like crown of thorns, is a euphorbia and could have been included here, but is grown in another part of the garden. Farther along is a mangrove swamp, bordering a lake in which coots are diving. Both are distinctive units—or, to be really technical—groups of units or niches, for one can easily subdivide the lake and swamp communities, but for our purposes it's enough to treat each as an entity. The lake includes not only coots and other water birds, but freshwater plants, fishes, crustaceans, frogs, snails, and aquatic insects. Near the mangrove swamp is a small sample of hammock growth, providing a characteristic world of its own, but we will look more closely at the life of mangrove swamp and of Florida hammock in later chapters.

I have mentioned, for the most part, only the plant life. In a natural environment, each of these worlds would be particularly attractive to specific insects, reptiles, birds, and mammals. For example, I would be almost sure to find a yucca moth in the desert planting if any yuccas were in bloom; and if I had time for a careful study, I'd certainly find other insects that belonged to the area, along with some ground lizards, no doubt. Red-bellied woodpeckers and Bahamian anoles are conspicuous on the palms. Warblers and zebra butterflies usually fly in and out of the deep shadows of the rain forest. Where there are flowers and more sun, a peacock butterfly may often be seen hovering over the blossoms.

What belongs where, and how one plant or animal affects another, can be a most absorbing study, but, aside from a few illustrations, the details are beyond the limits of this book. I shall, however, comment briefly on some of the birds of these parks. The most striking fact, again, is the greater number normally found where there is native growth. The Indian coral tree at Bayfront, with its flock of black-throated blues, was an exception. So were the Philippine pithecellobiums on the sea lane, although these are closely related to native plants. But on the whole, birds are most numerous in a natural environment where they can find the fruit, seeds, and insects that are part of their normal diet.

Because of this, aside from robins, blue jays, mockingbirds, cardinals, woodpeckers, and the non-native spotted-breasted oriole, I have never found too much on the lawns and shrubbery at Fairchild. The lagoons provide more of a natural habitat with native water weeds, frogs, crustaceans, fishes, and insects, and here one may well find a little blue heron wading slowly through the shallows, tilting his head from side to side at intervals for a better view of what lies below. From a distance, the little blue heron seems to be a uniform slaty color. Quite often another blue heron is feeding not far away, but while his size is the same, he has a white throat followed by a pinkish streak that extends down to the belly. All of his lower underparts are a snowy white. This is the Louisiana heron, Audubon's "Lady-of-the-Water." We may see him stalking along near the shore, extending one wing and whirling about, or again running suddenly ahead. The much larger great blue heron (ten inches bigger than the other two) has a statuesque look, standing immobile, with one leg raised, watching for the telltale ripple of a fish.

Swimming on the lake are coots, a common gallinule with its striking red bill, and a couple of lesser scaups. The last are fairly common bay and pond ducks, the male having a head, chest, and tail that are conspicuously darker than the rest of the body. Peterson says that on the water, it appears to be "black at both ends and white in the middle." The brownish female has a white area on the face around the base of the bill. This duck is the hunters' "little bluebill."

Matheson Hammock and Simpson Park

Matheson Hammock, a Dade County park, adjoins Fairchild Tropical Garden, and here the planting is largely native. During the morning hours, people are more likely to be gathered on the beach or at the marina, rather than on the nature trails or at the picnic grounds, and birds seem to occur in considerably greater number and variety than at Fairchild. The only exception is in the heart of the hammock where heavy growth and darkness discourage bird activity.

Near the shore in the mangroves, I find red-bellied woodpeckers, catbirds, great-crested flycatchers, and cardinals. On the edge of the hammocks, eating the berries of a strangler fig, are more catbirds and great numbers of myrtle warblers. Bird calls and swift flight can be seen and heard all through the grove of live oaks. I am sure there are more than I have identified, but I know that the trees hold cardinals, blue jays, flickers, red-bellied woodpeckers, mockingbirds, and palm, myrtle, and black-throated blue warblers. Close to 200 different birds have been counted in Fairchild and Matheson, but this has been since their establishment and the result of observations all through the year. I would certainly have found more had I gone early in the morning and at a time when I wasn't also thinking of plants.

Live oak groves are generally apt to provide good birding. Many insects find shelter in their rough bark, and even more crowd into the protecting leaves of their epiphytes. Rain water often collects in the leaf bases of bromeliads and this draws mosquito wrigglers and other kinds of insect larvae. Small tree frogs usually make their home here, and chameleons are likely to whisk in and out of the ferns, wild pineapples, and orchids. With such possibilities for food, it's understandable that birds flock to these trees.

The nature trails at Matheson Hammock Park wind through the heart of the hammock with the remarkable plant assemblage characteristic of these "tree islands" of South Florida. Hammocks will be described more fully in Chapter Ten, but I will note here that one of the best examples of a hammock is to be found in the Charles

Torrey Simpson Memorial Park right in Miami—the entrance is at S.W. 17th Road and Miami Avenue. Here, contained within a few blocks, is one of the most unusual parks of this region—a piece of "wilderness" preserved within the boundaries of a great city. Too few know it. The Gumbo Limbo Trail in the Everglades National Park and Matheson Hammock are often full of visitors, while I have almost always had the Simpson Park entirely to myself—a fact which greatly enhances its atmosphere.

A Scattering of Parks

It was in the live oak grove that I found most of the birds in the Hugh Taylor Birch State Park at Fort Lauderdale. This park also has much native planting, although it's been invaded by far too many casuarinas, a tree in which birds generally show little interest. I think it's because casuarinas dominate the place that I find the Cape Florida State Park a disappointment insofar as birds go. (It has other attractions, of course: a historic lighthouse, good fishing, and a beautiful beach.) Virginia Key has a small park in conjunction with its beach. Here it was buttonwood—old, gnarled, and in grotesque shapes—that drew birds. A flock of parulas and black-throated blues was all over it. Late in March the intense fragrance of citrus bloom at Redland Fruit and Spice Park (248th Street near Princeton) brings in many insects, and these, together with ripe fruit on other trees, makes the place highly attractive to birds, with such unusual species as white-winged doves and lark-sparrows. The park is also well worth a visit for its native and exotic fruit trees, all well-labeled.

In this brief survey, I am aware of many parks that I have not described. There is a delightful little garden on the MacArthur Causeway given to Miami by the Japanese government as an example of Japanese garden landscaping, with many plants that are native to Japan. This is the real thing—far removed from many American imitations. (I had forgotten that the bayberrylike pittosporum came from that country until I saw it here, looking entirely right with its twisted branches.) There are arched bridges, waterways, a stone pagoda and sculptured lanterns, a teahouse, and an overall feeling of restful retreat and quiet such as I found in the Rock Garden at Bayfront Park.

Then there is Greynolds Park in northeast Miami, with a colony of scarlet ibises; Myakka River State Park near Sarasota, with great flights of herons and flocks of wild turkeys; and Highlands Hammock State Park near Sebring, with catwalks through the cypress swamp. One of the giants here, a laurel oak, is 800 years old and has a girth of 31 feet. It was at Highlands Hammock that I first saw an armadillo in the wild, lumbering along by the roadside. Few animals seem more improbable than this prehistoric-looking armored creature. I also found here my first and only scrub jay, a big blue and gray bird without the crest or the conspicuous black and white markings of the blue jay, and finally it was here that I first looked upon a sandhill crane, the only crane that's at all common in this country. (Almost everyone knows of the battle to save the rare whooping crane—but that bird is found only in Texas and northwestern Canada, with a narrow migration route between the two areas.) The sandhill cranes were not actually in the park, but a ranger directed us to a nearby field where a little group could be seen feeding. If the armadillo seems prehistoric, this long-legged three-foot bird looks as if it belonged in Africa, and it was rather exciting to realize we had such an imposing native. From its size, sand-gray color, and bare red cap, the sandhill crane can hardly be mistaken for anything else.

More parks and gardens could be mentioned, for I have pleasant memories of a great number, but this should serve as a fair sampling and, I hope, provide more of an understanding and appreciation of all of these South Florida areas, whether specifically described or not.

Common and Scientific Names

African tulip tree: *Spathodea campanulata* Beauv.
aloe (true aloe): *Aloe barbadensis* Mill. (*Aloe vera* L.)
anthurium: *Anthurium andreanum* Lind.
Bahamian anole: *Anolis distichus distichus* Cope
baobab (bottle tree): *Adansonia digitata* L.
bird of paradise: *Strelitzia reginae* Banks
buttonbush: *Cephalanthus occidentalis* L.
buttonwood: *Conocarpus erectus* L.
cathedral bells: *Kalanchoe pinnata* (Lam.) Persoon (*Bryophyllum pinnatum* (Lam.) Kurz) (an air plant)

ceriman: *Monstera deliciosa* Liebm.

Ceylon senna (red cassia): *Cassia marginata* Roxb. (*Cassia roxburghii* De Cand.)

Chinese hat plant: *Holmskioldia sanguinea* Retz

coral tree: *Erythrina variegata* var. *orientalis* (L.) Merr.

dwarf poinciana: *Poinciana pulcherrima* L.

frangipani (red plumeria): *Plumeria rubra* L.

glory colvillea: *Colvillea racemosa* Bojer

herald's trumpet: *Beaumontia grandiflora* (Roxb.) Wall.

Indian tamarind: *Tamarindus indica* L.

kalanchoe: *Kalanchoe fedtschenkoi* Hamet & Perr.

leather fern: *Acrostichum danaeaefolium* Langsd. & Fisch.

pentas: *Pentas lanceolata* (Forsk.)

podranea: *Podranea ricasoliana* (Tanf.) Sprague

powder puff tree: *Calliandra haematocephala* Hassk.

prickly pear: *Opuntia moniliformis* Haw. (*Opuntia ferox* Willd.)

purple allamanda: *Allamanda violacea* Gardn. & Field

shell ginger: *Alpinia speciosa* (Wendl.) K. Schum.

staghorn fern: *Platycerium bifurcatum* (Cav.) C. Chr.

stiff-leaved wild pine (cardinal wild pine): *Tillandsia fasciculata* Sw.

thunbergia (sky vine): *Thunbergia grandiflora* Roxb.

ti plant: *Cordyline australis* Hook. f.

tree ferns: *Cyathea australis* (R. Br.) Copel; *Cibotium splendens* (Gaud.) Krajina (two of the tree ferns at Fairchild)

wild tamarind: *Lysiloma bahamensis* Benth.

yellow shower tree: *Cassia beareana* Holmes

References

Barrett, Mary Franklin. *Common Exotic Trees of South Florida.* Gainesville: University of Florida Press, 1956. 414 pp. O.P.

Neal, Marie C. *In Gardens of Hawaii.* Honolulu: Bishop Museum Press, 1965. 924 pp. In spite of the title, this is an excellent general reference work on tropical and subtropical plants.

Part III
Inland Trails

Typical of the Florida cypress swamp is the limpkin, shown here with the empty shells of pomacea, the apple snail, its favorite food. Although uncommon birds, limpkins are also found in marshy areas throughout South Florida.

Previous page:
Spanish moss curtains the foreground in this view of the Peace River, a stream flowing from Lake Hancock (at the northern edge of our area) southward through heavy jungle to Charlotte Harbor, where it enters the Gulf of Mexico.

9

The Cypress Swamp

The bald cypress, and the life that has grown up around it, is the story of this chapter—and it will lead us into the remote past, for cypresses had their beginning at the very end of the Mesozoic, the Age of Reptiles. Cypress and sequoia came into the world more or less together. They are related plants and probably had a common ancestor. Both were spread widely over the Northern Hemisphere throughout much of the Cenozoic (certainly from the Miocene on), and the buried remains of bald cypresses can be found today in peat bogs in Maine and New Hampshire. Undoubtedly they were growing in New England during one of the interglacial stages, probably a recent one.

There is something very moving about the near extinction of any plant or animal that has for centuries been widespread. Cycads and gingkos once nearly covered the earth and were among its most conspicuous plants. Cycads, as we have seen, are now merely a remnant of that overwhelming abundance, and gingkos no longer grow anywhere in the wild. They were followed as dominant plants by sequoias and cypresses, and these in their turn were dethroned—sequoias being limited now to the coasts of Oregon and California and the mountains of California, bald cypresses today living primarily in the coastal belt of the South Atlantic states and along the Gulf coast. I have seen cypresses as far north as the Pocomoke Swamp of Maryland, and some finger through Tennessee and Kentucky into Indiana and southern Illinois, and into Oklahoma, Arkansas, and

Missouri, but the typical cypress growth is to be found from the Carolinas down to Florida and along the Gulf in Alabama, Louisiana, Mississippi, and Texas. A related species is found in Mexico and another in China, but with these two exceptions, there are no other native taxodiums left in the world today, and the millions of acres of bald cypress that once grew in the southeast are now sadly reduced.

The tree is a stately and beautiful one, commonly reaching 50 to 80 feet in the South, at times towering as high as 150 feet. For the first 30 to 40 feet in a mature tree, the trunk is a straight column unbroken by any branches. Then high in the air, the limbs reach out, sometimes horizontally, sometimes drooping. Short yellow-green needles cover the tree except in winter—as I've said it's deciduous— and a thin veil of green creeps over the younger growth in mid-February, resembling the early delicate green that first touches our weeping willows in the North, then brushes the tops of the forest trees and spreads like a film through the underbrush. In the South, with its persistent year-round greenery, that echo of our northern spring is very welcome.

The bald cypress often grows right in the water and is one of the few trees with wood tough enough to withstand such constant wetting. Flaring buttresses spread out like skirts, and cypress "knees"—odd, conical growths covered with bark, though without branches or leaves, rise up from the roots whenever the parent tree is normally surrounded by water. To date their function has not been established. When the bark is removed, a satiny undersurface is exposed, and polished "knees," in a variety of fanciful shapes, are often to be found in souvenir shops.

In winter, when the tree stands bleak and bare, many times half-smothered, it would seem, in Spanish moss, it has a curiously desolate look—like an ancient skeleton. The fact that everything else is green gives it the appearance of death. Most cypresses are not dead, of course, since they do attain great age. Comparatively small trees with a diameter of only 20 inches may be 200 years old. One giant at Corkscrew, whose head was wrenched off by Hurricane Donna but whose base is surrounded by the boardwalk, is estimated at 700 years. Many others there have reached from 400 to 600 years, making them among the oldest trees in eastern North America. The oldest known taxodium on our continent, one at Tule, Mexico, is thought to be between 2,000 and 4,000 years old.

Today the best known cypress swamp is that of the Corkscrew Swamp Sanctuary, preserved for us through the efforts of the National Audubon Society, but this is by no means the only one. Okefenokee Swamp in Georgia is another magnificent example of this type of watery forest. The Cypress Gardens were built in the remains of an old swamp; handsome trees can be found at the Highlands Hammock State Park, and a patch of cypress swamp was included in the Caribbean Gardens. More cypresses can be found in the Everglades National Park and along that part of Alligator Alley that lies in Collier County, while a good part of the Tamiami Trail runs through scrub cypress. Motorists traveling the Sunshine State Parkway may also enjoy the beauty of these trees.

The world of the cypress swamp is also the world of heron, ibis, and anhinga; of coot, gallinule, and pied-billed grebe; of barred owl, pileated woodpecker, and the swamp-loving warblers. The Tamiami Trail, between Miami and Royal Palm Hammock, is often a birding adventure, for when the roadbed for the Trail was constructed, a ditch was dug at one side to provide drainage and furnish stone for the road. Much of this limestone was fossiliferous and the building of the Trail revealed the "Tamiami Formation," dating probably from the late Miocene, but of this I shall have more to say later on. The ditch, or canal, drew water birds, particularly during the dry season when the water level dropped in the Everglades and in the cypress swamp. And thus it is that in winter one can drive for miles along the Trail with a constant array of beautiful birds just a few feet away.

Some of these, I hope, by now are familiar. Among the first to be seen are coots, those little black fellows with white bills that were swimming at the Caribbean Gardens and at Fairchild. They are abundant here, nodding their heads as they paddle, diving for water plants with a little upward jump before they go down, occasionally taking flight, and pattering along the surface of the water before being airborne. Occasionally a common gallinule can be seen with the coots, but more often their companions are pied-billed grebes, squat little brownish birds only nine inches long (the coot is twelve), with chickenlike bills. The grebes are constantly diving, too.

On the edge of the canal are herons, and my first one today is the great blue, standing hunched together on a log. He is so close that I can see his white head, with the black crest streaming out behind. At a distance, none of this shows and the bird seems a uniform slaty-blue.

As I approach, he lifts his magnificent great wings and sails effortlessly overhead. The great blue is one of our commonest herons, not only in the South, but along northern lakes and rivers as well. Often he lingers along the Delaware River until late in November or even into December.

Snowy egrets are common, and many are perched high in young cypress trees, their feathers startlingly white against the dark limbs. Every so often I see one wading in the canal—there are stretches where half a dozen herons are in sight at once. Here is a snowy, lifting his conspicuous yellow feet daintily out of the water as he stalks up and down, while a Louisiana heron, in deeper water, is fishing with outstretched neck and bill close to the surface. A second Louisiana runs through the shallows hoping to stir up fish. Beyond, a little blue heron is flicking his wings very slightly as he eyes the water. There in the water is another snowy, and then a statuesque common egret moves slowly and deliberately through a patch of yellow pond lilies. He holds his head so utterly still that it looks as if he were balancing something on it.

The different egrets are easily recognized: the larger common or American egret (thirty-two inches in length) has a yellow bill and black legs; the snowy is twelve inches smaller and has a black bill, black legs, and yellow feet. The cattle egret, a land rather than a water bird, is less frequently seen along the canal and can be readily distinguished by his small size—smaller even than that of the snowy. This relative newcomer to Florida has a yellow bill, pinkish or yellow legs, and, in breeding plumage, pinkish or buffy-orange on his head, breast, and shoulders. Like the great blue, some of the common egrets go far into the northern states to breed.

Bordering the canal are the cypresses—miles of them. On the edge of the cypress swamp, they stand in the midst of saw grass. Farther along, scrub willows are also in evidence, with an occasional coco plum, a low tree with rounded, glossy, somewhat leathery leaves. Most of the cypresses are dwarfed and they are adorned with bunch moss, an air plant similar to Spanish moss (the two are closely related), that grows in a ball or bunch.

Around Willie's Indian Camp the trees are larger, and wood storks by the hundred are perched on the limbs. They are so spectacular it's impossible to pass them by, and I pull off the road for a better look

Bird books still call this extraordinary-looking bird a wood ibis, although admitting he's a stork; but anyone tutored by Alexander Sprunt, Jr. wouldn't dare use any name other than that of "wood stork," so a "wood stork" he shall be in these pages. He's a big creature—almost as large as the great blue heron (his wing span is five feet), with a long, very heavy bill, quite like that of his European relative who is so well-known for his baby-fetching activities. His head is bare and wattled, something like a vulture's; the body and forepart of the wing are white, the remainder black. When perching, he seems largely white except for his dark stilt legs, dark head, and bill. In flight, however, the black areas in the wings are conspicuous.

With the wood storks are common and snowy egrets and a few white ibises. In fact, my impression is of a tremendous flock of snowy white birds. The white ibis is smaller than the wood stork and has a red face, red downcurved bill, and red legs. Both the wood stork and the ibises fly with outstretched necks. Herons, on the other hand, hold their heads in, curving their necks to do so. With a little practice, one can tell whether it's a heron or an ibis in flight, even from a distance.

As I proceed along the Trail, the canal is full of chunks of limestone—it looks like fossil coral—and all the herons are perched upon these rocks. Overhead, kingfishers rest on the wires, watching the water quite as intently as the herons. With their big heads and bills, ragged crests, and blue-gray color, they are unmistakable. Mile after mile we go, always with the herons and kingfishers by the canal, always with cypresses intermixed with live oaks, palmettos, occasionally pine, all with an understory of ferns and shrubby growth.

Sometimes I see an anhinga, or snakebird, with wings outstretched to dry. Another name for him is "water turkey," because of his long black tail. "Snakebird," though, probably fits him best, for his neck is long and serpentine. Anhingas are distantly related to cormorants, and they have much the look of a cormorant except for the longer neck, longer reddish bill, and silvery patches on their long black wings.

I come to another halt in a big cypress head not quite a mile west of Monroe Station. A cypress "head" or "dome" is a rounded stand of cypresses that has been nourished by a pool of water often not visible to the passerby. Here there is also palmetto and live oak, and the oak is covered with bunch moss and wild pineapple. The giant cypresses, however, shrouded in curtains of Spanish moss, dominate the scene. At their feet is water so dark that it seems to lie on a black bottom except where the glinting of sunlight turns it to burnished copper. Long strands of green threadlike algae drift at the edge of this woodland pond, and farther out are great masses of lavender water hyacinth, blue pickerelweed, naiads, and other water plants. In their midst a green heron crouches motionless, while on a branch above him, equally still, is a common egret. Swaying fingers of moss trail down beside the herons, just brushing the water. There is a feeling of age-old mystery here, of a timelessness that goes back into the far reaches of the past. I am reminded of the ancient lineage of the cypresses—from the end of the Mesozoic—and of the fact that many of the birds of the cypress swamp—the herons and ibises, the anhinga, the kingfisher, the coots, and gallinules—are almost as old, having evolved either at the end of the Mesozoic or at the very beginning of the Cenozoic.

For a moment I am carried back to that dim early world, but then the notes of smaller and, generally speaking, more modern birds break in. The cardinal, Carolina wren, and white-eyed vireo are singing, and these belong in the swamp today as much as the heron and ibis. A yellowthroat with black mask flies chipping from a clump of leather ferns. A gnatcatcher springs from a branch in pursuit of an insect, and a palm warbler teeters on a twig. The calls, the swift movement of these little birds, are in sharp contrast to the brooding stillness of heron and cypress. And then out of the depths of the swamp comes the bellow of an alligator, and this, too, has a primeval quality.

The Corkscrew Swamp Sanctuary, maintained by the National Audubon Society, is less awesome and less mysterious than one might expect, for whenever I have been there, an almost constant parade of people broke the stillness, with women's heels clicking along the 5,800 feet of boardwalk, and frequent exclamations over the alligators. In the early morning I am sure it is quieter, although one can't go in too early since the park is closed at night to avoid possible encounters with bears and cougars. Here, at least, some of the larger carnivores can still be found, while bobcats and raccoons are abundant, although rarely seen during the day.

Corkscrew is actually a "cypress strand" as distinct from a "head."

A strand is a long narrow band of the trees, bordered usually by wet prairies and pine flatlands. The entrance to the sanctuary, in fact, is adjacent to the pinelands, and the first boardwalk crosses the prairie. The Corkscrew strand is the largest stand of virgin cypress left in the world. It's composed of bald cypress, the giants of the swamp, and the lower, slenderer, pond cypress, now considered a variety or subspecies of the bald cypress.

The best way to see Corkscrew is to allow a full day for it. On my first trip—a tour led by Alexander Sprunt, Jr.—we had to leave for lunch and the time allotted was too brief. Nowadays I take lunch along so that I can proceed at a leisurely pace.

Once when I was dawdling in this way, I lingered long enough at the gatehouse to see wild turkeys come out of the pines and pick up corn at my feet. They were definitely turkeys, but much trimmer than our domestic fowl. I am told they are no longer resident, but it is to be hoped they will come back.

I turned from the turkeys to the pineland with its typical growth of slash pines and saw palmettos. Wax myrtle is growing here, too, and on the floor of the pinewoods I find coreopsis and a small rudbeckia, looking like a black-eyed Susan. There are a few cabbage palms and a red-belly is talking loudly from one of them, while a palm warbler scolds near by. Behind them, a flicker drums on one of the pines and then we hear the sharp, distinctive call of a red-cockaded woodpecker. This rather small woodpecker has the most sober coloring of any of his tribe. The red cockade is there but hard to see, and what is generally visible is a black head, a "ladder" back of black and white bars, and a white eye patch. One of the less common of the woodpeckers, he is limited to the southern pinelands, and I have never found him except here. Many naturalists come to Corkscrew especially for this bird, and many, also, fail to find him, for it usually takes leisurely wandering through the pine woods, scanning every tree trunk for an inconspicuous form, listening for a sharp, unfamiliar cry. There is an extra dividend for all of this. If you have looked over a lot of pines, you will discover another of the rare birds that breeds here, the brown-headed nuthatch, also small and sober-looking, and generally found in the southern pines along with the red-cockaded woodpecker. His call is also distinctive—"kit-kit-kit," or a squeaky, twittery, "ki-dee-dee." Once my ears are attuned to the two cries, I often find that the woodpeckers and nuthatches are all around.

From the pinelands, we go back to the main trail and the wet prairie. Grassland stretches away on both sides of the boardwalk, broken only by pondweeds: duckweed in watery areas, arrowhead, pickerelweed, green arum, cattails, and the like—and the shrubby wax myrtle. This last I have mentioned before, and it grows so abundantly in the South it should be better known. I have generally found it as a shrub, although it can be a small tree, and I know it best by its narrow lance-shaped leaves, carrying a few widely spaced teeth toward the tip and dotted with orange flecks on the underside. When I can find the small berries growing close to the branch, much like bayberry (the two belong to the same genus), I am sure of it. The leaves are a shiny green and the bark a silvery gray.

Overhead, blue sky reaches away into the distance. Vultures circle on high, and a wood stork soars above the tree tops. I have come from the closed-in world of the pines, and ahead stands the gray mass of the cypress forest, but for a moment I have the spaciousness of the prairie, even though it's a little one. A fox squirrel is running along the railing now, pausing to look anxiously at me with his extraordinary big eyes. He seems to be asking for food, but there are "Do Not Feed" signs posted.

And now within minutes we are engulfed by the cypress swamp. This first stretch of trees (mostly pond cypress) has little moss, but the air plants—wild pineapple and orchids—make heavy bunches, some as bulky and big as crows' nests. Every so often I find the flaming bract of the cardinal wild pine. February is early for them but they are beginning to come out. The orchids at Corkscrew are among the most interesting flowers, although the time to see most of them is later in the year. Today, only the delicate brown epidendrum is in bloom, and I'd have missed the half-inch greenish-brown flowers completely if a ranger hadn't pointed them out. I can spot the cowhorn or cigar orchid because of its curious long pseudobulbs up to a foot in length, looking very much like a pointed cigar or, when bent, like a cow's horn.

Many tropical orchids have thickened leaves, and some have developed swollen stems in order to store food and water against the dry season. The "pseudobulb" is this swollen stem. Often it appears to be just the swollen base of a leaf, but in the cigar orchid, the pseudobulb has a leaf only when young, and the odd "cigars" are quite noticeable. Later on—in March and April—great bunches of flowers will be produced on a stalk that may be from three to five feet long. While the individual blossoms are small, the whole effect is very showy, with the frilled yellow orchids spotted and splashed in shades of red and brown.

When I entered the sanctuary I asked where I might see the whippoorwill. There are numbers along the railing for use with the "Self-Guided Tour." These numbers help to place the sleeping whippoorwill and various bird nests. The whippoorwill is so motionless and so well camouflaged by his mottled feathers that one needs to know exactly where to look for him, even though he's resting on a limb at eye level only a short distance away.

These birds are not limited to swamps nor to the South, although one is commonly found at Corkscrew, and I have learned to look for them in such areas. Many a time I've gone to the Pocomoke Swamp (that northern outpost of the cypress swamp in the Delmarva Peninsula) to hear the whippoorwills calling at night and to listen to the hooting of a barred owl. The barred owl is here at Corkscrew, too, and since these owls begin to nest in late February, I hear a short note every so often, even though it is daytime, and I may see the bird perched on a branch peering down.

But neither whippoorwill nor owl is as good a find, nor as dramatic, as the pileated woodpecker. A heavy drumming on wood, a flickerlike call, or even the sound of a big bird moving through the underbrush reveals him. Often I have found him just a short distance from the boardwalk, working on a fallen tree. The pileated has a red crest—a magnificent one—above his black and white head, and a solid black back.

Today whippoorwill and woodpecker are in the first-numbered stretch, between three and nineteen. As I leave this behind, the forest opens out and the boardwalk crosses a lake filled with water lettuce. There are such masses of this floating water weed that it seems like solid matter—a kind of green prairie, not a lake. Massive cypresses ring the pond, with gray banners of moss that sway in the wind. It's often windy at Corkscrew (or has been when I've been there) and the trees have been talking all along the way. Near at hand are pond or custard apples, gnarled and twisted trees with leathery leaves, trees moss-hung and bearing orchids. It was on one of these that I saw the brown epidendrum and a tiny gnatcatcher darting in and out. A yellowthroat is poised on the broad leaf of a pickerelweed and a white-eye is singing not far away. This was my trio from the cypress head and they are all here again. The green heron is here, too. I see him at the far end of the lake, surrounded by water lettuce, crouching low, motionless. He isn't usually green (another case of a misleading name). His head and all but the front of his short neck are dark red, his back is dark blue, and his legs—seen in flight—are yellow or orange.

On the other side of the boardwalk, alligators lie basking on logs. One huge old fellow has drawn the attention of most of the visitors. Beyond him is a stately blue heron and, always in the background, the cypresses. Almost no water is visible, but close at hand there are masses of pickerelweed and arrowhead. There is a tropical luxuriance here, with custard apple intergrown with red bay (one of the laurel family), the two intertwined with woodbine and bullbrier, and resurrection fern growing on the limbs of the custard apple. (Resurrection fern shrivels up in dry weather, but springs up green and beautiful at the first wetting.) Boston fern surrounds the base of the custard apple and even grows a little way up the trunk. Farther along is leather fern framing a big tussock, while on the tussock itself is strap fern with its long, arching, swordlike blades.

The walk leaves the open world of the lettuce lake and reenters the dark scenery of the cypress swamp. On every side are big trunks, flaring at the base, standing in water. Ferns are abundant: Boston, royal, swamp, leather, many others. There is heavy undergrowth of young red maple, pop ash, buttonbush, wax myrtle, elder, and always the dark-brown, mysterious-looking water. At times the heavy root of a strangler fig hangs down beside the railing. Here in a small tree, lying along a slender branch is a beautiful little snake, half-hidden among the leaves. It's a harmless yellow rat snake, a young one, not much thicker than a pencil, with a handsome pattern of thin dark lines on a tan background. From deeper in the swamp come the ringing notes of a Carolina wren.

Farther along, there is another lettuce lake edged with masses of swamp lily as well as pickerelweed. In the background are swamp maples and custard apples intermingled with cypresses. In the middle of the lake a little blue heron is walking right on the water lettuce, picking up insects and small fish, and a white ibis flies overhead. A wooden seat offers a chance to sit down, and I settle on it to watch quietly for what may come out. Because it's noontime, there is a lull in the stream of visitors. For a little while everything is still, and then casually a brown head with a long bill and fairly long neck sticks out from the pickerelweed. A brown body follows—it's about the size of the little blue heron—and the bill probes steadily in among the water weeds for snails. This is a limpkin, the last of the six birds I particularly hoped to find at Corkscrew. The herons, the wood stork, and the ibises are commonly seen beside the Tamiami Trail and close to the Alligator Alley. I have come upon the limpkin on the Tamiami Trail near the Shark River loop, and also along Route 78 on the northwestern side of Lake Okeechobee. The pileated woodpecker can sometimes be found in the Caribbean Gardens and I've seen one on Route 92 going to Marco. But Corkscrew is the place to be sure of limpkin and pileated woodpecker, and the only place in the South where I've seen the red-cockaded woodpecker, the brown-headed nuthatch, the whippoorwill, and the barred owl.

Normally Corkscrew Swamp Sanctuary is not a place for many different birds. It does have a spectacular rookery of wood storks—the largest in the United States—with as many as 4,700 pairs nesting here at times. And this sight, together with the six uncommon birds that I've mentioned, draws birders from all parts of the country.

The limpkin, meanwhile, has been coming nearer and nearer. I have been careful not to move nor to speak above a whisper, and the bird is either unaware of me or surprisingly fearless. For half an hour he probes for the big bullseye snail (pomacea), his favorite food. Every so often he finds one and eats it with apparent satisfaction. He comes so close that only the boardwalk and a couple of feet of water separate us, but then the tread of shoes on the boardwalk, voices, and laughter disturb him and he vanishes among the heavy leaves of pickerelweed and arrowhead.

As I continue on, an anhinga soars high over a moss-covered cypress. I know him from his long tail, outstretched neck, straight bill (an ibis's would be curved), and black color. A red-shouldered hawk screeches noisily. He, too, is flying somewhere overhead. I have heard his call throughout the day here in the swamp, and I am happy to know that he is still thriving in Florida. Ten or fifteen years ago we had red-shouldered hawks in eastern Pennsylvania, but pesticides and shooting have destroyed almost all of them. This is still the common big brown hawk of southern Florida.

There is another sound that I have heard off and on all day—the bellowing of a bull alligator, rousing to the feel of spring and the urge for mating. This, too, has a quality of belonging; it's in keeping with the ancient, primeval atmosphere of the cypress swamp.

I follow the trail, now, through more cypresses and ferns, with the occasional call of a white-eye, a cardinal's sharp chip, or the thin squeaky sound of a gnatcatcher. A "chameleon" runs along the railing and titmice fly through the lower growth of swamp maple and southern sweet bay. Sweet bay is one of the magnolias which later in the year will blossom with two-inch creamy white flowers that have a soapy fragrance. At marker "45" the wooden planking surrounds one of the greatest of all the giant cypresses—the 700-year-old patriarch that was killed by Hurricane Donna. Just beyond, the last section is barred off so that visitors won't disturb the nesting wood storks, but one can usually look off to the famous rookery and see the parent birds flying among the trees.

Their breeding season usually begins in November and activity around the nests continues into spring. Some years, however, this pattern is disturbed. One year when I was here, a severe drop in temperature killed the young birds, and it wasn't until late in the season that the parents started over again. Another year, because of drought and lack of food, many storks failed to nest. In 1970 there was too much water in the swamp, with the result that fish were not sufficiently concentrated to provide a ready supply for hungry nestlings. The storks must have sensed this (their young require quantities of food) and they didn't start breeding until mid-February. That time, I found, the big show was not at Corkscrew but on the Trail, where we must have seen a thousand storks along the way.

In 1968 the boardwalk ended at "56" and it was necessary to retrace one's steps, but the walk has been extended since then and one can now circle back to the entrance through a different part of the sanctuary. In 1970 I went back to Corkscrew to see this new section. The water was high, as I've said, and there weren't too many birds, but the swamp, with its narrow walk winding through the trees, had never seemed more beautiful.

Nowadays a spur leaves the boardwalk at "55," running some 300 yards to the right and ending in an observation tower that looks out over marshland. As I turn onto the new walk, a prairie warbler slips through the undergrowth at one side, now hiding behind some elder, now coming out onto a twig of pop ash. Some one ahead has just been lamenting the lack of birds—she was moving too quickly to see this—and I feel sorry.

Below me is the delicate white flower of an arrowhead, and on the water around it, myriads of tiny duckweeds, not much bigger than large pinheads. Farther along, a clump of thalia puts up huge long-stalked leaves. I took it to be pickerelweed until I noted the size of the leaves (one to three feet) and the rounded base. This is the conspicuous fire flag of the wetlands; in summer and fall it sends up lavender panicles on four- to ten-foot stems. The rest of the scenery is familiar: cypress, maple, red bay, leather ferns, moss-covered logs, ferns riding upon fallen trees. A gnatcatcher flicks from branch to branch; a yellowthroat looks at me from a cypress knee. The birds are here, but they are quiet today.

Now the walk runs through willow. I mount the observation platform and survey a tremendous sweep of saw grass, arrowhead, low scrubby willow—a section of the sanctuary I've never seen before. Later in the year swallow-tailed kites will soar above the marsh and the cypress swamp—as common a sight as the wood storks usually are in winter.

Returning to "55" on the original boardwalk, I turn left onto the new walk that will circle back. For awhile it is well-known territory: big cypresses first, then lower pond cypresses and more open growth, with a considerable amount of maple, red bay, and wax myrtle, until it emerges once again onto wet prairie—the same wet prairie that we crossed earlier near the entrance. I have been aware today of how much lichen there is on the trees—some the pale gray or whitish kind, but here where the pond cypress ends there are odd small patches of bright pink.

For some distance now the boardwalk runs along the edge of the prairie, and I can gaze into another ecological world: one of green algae and submerged pondweeds, with water lily pads floating on the surface, and half-inch fish darting from one shelter to another. An eight- or ten-inch bowfin, with long dorsal fin and a spot at the base of its tail, is herding some of the smaller fry, obviously guarding its young.

Scattered all over the prairie is pipewort—white buttonlike flowers on slender stalks—and, nearing the pinewoods at the end of the boardwalk, I am pleased to find purple butterworts with half-inch flowers easily recognized by their five deeply-cleft lavender petals. The leaves of butterwort have a sticky secretion to trap small insects, and the leaf margin can even roll over slightly to move an insect that has landed near the edge closer to the center. Once securely caught, the insect is dissolved by another secretion and absorbed by the plant. Sundews and pitcher plants are well known for their carnivorous habits, and butterworts can be added to this group. The last part of the walk winds through the pines over crushed Tamiami limestone, with Miocene fossil shells lying on either side of the roadway.

If we were circling the swamp in late spring, we would pause to look at swamp lilies and butterfly orchids (the latter greenish-brown, with a white lip adorned with a rosy center). In summer one of the most beautiful sights along the boardwalk would be the brilliant crimson flowers of swamp hibiscus, while later in the fall, there would be lovely shell orchids, partly yellow, partly dark purple or brown.

Whatever the season, though, and whether it be a good time for birds or not, the essential quality of Corkscrew remains, and anyone who recognizes and enjoys that atmosphere can never be disappointed in the cypress swamp.

Common and Scientific Names

Boston fern: *Nephrolepis exaltata* (L.) Schott
brown epidendrum: *Epidendrum anceps* Jacq.
bullbrier (chinaberry brier; catbrier): *Smilax bona-nox* L.
bullseye snail (apple snail): *Pomacea paludas* (Say)
bunch moss (ball moss): *Tillandsia recurvata* L.
butterfly orchid: *Epidendrum tampense* Lindl.
butterwort: *Pinguicula pumila* Michx.
cowhorn orchid (cigar orchid): *Cyrtopodium punctatum* (L.) Lindl.
crisped-leaf naiad: *Najas guadalupensis* (Spreng.) Magnus
Dominican cattail: *Typha domingensis* Pers.
fire flag: *Thalia geniculata* L.

Florida elderberry: *Sambucus simpsonii* Rehder
giant arrowhead: *Sagittaria lancifolia* L.
green arum: *Peltandra virginica* (L.) Kunth
pipewort: *Eriocaulon compressum* Lam.
pond cypress: *Taxodium distichum* var. *nutans* (Ait) Sweet
pop ash: *Fraxinum caroliniana* Mill.
royal fern: *Osmunda regalis* L.
rudbeckia (orange cone flower): *Rudbeckia fulgida* Ait.
shell orchid: *Epidendrum cochleatum* L.
southern pickerelweed: *Pontederia lanceolata* Nutt. (for many years it
     was assumed that there was just one species, *P. cordata* L., but
     now a southern species is recognized)
strap fern: *Campyloneuron phyllitidis* (L.) Presl.
swamp fern: *Blechnum serrulatum* Rich.
swamp hibiscus: *Hibiscus coccineus* Walt.
swamp lily (spider lily, ribbon lily): *Crinum americanum* L.
sweet bay: *Magnolia virginiana* L.
tickseed: *Coreopsis leavenworthii* T. & G.
valdivia duckweed: *Lemna valdiviana* Phil.
water lettuce (water bonnet): *Pistia stratioides* L.
wax myrtle: *Myrica cerifera* L.
woodbine (Virginia creeper): *Parthenocissus quinquefolia* (L.) Planch.
yellow pond lily: *Nuphar advena* R. Br.
yellow rat snake: *Elaphe obsoleta quadrivittata* (Holbrook)

References

"Corkscrew Swamp Sanctuary: A Self-guided Tour of the Board-
     walk." National Audubon Society, 1968. 28 pp.
Meyeriecks, Andrew J. "Diversity Typifies Heron Feeding." *Natural
     History* LXXI (No. 6, 1962).
Reid, George K., Zim, Herbert S., and Fichter, George S. *Pond Life.* A
     Golden Nature Guide. New York: Golden Press, 1967. 160 pp.
Robbins, Chandler S., Bruun, Bertel, and Zim, Herbert S. *Birds of
     North America.* A Golden Field Guide. New York: Golden
     Press, 1966. 340 pp.
Sprunt, Alexander, Jr. "Emerald Kingdom." *Audubon Magazine* 63
     (No. 1, 1961).
Sprunt, Alexander, Jr. *Florida Bird Life.* New York: Coward-McCann,
     1954. 527 pp.

Snowy egret

10
The Everglades

"The Everglades is a river of grass." This has been said so often, it seems trite to repeat it, but the newcomer to southern Florida may still expect (as I did once) woodland glades, or, if not that, tropical jungle. In short, a forest of some kind. Instead he finds grass—a seemingly endless sea of grass in the true Everglades—growing in a few inches to a couple of feet of water. The "grass," which is actually a sedge, is high and coarse, with cutting edges—hence the name "saw grass"—and it covers much of the central section of southern Florida. That part within Everglades National Park is big enough—almost 200 square miles—but it's only a fraction of what is properly considered "the Glades." The entire area today may cover 2,500,000 acres (it was once 3,000,000). And there is nothing else like it in the world.

Just what is this central section of southern Florida, and how did it come to have such marked characteristics? Quite simply, there is a broad but slight depression in the flatlands reaching from Lake Okeechobee to the southern coastline. The channel is irregular: it bulges out toward West Palm Beach and in places is seventy miles wide, although in general the width is about forty miles. A very gradual slope occurs—an average of less than three inches to a mile—and through this wide slough, as it should be called, occasional overflow from Lake Okeechobee used to spill out and then proceed at a very sluggish pace to the sea. Most of the flow, however, came from the summer rainfall, and through this means the whole area got a good wetting. During the winter—the dry season—water would gradually become concentrated in ponds, or smaller sloughs, within the big one. But each summer would normally bring the renewed flooding that was essential to the plants and animals of the area.

This is a broad general outline and there are details, of course, to be filled in. First let us look at its boundaries. To the north is the lake, and actually the Everglades surrounds Lake Okeechobee almost halfway up on either side. To the west lies the great cypress swamp of Collier County, along with sandy coastal plain; to the east is a narrower, sandy coastal belt; and to the south, in good part, mangrove swamps.

The floor of this tremendous slough, underlying a crust of peat and marl, is limestone—Miami oolite—formed in that shallow, subtropical sea which covered all of southern Florida some 100,000 to 150,000 years ago. As I mentioned earlier, the rock rises up in a low ridge along the southeastern edge, making a rim that stretches from Fort Lauderdale down to Long Pine Key in the National Park. Almost everywhere, the limestone is eroded and full of potholes. It was just 10,000 years ago, geologists speculate, that the shallow trough, stretching from Lake Okeechobee to the sea, came into being. It was to be flooded again by the sea—the last time was probably a mere 5,000 years ago—but the lines of the trough remained intact.

The cover isn't all grass (or sedge) by any means, although saw grass lies over the major part of the true Everglades; the river of grass is spotted with hammocks—very small hillocks—in the otherwise flat ground. These hammocks are named for the dominant type of vegetation. Thus we may have "bay heads" where sweet bay (magnolia) or red bay predominates, "cypress heads" where there is cypress, and finally "willow heads." All are temperate climate trees. In such "tree islands" we are likely to find also wax myrtle, pond or custard apple, buttonbush, dahoon, and coco plum. If the dominant tree is a tropical hardwood, it's called a "mahogany hammock" or a "gumbo-limbo hammock," and in its strict use, "hammock" is limited to these two, "heads" being the proper term for hammocks dominated by temperate growth. Mahoganies and gumbo-limbos occur in the southern part of the Glades and are surrounded by truly tropical vegetation. Here there may well be strangler figs, wild tamarinds, poisonwood, false mastics, and, on occasion, royal palms. Mahoganies and royal palms once were common in these parts but have been sadly reduced because of their commercial value. As many as 35 kinds of trees and more than 65 different shrubs can be found in some of these hammocks.

The vast saw grass area is broken not only by hammocks, but also by open stretches of water. These may be ponds, canals, or other types of waterways. The alligator has played a very important role in the ecology of the Glades by keeping open thousands of ponds formed in old solution holes.

In this river of grass, which the Indians called "Pa-hay-okee"— "grassy waters"—great numbers of wildlife once flourished. Alligators were counted in the hundreds of thousands (possibly as many as a million at one time). There was an unlimited supply of fish, great clouds of birds—herons, ibises, and ducks could be seen overhead—and larger mammals—black bears, cougars, otters, white-tailed deer, raccoons, and opossums—were abundant. The native Indians—Calusas and Tequestas—hunted and fished here without disturbing the balance of nature or causing any great harm to the wildlife. This continued to be true when the land became a Seminole reservation. But at the end of the last century, civilization descended upon the Everglades, and in one way or another has been endangering it and many of its species ever since.

The story of the egrets is too well known to need more than a passing mention. For years, fashion decreed that women's hats should be adorned with bird plumage, and the beautiful feathers of herons stood high on the list. Most sought after was the breeding plumage of the white egrets: the little snowy and the American, and, though less frequently, the feathers of the great white heron. Since the greatest concentration of nesting egrets and herons was in the Everglades and on the Keys, this was the area to which most of the hunters came. It seemed for a time as if both the snowy and the common egret were doomed because, even when laws were passed for their protection, poachers persisted in taking these exquisite birds for their feather value. Finally, one Audubon warden was deliberately shot down off Flamingo, while a second was killed three years later, and public outrage ended the slaughter. If bird plumage on hats was to result in murder, many women decided they could do without feathers. The Audubon Society assumed a leading role in the wave of protest and, before long, state legislation and other state laws completely stopped the trade in our country.

Today, it looks as if the popularity of alligator bags and shoes may well destroy the alligators of southeastern Florida. Again the problem is one of poachers, and once again, an end to such destruction would be public willingness to remove temptation. If we would forgo all articles made of alligator or crocodile hide, if we would refuse to buy stuffed animals or the live babies, then we would be well on the way to saving these interesting and valuable reptiles. The recently enacted federal ban on interstate shipment of hides, and the New York law forbidding the sale of alligator products, should provide some protection. If other states, including Florida as perhaps the most important one, will follow suit, alligators and crocodiles may have a chance to recover, but again, public support is needed for such legislation. From an estimated one million, the animals are down to about 10,000, and without adequate safeguards their end seems near.

The alligator has had other problems to contend with besides that of being overhunted, but that story involves the whole life of the Everglades. Back in 1906, the rich lands south of Lake Okeechobee caught the eye of farmers. New railroads were making truck farming, with fast shipment to northern cities, a highly profitable business—at least when there wasn't an unseasonable frost. As a result, a large area was drained—some for truck farms, some for sugarcane, some for cattle.

Settlement on flood plains is an old story in this country. Again and again, rich, alluvial land, nearness to a waterway—a lake or river—and a flat terrain, have resulted in extensive development. Farms, industrial plants, and sometimes even towns and cities have come into being, and, again and again, the plain has been flooded, lives and property have been lost, and the state or nation has been called upon to stop such ravages—only too often at an exorbitant cost. Slowly a new idea is taking hold. Maybe in the future people shouldn't be allowed to settle on flood plains where destruction is so likely.

But in the first half of our century, no one questioned a man's right to settle where he would and to be protected from floods. Nearly 500 miles of canals were dug, and 47 miles of levees built to safeguard the truck farms and settlements in the Everglades. In normal years the lake seldom overflows to any extent, but in 1926 and 1928, hurricanes brought the waters of Lake Okeechobee pouring down over the reclaimed land with great loss of life and property. The federal government was called upon for help and in 1937, alone, the cost for levees, gates, and canals was 16 million dollars. One of the unexpected side results of the loss of natural water flow was the fearful burning of great sections of the Glades, as fires swept through dried-out grass and peat, destroying all wildlife in their path, and sending clouds of smoke southward toward Miami. And still people were fearful lest the farmlands, cattle, and human life might be endangered from floods; so, as a further step, in 1948, a large part of the Everglades was set aside as a conservation area in which the overflow from the lake was to be stored. The Central and Southern Florida Flood Control District was created for the dual purpose of protecting life and property, and for regulation of the water supply in times of drought. The state authorities have worked with the U.S. Corps of Engineers in carrying out this plan.

Up until 1962, a more or less normal amount of water was still allowed to flow through the undrained, "unmanaged" section of the Everglades, but at the end of 1962 this was cut off, as the last conservation areas were completed. Apparently, water for agricultural purposes was one thing, for wildlife quite another, and the releases made were irregular and not adjusted to need. In 1965 during a severe drought, the Everglades National Park was given only 140 acre-feet of water in the month of April, while 280,000 acre-feet were released directly into the sea—as "unneeded excess." An enormous loss of wildlife resulted and there has been growing public concern over what seems to be plain water mismanagement. Much needs to be done, but we can hope that this needless kind of destruction will be stopped before too long.

Meanwhile let us see just how the Everglades is divided up right now. Forty-four percent has been drained for farming or residential purposes; forty-nine percent is in the conservation area, and only the remaining seven percent is assured to the public as that part in which the true Everglades will be preserved—*if* it's given enough water. The Everglades National Park was formally opened in 1947 and represented years of effort by individuals and the state of Florida to acquire enough land to make a national park possible. Even though so much of the Everglades is marked for uses other than that of preserving its original character, a vast area—far beyond that in the Park—is still saw grass country, with conspicuous hammocks and heads rising up all over it. Part of Alligator Alley, running from Fort Lauderdale to Naples, and of the Tamiami Trail go through the Everglades, and part of U.S. 1, between Homestead and the Keys, is also in this area.

Drainage, road and canal-building, water impoundments, heavy traffic, and hunting may not have altered the plant life or the look of the Glades too much as yet, but what have they done to its animals? Black bears and cougars are rare, which is hardly surprising since the larger carnivores are being rapidly eliminated in our country. Alligators have suffered heavily, although, in all fairness, it must be said that nature has played an important role in this decline. Fires, droughts, and Hurricane Donna in 1960 all took their toll, but alligators are prolific breeders. With reasonable flooding of their haunts and protection from poachers, there is no doubt that they can make some sort of comeback.

Another species which has suffered at the hands of man is the tree snail liguus, one of the most beautiful of its kind in the whole world. Liguus was originally found throughout the hammocks in the Glades. Furthermore, the pattern of the shell varied from hammock to hammock, many having a snail with distinctive markings. Unfortunately, liguus became a prized item for shell collectors, with a complete assemblage of all the different forms a greatly-desired goal. Snail hunters ravaged the Glades, entirely wiping out some of the forms. Today liguus is protected, but the laws came too late to save some colonies, and the total number has been greatly reduced.

For a brighter note in the picture, we can say that the snowy egret has made a remarkable recovery and is now present in very considerable numbers, although not in the enormous flocks of the last century. The great white heron was still a rare sight when I was on the Keys in 1961. In 1968 I found them everywhere.

I have mentioned the relatively new science of ecology. During the latter part of the eighteenth century and through the nineteenth, naturalists in general were too busy naming the various species and collecting specimens for zoos, botanical gardens, and museums to give much thought to the communities from which those specimens had come. During the nineteenth, however, the science of ecology came into being, and today we are looking more and more at the picture as a whole, not at the individual items. This is why I prefer my barnacles, limpets, and rock purples where they belong, at the tide line, rather than in a collection. I am much happier with an orchid that blooms on a tree trunk in its native habitat than with one in a greenhouse, and I would like once again to be able to see a liguus snail crawling below it. An alligator, finally, should be found basking in a sunlit pool in the Everglades instead of being confined to a pit in a zoo.

The alligator's role in his community is an important one, and provides a good illustration of what may happen when one member of an interdependent group is taken away. Before man interfered in the ecology of the Everglades, summer rainfall and the overflow from Lake Okeechobee usually gave the saw grass country a thorough wetting between June and November. From November until May, however, there was normally a long, dry season, during which the water gradually retreated into sloughs, ponds, and sinkholes. The ponds and sinkholes were kept open by the alligators, and they still carry out this important function for those still in use. As the dry season returns each year, vast numbers of fish crowd into these water holes. Along with them are protozoans, crustaceans, amphibians, and reptiles. The ponds also provide a survival area for many ferns and flowering plants, as well as feeding grounds for birds and mammals. There is a complex food chain here, with the two-inch gambusia entering the ponds first in pursuit of mosquito larvae; sunfish following gambusia; bass feeding on sunnies, and garfish—the chief food of the alligator—on bass. Wading birds and otters feast on the great concentration of fish, and snakes come in for frogs and crustaceans. In "The Role of the Alligator," F. C. Craighead, Sr., says: "The productivity of these ponds is phenomenal, no small part of which is directly attributable to the alligator . . . He is a sloppy feeder and as he crunches his prey, leaves many 'crumbs' for other inhabitants."

For over 2,000 years this has been the life pattern of the Glades, and many of the fish-eating birds depend upon this overabundance to feed their young. The fact that mammals, birds, and reptiles all concentrate upon the ponds and smaller sloughs has also made it possible to offer the winter visitor real spectacles and, in consequence, to make possible a national park.

The Everglades and the Park are not really synonymous, and it's time to separate them. As I've said, the Everglades—drained, channeled, as they may be—far exceed the Park. On the other hand, the

Park, in spite of its name, takes in far more than the Everglades. Some 2,100 square miles lie inside the Park, an area greater than the state of Delaware. Of that total, only 192 square miles are saw grass and hammocks. The rest is pineland (a small part), cypress swamp (also small), mangrove swamp, Florida Bay and some of its little keys, and, reaching up the Gulf coast, a good part of the Ten Thousand Islands.

It follows that the wildlife of the Park is much greater than that of the Glades. It includes the crocodile, a creature of salt marshes and mangroves (alligators live in fresh water), and the loggerhead turtle which lays its eggs on Cape Sable. It takes in the manatee of Florida Bay and the salt water estuaries, as well as dolphins, many marine fishes, and other kinds of sea life. The roseate spoonbill and the great white heron nest on keys in Florida Bay and hence really belong to the Park, but not to the Everglades, and we can hardly claim for the Glades such true sea birds as the pelicans, skimmers, cormorants, terns, and sanderlings.

The true saw grass community is best seen in the Shark River Slough, which has a fourteen-mile road semi-circling through it. The entrance is off the Tamiami Trail near the Mikasuki Restaurant and it used to be possible to drive around the whole loop, making stops along the way. Now closed for repairs, the road is expected to be in use again in late 1971, and permission is sometimes given to individuals or groups by the Park ranger for limited access. To the left of the entrance, the wide grassy plain is often covered with white ibises, which rise in the air like a cloud taking wing. White ibises provide the memorable flights in the Everglades, just as wood storks do for the Cypress Swamp. As I watch them, I think of their relative, the sacred ibis of Egypt, once supposed to be the god Thoth, the recorder of human affairs. Often I see immature birds here, with a black tip to the otherwise reddish bill and face, and black legs. Head and neck are brown, with darker wings and tail; the belly, in contrast, is snowy white.

The usual canal borders the road, and along road and canal are the familiar scrub willow and coco plum. Herons are abundant. So are kingfishers, and every so often an alligator can be seen lying motionless in the water. This is an infrequently traveled road—it has the feel of a country lane—and its wildlife has little fear of man. Once when I was on foot, and the herons seemed unaware of my presence, I heard them talking back and forth with grunts and hoarse calls. I felt as if I were eavesdropping on a private conversation.

Not far from the entrance, a trail leads off to a hammock. Here a narrow woodland path, winding through willows, crosses and recrosses a little stream. The air is deeply scented with the smell of the water and of ferns—leather, swamp, and royal—some growing right in the course of the stream along with yellow bladderwort and masses of arrowhead. The brook runs over a dark-bottomed floor—the peat and muck of the Everglades—and it's stained with tannin just as it was in the cypress swamp. Here, too, the sun ripples over the water, making patches of amber. A black and white warbler works his way up the trunk of a willow and a yellowthroat (that denizon of wet places) scolds from a twig just a foot or two above the ground.

Now we come out into the sunlight and there is an abrupt change of scene. A brilliant red gulf fritillary sails up in front of us. A moment later a dragonfly, with green foreparts (head and thorax) and black and yellow abdomen, zooms across the path, while drifting in and out of the heavier foliage is a zebra butterfly with exotic patterning in yellow and black. Beyond, a long-tailed skipper with handsome green body sips honey from the Spanish needles and heliotrope. It's the world of my sea lane—fragrant, sun-warmed, busy with insects—and I pause for a moment to savor its alluring quality.

The hammock lies just ahead and it, too, is different, as different as the pathway of the ferns was from the pathway of the insects. Big trees—live oak, pigeon plum, and gumbo-limbo—make a canopy above the stony platform of oolitic limestone. The rock has been deeply eroded—there is said to be a cave below it—and sinkholes go down, some as large as small wells. This is the hammock of the "Otter Cave," and I peer down the largest of the holes into darkness. Nothing can be seen except the ferns growing among the rocks.

Back on the loop, however, a couple of otters hump themselves across the road in front of us, so perhaps they really do make use of the holes. Now the canal widens into a small slough, lush with arrowhead, green arum, cattails, and pickerelweed, and a lovely white peacock butterfly hovers over the blue pickerel flowers. In the water, sunfish swim below the quiet ripples, and the lacy green of pondweed (southern naiad) billows out in the current. The brown shells of the orb snail lie on the bottom of the pond, while nearby on dry ground are empty pomacea shells—that snail the limpkin feeds upon. Pomacea is the largest snail in this country and is the only food of the now rare Everglade kite. Because of this, it's now protected.

A school of gambusia (mosquito fish) suddenly dart into sight and as quickly disappear. As I watch them, a black snake glides over the ground into the weeds. He is as intent on his business as I am on mine and neither of us is disturbed by the other. I do know from the shape of his head and sleek form that he isn't a moccasin. From his white chin and throat I guess that he's an Everglades racer.

People are often afraid of snakes and quite needlessly so. A good part of my life has been spent out of doors, frequently in uninhabited country, and I have seen only two uncaged poisonous snakes in the course of walking some thousands of miles. Nonpoisonous snakes, on the other hand, are reasonably common. My own list runs into a considerable number, and I am always pleased when I can add another such as the Everglades racer. It is true that in Florida, where the dangerous coral snake is to be found, and where rattlers and moccasins are considerably more common than in the North, it's foolish to step into high grass or weeds where the ground underfoot can't be seen. I therefore stick to pathways, roads, and cleared ground, knowing that the likelihood of meeting a poisonous snake is small. Among other things, alligators dispose of a considerable number of the water-haunting snakes, and most of the poisonous ones have also been removed from park areas where people commonly walk.

Following the loop again, we see hammocks rising out of the saw grass on our left, often with the light mottled bark of pigeon plum very apparent in the distance. On the right is the canal, with soft-shelled turtles sunning themselves on rocks and logs. Big red-bellied sliders—granddaddies of turtles—are here, too, and, of course, there are alligators, both big and little ones, for the Shark River slough is a favorite gathering place during the winter months. Always, too, there are the herons: great blue, little blue, Louisiana, common, and snowy egrets—all that we have seen before—and sometimes a green heron goes squawking up the canal with orange legs trailing behind.

And then halfway round the loop is the Observation Tower, with its wide view of the saw grass country, and directly below it, the amazing sight of alligators by the score (at times reaching a hundred), concentrated thus mostly because of garfish. Alligators feed on gar, and gar in their turn make heavy inroads on many of the other fish of the Glades. Were it not for alligators, garfish would get out of bounds, but as it is, a workable balance is maintained. I had earlier seen the gambusias and the sunnies which feed on them. One or two bass had also been in evidence. (Bass take sunnies and are themselves food for garfish.) Now the canal is full of long-nosed gar, curiously elongated, cylindrical fish which look like prehistoric relics, and are often referred to as such, but in actual fact are quite modern as fishes go, dating merely from the Eocene.

As I watch the gars, I become aware of a great variety of calls coming from the swamp behind them. There are grunts, clucks, and sounds that are just indescribable. Red-winged blackbirds fly over, giving their musical "oak-a-lee," but the really odd noises come from the marsh and are the chatter of coots and gallinules. In all of the commotion I can also pick out the peculiar grunt of a Virginia rail, and even as I name it, the rail flies out calling "kid-ick, kid-ick, kid-ick."

Overhead there is another big flight of white ibises, swirling in the sky, banking, making patterns against the blue. More white ibises can be seen on the return stretch of the loop where the birds are gathered in a wide shallow pond. Herons are here again, along with anhingas. Pied-billed grebes and coots paddle around, joined now by blue-winged teal. The male of this small duck has a white crescent on the side of his face. Hundreds of yellow-legged sandpipers are busily feeding in the shallows, and there is another ibis, the glossy, that I have not encountered earlier. He has the familiar downcurved bill and is dark purple in color.

I have one last memory of ibises in flight—one that cannot be ignored—that took place in a very different part of the Glades. The Loxahatchee National Wildlife Refuge, covering more than 145,000 acres, is in Palm Beach County on the east coast. It came as a surprise that the typical slough and saw grass country exists so far to the east, with many of the birds of Shark River and the Anhinga Trail on view. In addition, the big ponds draw ducks and sandpipers. A total of over 200 birds have been recorded in the refuge, but when I was there it must have been an off time, and I noted only the customary herons, gallinules, coots, glossy ibises, blue-winged teal, and mottled ducks.

The white ibises alone, however, made the trip worthwhile. By the hundred they rose from the swamp of pickerelweed, arrowhead, and yellow primrose-willow. Flight after flight went directly over my head, so low that I could hear wingbeats and clearly see hooked red bills, red legs, and white bodies just touched with black at the wing tips. Each flock advanced perhaps thirty feet, then sank with noisy grunts into the marsh, vanishing among the high weeds.

Shark River and Loxahatchee both offer good displays of marsh birds, but the best spot for them—and the most famous—is the Anhinga Trail. This is in Everglades National Park, only a few miles from the main entrance. On entering, stop briefly at the Visitor Center with its fine planting of mahoganies and long line of fernlike coonties leading to the information building. Many excellent guides may be bought here, and some might well prove helpful in pinning names to plants, insects, and birds.

I would like to think, though, that by now the herons, anhingas, grebes, coots, and gallinules, at least, are old friends. Many a newcomer to Florida has to learn what must seem like a lot of new birds and plants. The thing is that they keep reappearing. Once learned, one has the key to the birds of the Tamiami Trail, Alligator Alley, the Cypress Swamp, and the Everglades, and the total number of common ones isn't more than a dozen. There are more plants, but here again, a few dominate the landscape, with the others coming in merely as accent notes.

The Anhinga Trail and the adjoining Gumbo Limbo Trail are only a short distance from the Visitor Center. Both are part of Royal Palm Hammock, the site of Florida's first state park, and the area originally described by W. E. Safford in his "Natural History of Paradise Key." An unusual concentration of marsh birds occurs along the Anhinga Trail, and as the boardwalk crosses Taylor Slough in several places, they are easily seen. Like many of the walking trails in the Park, this one is only a third of a mile in length. It is bordered by scrub willow, the tree that follows so many of the southern canals. On the other side of the waterway I can see phragmites, that feathery common reed which is said to be "the most widely distributed flowering plant in the world." Shrubby groundsel tree or salt bush is here as well, and morning glory grows in among reeds and bushes. All along the boardwalk are custard apples laden with epiphytes, and with heavily buttressed trunks. Their wide-spreading branches are twisted and contorted, making them look like age-weary trees. They also serve as perches for the anhingas as they spread their great black wings to dry. Curiously enough, cormorants and anhingas lack the highly water-repellent feathers of other water birds, and because of this must dry their wings after a wetting.

At the end of the boardwalk a purple gallinule is walking over the lily pads, and a photographer, armed with tripod, camera, and a great deal of equipment, is taking his picture quite as if he were the star of the show—as, in fact, he is. The common gallinule is often seen, but the purple gallinule exhibits himself rather rarely, and with his brilliant color, he is outstanding. A little further there is an even more surprising sight, for I look over the railing at a sora rail that is pecking a big water snake. This is truly a David and Goliath performance, for the snake is several feet long while the sora is smaller than a bobwhite. Again and again the sora comes back to the attack, but the sluggish snake moves only an inch or so, then lapses again into immobility. Is the snake, in the bird's eyes, an enemy? I have no idea, and the chances are slim that anyone else will ever see a sora battling a snake at this particular spot or hour again. (Soras are rarely seen at any time, and when they do appear, it's more likely to be at dawn.) But the likelihood is great that anyone interested in wildlife and alert to what is happening may see something just as interesting.

The nearby Gumbo Limbo Trail offers hammock in contrast to swamp life. Tropical hammock plants often have intriguing names, with gumbo-limbo probably heading the list, but others that come to mind are false mastic, satinleaf, stopper, poisonwood, and paradise tree. How often have I read of myrsine, lancewood, fiddlewood, and marlberry, rolling the names over my tongue as I did so. The Gumbo Limbo Trail is an opportunity, through the labels identifying the plants along it, to put a few of the names and plants together. But before I do so, I would like to see what it is that makes a hammock so distinctive. In trying to pin down its elusive quality I mean to look not only at the Gumbo Limbo Trail, but at the hammocks in Matheson Hammock Park and in the Charles Torrey Simpson Memorial Park. Matheson I mentioned earlier—it adjoins the Fairchild Tropical Garden. The Simpson Memorial Park, dedicated to the great Florida naturalist, is in Miami with the entrance at S.W. 17th Road and Miami Avenue.

Standing in the sunlight outside one of these tree islands, it's the darkness that is most striking. Beside the Simpson Park I feel as if a piece of night had been imprisoned here, held tight within its fence. Matheson and the Gumbo Limbo Trail aren't quite so black, but as I look now at the trail's hammock, a solid wall of vegetation seems to rise up on its outer edge. Few tree trunks. No, the wall is of flimsier stuff, with weeds and ferns at the bottom, then shrubs such as wild coffee and myrsine, vines—woodbine, grape and bullbrier—and finally wild pawpaw and gumbo-limbo rising above them.

Within the hammock there is a different look. I am conscious of crowded growth—for the most part, hundreds of small trees, often with crooked trunks—but it isn't impenetrable, as in the jungle of travelers' tales. Ferns (bracken, shield, wood, sword, Boston, halberd, and leather) cover the floor of this little forest, and one could walk through it were it not for the leaning trees and the vines. Many of the latter belong to the temperate zone. I have spoken of woodbine, grape, and bullbrier, but poison ivy is here, too. Some, of course, are strictly southern, such as love-vines, which trail over some of the weeds looking much like orange dodder. Strangler fig sends down its heavy loops and hanging arms all through the hammock, but as a massive jungle vine, it's outdone by a true liana, hippocratea, named for the "Father of Medicine." This plant has stems as big as a man's arm and would serve Tarzan remarkably well. Its giant coils could easily throw a man, and its weight on the crown of a tree has brought many a handsome specimen to the ground.

Along the Gumbo Limbo Trail, overarching shrubs and small trees form a canopy above the path. When the light gets through, it makes dappled patterns underfoot, but mostly the atmosphere is dim and subdued. Few birds sing and it's rare that an insect comes into sight. If birds or insects are about, they are flying in the tree tops. Air plants, of course, are abundant—they are a part of all tropical hammocks. In the Simpson hammock the floor of the path is of rough oolite, and heavy roots sprawl across it, so that it's hard walking. Most of the roots belong to a strangler fig—that variety that develops into trees—but some of them come from gumbo-limbos. In the Matheson hammock there are the same roots and the same eroded limestone. Only on the Gumbo Limbo Trail have the paths been made smooth before our feet.

Other things come to mind as I think of the hammocks. One is the rain of falling leaves, especially during fall and early winter months, and this I noticed particularly in Simpson Park. The ground in spots is thickly carpeted with them. Many a time I've had this area to myself, and the sound and sight of drifting leaves was notable. I've also been startled here when the silence was broken by the sudden snapping of a twig. A squirrel or wood rat, perhaps. Perhaps the natural breaking of a branch.

There is a woodsy fragrance in all these places, one that's mingled every so often with a slightly skunky odor—the smell of a white stopper. "Stopper" is another name that has come from the British West Indies and is applied to all of the eugenia species—small trees with aromatic leaves (cloves are the flower buds of one of them). The only one I can identify is the white stopper and then only by its smell. It's curious that several plants have this slightly acrid odor. I think of skunk cabbage, for example, and crown imperial.

On the Gumbo Limbo Trail, the labels carry much interesting information, quite aside from names. For instance, they point out that the leaves are nearly all smooth-pointed and elliptical in shape (that bewildering similarity that I've noted before). They are drip-tip leaves—streamlined in order to let the plants rid themselves quickly of the enormous amount of rain that falls here in summer. They also tell me that the wood of gumbo-limbo is very light and used for fishnet floats and for merry-go-round horses, while a medicinal salve and a cold remedy have come from its resin and bark.

I have read often of the big trees of the hammock—of mahogany, royal palm, live oak, pigeon plum, gumbo-limbo, wild tamarind, and false mastic. But on this trail, at least, the smaller trees play a dominating role. Mahoganies and royal palms were cut out, of course, in the early days. I find just one false mastic with the help of a ranger, who points out the crinkled edges on the yellow-green leaf and the size of the trunk—some trees are three feet in diameter. Pigeon plum is here—I recognize its mottled bark, to me like that of sycamore. The live oak is adorned with resurrection fern, which always helps to place it. Gumbo-limbo and the feathery wild tamarind are easy, and I add one new name, the paradise tree, related to the ailanthus and somewhat similar, with alternate, leathery, oblong leaflets.

The giants of this forest are in truth few in number, and I shall do better to learn some of the shrubs and small trees. Another label states that there are 75 different kinds of woody plants along the trail. This is a phenomenal number for a natural area in just one-third of a mile. It's a reminder that we live in a geological period that has an extraordinary diversity of plant life, and, to go a little further, that southern Florida has a range far beyond that of a northern forest. An ecologist would call this area "poor rain forest," but I'm thankful that I need not cope with the luxuriance of the true rain forest.

I shan't attempt to name more than a very few of the plants, but as on the streets and lawns of Miami, I found that a little knowledge added amazingly to my enjoyment of the scenery. And some are quite easy to pick out. Take satinleaf, for instance. Its leaves are a dark green above, a velvety copper-brown underneath. When a breeze catches them and the undersides come into view, it's a lovely sight.

Then there is lancewood, like red bay, a member of the laurel family. The leaves of these two have the look of laurel, but that of lancewood is long, very narrow, and hangs downward, while the red bay's is wider and shinier. Wild coffee I learned to recognize in the Parrot Jungle, and I have found it in many places since then, not only in the Everglades, but at Matheson and in the Hugh Taylor Birch State Park. It's a small shrub—a true coffee—and the common species has "lacquered vivid light green leaves with very deep veins" (*Guide to Plants of the Everglades National Park* by Alex D. Hawkes). This description is good and, once seen, the plant is easily recognized.

Another distinctive leaf is that of the Florida tetrazygia. The prominent veins run lengthwise of the narrow leaf—a center one and one bordering each edge. Smaller cross veins run between them at right angles to the main nerves. Charles Brookfield, one of the well-known present-day naturalists of southern Florida, calls this our most beautiful native flowering tree. Its white panicles with the curious yellow stamens of the melastome family can be seen in late spring and summer. Later on the paradise tree will also have great clusters of yellow flowers, followed by scarlet and purple fruit. Lancewood will produce small, sweet-smelling whitish blooms, and the fishpoison tree will be gay with lavender pea-like flowers.

Poisonwood, belonging to the same family as poison ivy, is also a common small tree. This is sometimes included among the "big trees"—it can reach 40 feet—but those I have seen were much smaller. Its pinnate leaves have from three to seven shiny dark green leaflets with tiny dark specks. Often dark blotches are present on the trunk where sap has oozed down the tree. This plant is quite as poisonous as poison ivy, and care should be taken not to touch it. The much more dangerous manchineel occurs in the Park but has been largely removed from those parts that are frequented by visitors.

The last shrub or tree I shall mention is also a common one—*Guianea rapanea,* or, to use the name I prefer, myrsine—and this, like the cultivated pittosporum, reminds me of bayberry. Leaves, shape of branches, and clustered berries—the last close to the stem—are all like bayberry, even though the two are not related. Myrsine, in fact, resembles our northern bayberry far more than wax myrtle, which does belong to the same genus.

Leaving the Gumbo Limbo Trail, I continue on State Route 27 which runs through the Park for a distance of 38 miles, ending at Flamingo. Today, however, I shall follow it only halfway, since most of the other part is in the mangrove country. Four and a half miles beyond the turnoff for Royal Palm Station is the Pineland Trail on Long Pine Key. I was expecting this to be typical piney flats, and am surprised when I find mixed pine and hammock growth. The answer (provided by the Park rangers) is that in nature the pinelands of the Miami oolitic ridge survive only when they are periodically ravaged by fire. What we see here is a case of invading hammock life, which, if left unchecked, will eventually replace the pines. Today myrsine is one of the predominant shrubs, and wild tamarind is widespread. Towering above them, though, the pines still stand, with their fragrance filling the air. As I walk under them, the wind soughs through their branches, making a constant murmur overhead. By the side of the path, too, are many of the characteristic flowers of the Florida pinelands. Their bloom will come at various times of the year—only a few are performing now—but spring and summer will offer quite a show. Among the plants are Bahama senna, rattleboxes, St. John's-wort (all three with yellow flowers), grass pinks (a delicate ground orchid), lilac meadow beauties (another melastome like tetrazygia), and wild allamanda with tubular dark-yellow flowers.

The Mahogany Hammock, ten miles farther along, still preserves many of the big mahoganies, although a large part of its wonderful collection of orchids and other air plants was destroyed by Donna. A boardwalk winds among these patriarchs, letting us see what the "big trees" were like. Paurotis and cabbage palms grow among them with quite a bit of satinleaf. I know by the smell that white stopper is here, and as always there are the ponderous leather ferns. The whole hammock is curiously different from that of the Gumbo Limbo Trail; it has another feel to it. With its many smaller trees, the Gumbo Limbo was a lighter, more graceful woods. This is massive, cathedral-like, and imposing. I know more about hammock life from having explored all three trails.

Hammock land also exists farther up the eastern coast, and outside the exact province of "the Everglades." Not long ago an analysis of the plant and animal life found in a live oak-cabbage palm coastal hammock near Vero Beach appeared in *Audubon Field Notes* (Vol. 22, No. 6, December 1968). It was part of a study made by the Entomological Research Center at Vero Beach, and while their hammock was in Indian River County to the north, it is still within the section covered by this book and it's likely that many of their plants and animals would also be found in the more southern hammocks. I noted with interest that wild coffee was the commonest shrub, and that the second most common tree was myrsine. The latter has not received the popular recognition its abundance deserves.

Some of their figures are worth reporting. The most abundant tree was live oak with 621 individuals. Next came myrsine, 310; followed by Brazilian pepper (Florida holly), 200; twinberry eugenia, 176; shore bay (a small tree related to red bay and found near the coast), 146; and cabbage palm, 116. I am omitting less common trees. The wild coffee shrub totaled 374. Fourteen mammals (other than dogs and cats) came into the hammock and the variety was interesting. Mammals listed in the study were: Virginia opossum, nine-banded armadillo, eastern cottontail, marsh rabbit, eastern gray squirrel, eastern fox squirrel, hispid cotton rat, cotton mouse, oldfield mouse, raccoon, striped skunk, spotted skunk, river otter, and Florida bobcat.

In the Glades we would probably be able to add deer, domestic pig, and possibly bear. Twenty species of birds nested in the hammock, five others nested nearby, and twenty-three more were seen in the area, but many of these I have mentioned and won't list here. Reptiles and amphibians numbered twenty-one, and again a list will serve to give an idea of this type of hammock life: striped mud turtle, Florida box turtle, southern diamondback terrapin, gopher tortoise, green anole, broad-headed skink, ground skink, Florida 5-lined skink, banded water snake, eastern garter snake, rough green snake, yellow rat snake, southern blue racer, eastern indigo snake, eastern coral snake, eastern spadefoot toad, southern toad, eastern narrow-mouthed toad, green tree frog, southern leopard frog, and greenhouse frog.

Note that there were six harmless snakes to one poisonous species! Moreover, the coral snake, while extremely dangerous, is active only at night. "Coral snakes" reportedly seen during the day are likely to be scarlet king snakes.

A major part of our area has been covered in this chapter, including, as it has, the saw grass country, sloughs, hammocks, and heads. This is the Everglades, one of the most important features of South Florida.

Common and Scientific Names

Bahama senna: *Cassia bahamensis* Mill.
bladderwort: *Utricularia* sp.
Boston fern: *Nephrolepis exaltata* (L.) Schott
bracken fern: *Pteridium aquilinum* (L.) Kuhn var. *caudatum* (L.) Sadebeck
chicken grape: *Vitis rotundifolia* Michx.
common reed: *Phragmites communis* Trin.
dahoon: *Ilex cassine* L.
dragonfly: *Lepthemis vesiculosa* Fabr. (mostly bright green with black and yellow abdomen)
Everglades racer: *Coluber constrictor paludicolis* Auff. & Babb.
false mastic (mastic): *Mastichodendron foetidissimum* (Jacq.) (*Sideroxylon foetidissimum* Jacq.) (authorities are divided as to the correct common name; some use wild mastic; I am using false mastic since there is a European mastic totally unrelated to this tree)
fiddlewood: *Citharexylum fruticosum* L.
fishpoison tree (Jamaica dogwood): *Piscidia piscipula* Hitch.
Florida red-bellied slider: *Pseudomys nelsoni* Carr
Florida tetrazygia: *Tetrazygia bicolor* (Mill.) Cogn.
grass pink: *Calopogon pulchellus* (Salisb.) R. Br.
groundsel tree (saltbush): *Baccharis halimifolia* L.

halberd fern: *Tectaria* sp.
hippocratea: *Hippocratea volubilis* L.
lancewood: *Nectandara coriacea* (Sw.) Griseb.
love vine (woe vine): *Cassytha filiformis* L.
manchineel: *Hippomane mancinella* L.
marlberry: *Ardisia escallonioides* Schlecht. & Cham (*Icacorea paniculata* Sudw.)
meadow beauty: *Rhexia mariana* L. var. *exalbida* Michx.
myrsine (Guiana rapanea): *Rapanea guianensis* Aubl.
orb snail: *Helisoma duryi* (Wetherby) (the common helisoma of the Everglades)
paradise tree: *Simarouba glauca* DC.
paurotis palm: *Paurotis wrightii* (Griseb.) Britton
pigeon plum (dove plum): *Coccoloba diversifolia* Jacq. (formerly *Coccolobis laurifolia* Jacq.)
poison ivy: *Toxicodendron radians* (L.) Kuntze
poisonwood: *Metopium toxiferum* (L.) Krug & Urban
rattleboxes: *Crotalaria* sp.
St. John's-wort: *Hypericum* sp.
satinleaf: *Chrysophyllum olivaeforme* L.
saw grass: *Cladium jamaicensis* Crantz
shield fern: *Thelypteris normalis* (C. Chr.) Moxley
shore bay: *Persea littoralis* Small
shrubby primrose willow: *Jussiaea peruviana* L.
southern soft-shelled turtle: *Amyda ferox ferox* (Schneider)
sword fern: *Nephrolepis biserrata* (Sw.) Schott
tree snail: *Liguus fasciatus* Mull (although 50 varieties have been claimed for the Everglades and Keys, there are probably only 8 valid subspecies)
twinberry eugenia: *Eugenia dicrana* Berg.
water snakes, brown: *Natrix taxispilota* (Holbrook); green: *Natrix cyclopion floridiana* Goff; horn snake: *Farancia obscura* (Holbrook)
white stopper: *Eugenia axillaris* (Sw.) Willd.
wild allamanda: *Urechites pinetorum* Small
wild coffee: *Psychotria undata* Jacq. (there are several species, but this is a common one)

References

Beard, Daniel B. "Wildlife of Everglades National Park." *National Geographic* XCV (No. 1, 1949).

Brown, Andrew H. "Haunting Heart of the Everglades." *National Geographic* XCIII (No. 2, 1948).

Blackwell, Harriet Gray. "Trailing Our Most Beautiful Land Snail." *Natural History* LXXV (No. 9, 1966).

Carr, Archie. "Alligators—Dragons in Distress." *National Geographic* 131 (No. 1, 1967).

Craighead, Frank C. "The Role of the Alligator in Shaping Plant Communities and Maintaining Wildlife in the Southern Everglades." *Florida Naturalist* 41 (Nos. 1, 2, 1968).

*Douglas, Marjory Stoneman. *The Everglades: River of Grass.* New York: Rinehart, 1947. 406 pp.

*Hawkes, Alex D. *Guide to Plants of the Everglades National Park.* Coral Gables, Fla.: Tropic Isle Publishers, 1965. 51 pp.

Needham, James G., and Westfall, Minter J., Jr. *Dragonflies of North America.* Berkeley and Los Angeles: University of California Press, 1954. 615 pp.

*Robertson, William B., Jr. *Everglades—The Park Story.* Coral Gables, Fla: University of Miami Press, 1959. 95 pp.

Safford, William Edwin. "Natural History of Paradise Key and the Nearby Everglades of Florida." In *Smithsonian Institution Annual Report, 1917,* pp. 377-434 plus 32 pp. plates. Washington, D.C.: Government Printing Office, 1919.

Schneider, William J. "Water and the Everglades." *Natural History* LXXV (No. 9, 1966).

Truslow, Frederick Kent, and Vosburgh, Frederick G. "Threatened Glories of Everglades National Park." *National Geographic* 132 (No. 4, 1967).

*Zim, Herbert S. *A Guide to Everglades National Park and the Nearby Florida Keys.* New York: Golden Press, 1960. 80 pp.

A cut in the Key Largo limestone displays fossil corals. This limestone underlies Miami Beach and much of the Keys.

11
Evidences of the Past

Many a time as I wander along Florida beaches or explore the inland paths, scenes of the past rise up before me, some highly familiar, others startingly strange. Evidence of that ancient history is all around—a fossil shell or bone, a portion of a reef, an old sea terrace, or the remnants of the inland sea that is now Lake Okeechobee. In my "Afternoon and Evening at Naples," I conjured up a little of the scenery of bygone times, but it is time now to look at the whole great spread of prehistory in Florida—of all that happened here in ancient days.

It is true that the visible signs of the past come mostly from the Miocene, Pliocene, and Pleistocene epochs, but these need to be set in a larger framework. Most of the prehistoric life that we know can be fitted into three major eras: the Paleozoic, literally the time of "old life," when seas were widespread and the most advanced animal forms were those of fishes and early amphibians; the Mesozoic ("middle life"), when dinosaurs roamed the earth and even took to the air as flying reptiles; and the Cenozoic ("recent life") when mammals came to dominate the land.

Dr. Robert Dietz of the Environmental Science Services Administration's Atlantic Oceanographic and Meteorological Laboratories has recently advanced a new theory as to the formation of the lower third of Florida—the part of which I have been writing—and it is so extremely interesting that I will try to outline it briefly. Under this theory, all present continents were joined in one supercontinent,

Pangaea, during the Paleozoic. Some time at the end of that era–around 200 million years ago–a crack appeared in this single great land mass, a crack that began just southeast of what is now Florida. As it widened, an inland sea was formed, one that was surrounded by the future continents of North America, South America, Africa, and Europe. At this point, for reasons still unknown, the breakup of the original land mass was halted for 30 million years. Throughout this time, sediment from the rivers and calcium carbonate from the sea piled up in the inland "lake" until three to five miles of limestone rested on top of the underlying sediment, forming the Bahama platform and what is now the lower part of the Florida peninsula. When movement started again and the continents began to drift apart, the Bahama platform and southern Florida became attached to North America and moved with it on its long 5,000 mile journey to the northwest.

Any detailed explanation of the reasons for the crack or of the evidence (and there is a great deal of it) for continental drift is beyond the scope of this book. It is enough to say that geologists today are giving wide acceptance to the idea of a continental breakup and the separation of the continents, and that this new concept of an inland sea lasting for 30 million years and the gradual building of a small land mass within its boundaries seems to be a logical and needed explanation for the existence of southern Florida and the Bahamas. During the Mesozoic, our area was still under water–a great submerged platform–but during the Cenozoic it began to rise.

The three eras are subdivided into periods, which are further broken down into epochs; but since we are concerned from here on only with the age of mammals, we will not backtrack any further. There are six epochs in the Cenozoic: Palaeocene, Eocene, Oligocene, Miocene, Pliocene, and Pleistocene. These names are built upon the basic Greek word, "kainos"–"recent"–anglicized to "cene." So we have, going backward, Pleistocene, "most recent"; Pliocene, "more recent"; Miocene, "less recent"; Oligocene, "little recent"; Eocene, "dawn recent"; and Paleocene, "ancient recent." Translated thus, the names seem very unimaginative and awkward, but this is what we are stuck with.

During the first half of the Cenozoic, the mammals were generally archaic, and some, particularly in the Oligocene, reached a gigantic

ERA	PERIOD	EPOCH	DISTINCTIVE FEATURES	DURATION in millions of years
CENOZOIC	Quaternary	Pleistocene	Widespread glaciation. Early Man.	0-1.5/2.0
	Tertiary Neogene	Pliocene	Many large mammals Land bridge between N. and S. America.	1.5/2.0-7
		Miocene	Widespread grassy plains. Grazing mammals.	7-26
	Palaeogene	Oligocene	Large running mammals. Increase in rodents. Dog and cat families developing.	26-37/38
		Eocene	N. and S. America separated. 1st primitive horse. Archaic mammals.	37/38-53/54
		Paleocene	Small archaic mammals.	53/54-65
MESOZOIC	Cretaceous	(Epochs in Mesozoic and Paleozoic Eras are omitted.)	Climax of dinosaurs and their extinction. Flowering Plants.	65-136
	Jurassic		First birds and mammals. Dinosaurs abundant.	136-190
	Triassic		Early Dinosaurs. Turtles and crocodiles. Cycads and conifers abundant.	190/195-225
PALEOZOIC	Permian		Dying out of many marine species. End of the great coal forests. Glaciation and mountain building.	225-280
	Carboniferous Pennsylvanian Mississippian		Coal forests with scale trees, horsetails, and seed ferns. Many amphibians. First reptiles.	280-345
	Devonian		Fishes abundant. First amphibians.	345-395
	Silurian		First land plants and animals. Invertebrates still dominant.	395-430/440
	Ordovician		First fishes. Marine invertebrates abundant.	430/440- ca. 500
	Cambrian		Ample documentation of a rich marine life, although many forms were still primitive. Prior to the Cambrian the record is sketchy owing to an absence of hard parts.	ca. 500-570

The time scale in this chart was taken from that of J. Laurence Kulp, as revised by a Geological Society of London symposium in 1964. Although accepted by eminent geologists here, some of the dates have already been altered by European paleontologists, and it's quite possible that there will be more revisions in the future.

size. Many of our familiar plants, on the other hand, would have seemed quite at home in this landscape. Oaks, elms, and sycamores were common in various parts of the world and magnolias could be seen along with other recognizable flowering trees. Surveying the scene, we would have noted only that the leaves tended to be large and thick, and that, to our surprise, there was little sign of grass.

With the Oligocene and Miocene came a change in climate. The earlier part of the Cenozoic, particularly the Eocene, had been marked by lowland forests, swamps, and warm, fairly humid weather conditions. But now the land, generally, rose and the climate became much drier, although it was still warm—warmer than at present. At times during the Miocene it was even semi-arid in Florida and we find desert rodents and snakes putting in an appearance. Widespread grassy plains came into being and the earlier mammals, which had browsed upon leaves of trees, shrubs, and herbaceous plants, were replaced in good part by grazers, some of them feeding in great herds. Could we step back in time to the Florida of this period (or possibly a little north of our area, for much of southern Florida was underwater then), we would look out on bands of horses—a smaller, more primitive-looking animal than that of today. Diminutive camels would also run in herds, and stalking them might well be a pack of coyote-sized dogs. Tapirs and peccaries would seem strange in Florida, but they were indeed natives and quite common. So were rhinoceroses and amphicyon, the bear-like carnivore, the largest flesh-eater around. Kites might be circling overhead and doves flying in and out of the bushes. Only the larger mammals would really tell us that we have strayed back into another world.

For me, this vision of the past colors all the present scenery of Florida. I look on the fossil evidence of a shallow Miocene bay—and see the extraordinary parade of animals that walked along its shores or were trapped, perhaps, in its quicksands. This is as much a part of its history as the more recent landing of the Spaniards and the Indian wars.

During the Pliocene, the average temperature dropped, although it wasn't as cool as today. We still have immense herds of horses and camels, but the horses are a little bigger, and one archaic member of the family, moropus, with clawed feet and a long neck, has died out. Peccaries and tapirs are still here and there are a number of dogs and wolves as well as a large bear (a true bear, at last.) Pronghorned antelopes have appeared—they are new on the scene—and on the plains, now, we might well see a sandhill crane, looking exactly as he does today, for this is one of the oldest bird species still in existence. But the period has real surprises in store. Imagine for the moment that we are watching a river bank—the common meeting ground of many animals. We may hear a noisy trumpeting, followed by the crashing sound of underbrush trampled heavily underfoot, and then the appearance of a full-sized mammoth or mastodon. These beasts had entered North America by way of the land bridge, through the Bering Straits, back in the Miocene. They were not uncommon in the West toward the end of the period, but apparently didn't reach Florida until the Pliocene. In the river itself is one of the hornless rhinoceroses, for this animal has taken to the water just as the hippopotamus has today.

But now for a very different scene let us go up to the northern part of our area. In what is today Polk County, southeast of the present Tampa but some thirty to thirty-five miles inland from the coastline that we know, a rocky shore marks the western limits of Florida. (This is during the early Pliocene.) It is desert country, with limestone cliffs descending abruptly into the sea, and it resembles part of present-day Peru. Big seabird colonies are established here, even as they are in Peru today, with rich guano deposits occurring as a result.

If we were to stand on these cliffs, we might look down on an ancestor of the great auk; on Wetmore's, cormorants, guano boobies, and Elmore's gulls—all close to modern species, although not the same. Curiously enough, a goldeneye duck (the Bone Valley species) paddles in the water below. Today the common goldeneye breeds in the far North and enters southern Florida only occasionally in the winter-time. On the rocky shore a godwit (one of the bigger long-billed sandpipers) stands on one leg, apparently resting. (This reconstruction is based on Professor Pierce Brodkorb's excavations in the bone beds near Bartow and the description of his discoveries in Fisher and Peterson's *World of Birds.*)

Toward the end of the Pliocene, another land bridge appeared—one that would change the whole look of our larger wildlife. This was the connection between North and South America. For millions of years, marine creatures had wandered freely between the Pacific and the

Atlantic oceans, while during the same period of time, a distinctive fauna had grown up on each of the two fully separated continents. Now the oceans were parted and the continents joined. Elephants, horses, deer, peccaries, tapirs, and camels all moved for the first time into South America. They were joined in their southward trek by our carnivores: dogs, wolves, bears, and big cats, and their invasion proved too much for the native ungulates, or hoofed mammals. All died out. But some hardier animals indigenous to South America moved northward, and three of them, the opossum, porcupine, and armadillo, we still have. The conspicuous newcomers to Florida were a giant sloth—20 feet high when he rose up to feed upon the tender leaves of a tree—and the heavily-armored glyptodont, a large relative of the armadillo, with a shell that was sometimes five feet long.

The land bridge connecting the two continents was part of a general upheaval that occurred at this time. While the bridge added to our land fauna, the end of the waterway and the emersion of the Florida plateau, which also took place at this time, had a profound effect on marine life. We find Pliocene mollusks in Florida whose nearest relatives today are in the Pacific. The massive upthrust in the Gulf, even though it was spread over a long period of time, resulted in the dying out of great numbers of mollusks, as well as of other marine forms. Perhaps an outer shelf rose first, enclosing a great inland sea. As this became landlocked, its salinity may have increased, or, if it was fed by freshwater streams, the water may have become brackish and then entirely fresh. In any event, many species of mollusks became extinct on the Atlantic side, although their cousins, or even their direct descendants, survived in the Pacific.

Meanwhile, however, land animals were flourishing. Sloth and glyptodont were widespread by the Pleistocene, and at that point there was such an abundance of game on the grasslands of Florida that the common comparison is with the Serengeti Game Preserve in Africa. Never before nor since has our country seen such hordes of the larger mammals. Bears, dire-wolves, and saber-toothed tigers fed upon the herds of horses, camels, deer, bison, and peccaries. Tapirs, capybaras, giant beavers were common, and elephants and mastedons could be found everywhere. Smaller creatures, such as dogs, foxes, pumas, raccoons, armadillos, as well as squirrels, rabbits, and opossums were all here, too. It's a pity that we can know it only through imagination. The actual sight must have been astounding.

It came to an end, of course, and no one quite knows why. All that we do know is that between 10,000 and 9,000 years ago there was an enormous dying-out of the bigger animals—an extinction almost as dramatic as the earlier one of the dinosaurs. Was climatic change the cause? The beasts died at the end of the last ice age when living conditions were improving. And they had survived more drastic upheavals in the Pleistocene. Did Stone Age hunters kill them off? Twelve thousand years ago some of the early Americans were making and using stone projectile points capable of killing big game: mammoths, big-horned bison, and horses. Small bands throughout America lived primarily upon these creatures, and so great was their dependence upon them that they, too, died out when their food supply was exhausted. But if they were the cause, why didn't later Indians destroy their buffalo herds? (They didn't, until they acquired guns and horses.)

This in brief is the history of Florida during the past 26 million years. Dates for the Cenozoic have been changing rapidly throughout the past decade or two, but the latest figures place the start of the Miocene at 26 million years ago. It is thought to have lasted 19 million years. The Pliocene began seven million years ago and lasted four to five million years. The Pleistocene has been lengthened from its original million to two or even three million years.

Only a remnant of the huge assemblage of the Pleistocene is left to us today. Many—the capybaras, tapirs, sloths, and llamas (descendants of camels)—survive only in Central or South America. But I still find it fascinating to realize that a venus clam from the Caloosahatchee River could have lived at the time of the sloth and the mastodon; that an older scallop grew to maturity in a world of camels, tapirs, and rhinoceroses.

Bones of the larger vertebrates are less common south of Tampa than north of it, and hence they will play a very minor part in my present story. Florida, however, has provided the major sites for Miocene land vertebrates east of the Mississippi, and in any natural history of the whole state, they would properly be given ample coverage. S. J. Olsen's *Fossil Mammals of Florida,* published by the Florida Geological Survey, is an excellent booklet on these animals and on the fossil sites. In our area, the phosphate pits of Polk County have produced Miocene and Pliocene vertebrate fossils (including the bird fossils mentioned earlier). Pleistocene remains have been found near Saint Petersburg and Bradenton, usually when dredging was being done for yacht basins or in connection with house-building, particularly on the islands. Some bones of a mastodont and of a primitive mammoth have been found on Alligator Creek in Charlotte County, and Peace Creek in De Soto County seems to be a likely spot for collectors.

One of the best booklets for the amateur on vertebrate fossils is *Let's Find Fossils on the Beach,* by M. C. Thomas, published by the Sunshine Press at Venice, Florida. The beach at Venice has proved highly productive, but other beaches, particularly between Saint Petersburg and Fort Myers on the West Coast, also yield fossil bones and teeth at times. Such areas are better collecting grounds for amateurs, both because specimens are more easily found, and because, being wave-worn, they are not of such value to professionals. It was on the Naples beach that I found my one vertebrate fossil from Florida—the tooth of the giant shark that I spoke of in Chapter Three.

My own great interest has always been in invertebrates—and these fossils are to be found throughout southern Florida. I mean to touch briefly upon some of the sites I have worked, but the best advice I can give is to keep a weather eye out for big piles of dirt—the spoil banks from canal-digging and house construction, the borrow pits from road-building. (A "borrow pit" is an engineering term for stone and gravel left for such purposes as road-building.)

When I first began to hunt for fossils in Florida, I was on the trail of the Caloosahatchee Pliocene, a formation described in almost every textbook, and one I had been reading about for years. Quite naturally, lacking other information, I turned to the banks of the Caloosahatchee River in Lee and Hendry counties. Piles of rock and sand dredged from the river were what I was looking for, but it seemed that every pile to which I was directed had been carted away before I got there.

My search led me through backcountry of a kind that I had never seen before. Ripe grapefruit brushed the car as I drove over narrow lanes, and from time to time I looked out on the river itself—a big, sluggish stream flowing past miles of citrus groves. Finally when I reached the vicinity of Fort Denaud in Hendry County, I realized that I had been driving over great numbers of marine shells—the very fossils

I had been looking for all day. They had been used for road fill or had bounced off heavily-laden trucks, and as I gathered them in, I had no question that I had come upon Pliocene at last. Massive chalky venus clams lay on the roadway, and beautiful big scallops were embedded in the ground not far away. As it happened, I was in rattlesnake country, and one actually slithered across the road in front of me; but fossils outweighed the danger of snakes, although I will admit I did most of my collecting well in the middle of the road.

It was some time before I realized that most of what had dropped from the trucks was Pleistocene and, for a geologist, comparatively recent stuff. The scallops, on the other hand, along with an ark shell I picked up, were from the famous Caloosahatchee formation. Actually there was nothing from their general appearance to distinguish my various specimens except that some of the pectens were much larger than modern scallops in the Florida area. What told me that most of my shells were probably a hundred or so thousand years old, rather than, let us say, two or more million years of age, was the fact that they were almost all modern species: cones, bubble shells, oysters, cockles, and arks that one might find today on the Gulf shore. The trouble was that the material had been dredged, and it's all too easy to combine layers when one is digging out a river bed.

A lot of mixing has taken place in South Florida. Both nature and man have taken a hand in confusing the picture, and it's often very difficult to tell from just what level a fossil has come. Many have already been dug out of lakes, rivers, ditches, and quarries; others have been turned up by bulldozers in leveling ground for developments. In addition, the seas have swept far inland, covering this area, time and time again during the last million years. There has been considerable erosion, too, and many fossils have undoubtedly been identified as from the "wrong period," because of the cutting of stream beds and the vast number of sinkholes that riddle much of the limestone.

Sheer accident—or a roving eye—led to my second discovery of fossils in Florida. I was walking over a golf course at Lehigh Acres, not far from Fort Myers, when I caught sight of a big oyster shell sticking out of the bank of a gully. I knew at once, when I picked it up, that it was no modern shell. In fact I'd never seen such a massive oyster, an inch thick, and almost four inches across. All other considerations vanished until I'd canvassed the whole development. Scattered fossils were everywhere, on banks and along the road, but I struck gold in a pile of marly rock and soil, pushed up by a bulldozer in leveling ground for a new building. Some 37 species came from the spot, with many large and beautiful shells. Big oysters dominated the site, and it was obvious that I had come upon an ancient patch reef or oyster community. Surely this was Pliocene—and Caloosahatchee!

There is always a story to be read from the rocks, if one can but read it aright. I found coral, and knew that the seas then had been warm, warmer than today. Some of the oysters were massive, as I've said, but mingled with them was a species that still survives—the eastern oyster—a mollusk that favors shallow, brackish bays. Some of the other fossils bear out this picture. There are great numbers of *Rexmela subcoronata,* a close relative of the crown melongena. The only time I've ever found crown melongenas in such quantity was on Sanibel, in the muddy brackish waters of Tarpon Bay. Quite a few worm shells (vermicularia) are present, and for a geologist they are important in placing the strata. Other shells are in such perfect condition—a pear whelk, lightning whelks, a murex—that it seems doubtful they were ever battered by the surf. One answer is that they came to rest on a quiet bottom, part sand, part marl, that was protected by an outlying barrier: an islet, a spit, or even a submerged sand bar. There are many barnacles, and these, too, are in accord with the brackish conditions. I note that one shell is covered with barnacles and has been bored both by a worm and by a boring sponge.

Great stretches of turtle grass may have covered the bottom then even as they now do in Biscayne Bay. Typical of the modern turtle grass community are such shells as the rose murex and the tulip band shell. The first is here, and I have the extinct *Fasciolaria apicina* which was very close to the tulip band. Knowing what could have been here, let me add a few more details: mangroves on the mainland shore, pelicans and gulls flying over the water, possibly some of the mammals I described earlier coming to the beach for fish or clams.

Two fossils are a little puzzling. They are freshwater snails, and I have alternative explanations for their presence. Possibly the ancient bay lay at the mouth of a river and the snails were washed into it from this source. Or possibly, since it seems to have been a time of rising land, the snails represent a stage when the sea had retreated and freshwater lakes dotted a marshy area.

There is more to be said about my fossil site, however, for in the above account I have ignored the massive oysters which led to my discovery of the Lehigh Acres' prehistoric fauna. Many of the shells belonged to an earlier period—these certainly did. Was there a more ancient oyster community? It seems likely. How many of the shells belonged to the earlier reef; how many to the later one? I couldn't be certain, although I knew that roughly half of the species were extinct, and the big oyster was the one I would find later at Tamiami sites, although the shells at Lehigh Acres were not quite as heavy.

On the map the part of Lee County embracing Lehigh Acres is shown as Miocene, and Axel Olsson, one of today's authorities on the Pliocene and Miocene of South Florida, thought (on the basis of my identifications, for he didn't see the actual specimens) that some of my fossils were Pinecrest; others from "Unit A," a formation not yet described in published form by Dr. Druid Wilson of the U.S. Geological Survey. The Pinecrest formation is earlier than the Caloosahatchee, and probably late Miocene. Dr. Wilson places the more recent "Unit A" in the early Pleistocene. This meant that I had not found the Caloosahatchee at Lehigh Acres, and I began to suspect that my scallops from Fort Denaud were also "Unit A."

My experience in the search for the proper sequence in the past provides a good example of a major problem that constantly confronts geologists—missing strata. Once upon a time Pliocene limestone almost certainly lay upon the Miocene rocks. And in many places it was all eroded away before the Pleistocene layers were deposited.

When I came back to Lehigh Acres three years later, the pile quite naturally had disappeared, and there were houses on my "dig." There didn't seem to be any other worthwhile spots, and by that time I knew exactly where to go for recognized Caloosahatchee—to La Belle and Clewiston.

The work of the Army Engineers in building an embankment at the southern end of Lake Okeechobee exposed some excellent Caloosahatchee fossils. A roadway of sorts runs along the embankment at Clewiston. Bordered by a canal lined with Australian pines, the setting is a very pleasant one for a collector, and fossils are scattered all over the road. Many are far more exotic than those from Lehigh Acres. (None of the typical Caloosahatchee fossils had appeared there.) The horrid vase shell is typical. A left-handed cone is one of the oddest things I've seen, and the problematical cowrie is another. I picked up a queen chank and Heilprin's miter, both very strange to a modern shell collector. One of the most delicate and beautiful of the fossils is the Wagner ark. There are no oysters here, nor melongenas, and it seems obvious that this was once a very different shoreline. Of course the fossils have been mixed from dredging, and hard and fast conclusions are dangerous, but it seems as if this had once been more of a marine community. I note that these shells are a chalky white, whereas mine from Lehigh Acres were a brownish-yellow. One venus clam had been bored by a snail, just as our modern ones are. I have a moon snail here. Was this the villain? It's not impossible.

On the road back to Lehigh Acres, I stopped at La Belle, headquarters for a huge quarrying operation. Fossils lay everywhere in the waste piles and on the outskirts of the quarry, so that I could collect without having to enter the quarry proper. The truly efficient collector, I am told, gets permission ahead of time and goes in with an inflatable rubber raft, by means of which he can maneuver around the water-filled holes, taking fossils out of their rocky sides. But I am well-satisfied with the piles of discarded material.

Many of the fossils here are the same as at Clewiston; others are like those of Lehigh Acres. I notice that I have melongenas again, though not the great number that were present three years ago at Lehigh Acres. With fossils, as with modern marine life, trying to understand the community seems to me fully as important and interesting as the mere collecting of specimens.

A number of Pliocene sites, including Ortona Locks, I have not yet visited, and I should like to go back to Fort Denaud. A new Pinecrest area at Kissimmee, in Highland County, is said to be good, and there are others that might well be worth investigating.

My discovery of Tamiami fossils was as accidental as my collecting at Lehigh Acres. I was in Naples and I was walking, by chance, along Gulf Shore Drive. "By chance" is really the wrong phrase, for I walk whenever I possibly can, watching and listening for everything along the way. But I wasn't expecting fossils, and certainly not the big gray-white scallops, oysters, and jingle shells at the side of the road. They were embedded in gray limestone and their chalky white dust covered my fingers. With them were barnacles and an occasional sand dollar. It was obvious that the stone had been brought in for the roadbed, and equally obvious that the fossils were unlike anything I'd seen before. In a short time I realized that I had more of the same gray fossils on the beach—as described in an earlier chapter—and my search for an answer to why led me to the public library, which had some excellent works on Florida geology. It also led to this book, because the librarian had been faced with questions such as mine for years and had sought in vain for something on a popular level that would explain the prehistoric life of Collier County (where Naples is), its fossils, and the rapidly changing views on the age of those fossils. I soon found that marine life needed similar coverage, and so did plants. Little by little, what had been a small project was expanded, but I have tried, in the larger endeavor, to give adequate information as to Collier County and its geological past.

What I was collecting in Naples was Tamiami limestone, first described by W. C. Mansfield of the U.S. Geological Survey. When the Tamiami Trail was built, a canal was dug beside it for the double purpose of providing drainage and fill for the roadbed. Dr. Mansfield noted the fossils and decided the formation was Pliocene, but earlier than the Caloosahatchee. In 1955, G. G. Parker put it into the late Miocene, and this dating is now generally accepted.

Parker also did some work at Buckingham in Lee County, just a few miles from Lehigh Acres, and he decided that the shells there also belonged to the Tamiami Formation. On my second visit to Lehigh Acres, I investigated Buckingham and was so fortunate as to find fossils in evidence. (Other geologists have visited the site when there was nothing to be seen.) Since the material I collected appears to be identical with some of that from Lehigh Acres, the site may be Pinecrest. The fossils are certainly not typical of the Tamiami Formation as it appears around Naples.

There are a number of recognized sites for the Tamiami, but one, the borrow pit at the junction of the Trail and Route 29, had been depleted by the time I found it, and a second pit to which I was directed, on the road to the Isle of Capri outside of Naples, had also disappeared. I had better luck, however, at the Sunniland Limestone Quarries on Route 29 north of the Trail. Again I hadn't obtained permission to enter the quarry proper and had to content myself with what lay outside of the fenced area, but I think I found most of the fossils normally collected there. Once more, I had huge oysters, big scallops, jingle shells, barnacles, and inner and outer casts of shells: cockles, arks, turret shells, olives, and venus clams. This is the rather modest reward of a collector in the Tamiami. I find it hard to explain the fascination of these fossils, but ever since I picked up my first gray oyster in Naples, I have been delighted with them. The result is only too often box loads of some of the heaviest fossils I've collected—because I find it hard to leave many behind.

As in the Pinecrest, I did almost as well on my own. A stop for a field of gladiolas due east of Naples gave me a perfect Miocene lion's paw in a double valve. Driving east on the Trail, the ponds eleven miles beyond Royal Palm Hammock caught my eye. It's confusing that there is a Royal Palm Hammock on the Tamiami Trail, and another in the Everglades National Park, but we have to make the best of it. I got out of the car to look for water birds and plants—wax myrtle was growing all along the cart track leading to the ponds—and stumbled over a big sea urchin of the Tamiami, as well as a particularly handsome scallop. A smaller pecten was covered with a mat of bryozoans, just as a modern shell might be.

A few years later I drove west from Miami to Naples on the Tamiami Trail and returned by the new Everglades Parkway (Alligator Alley). At the first rest stop I found myself surrounded by fossils—Pinecrest again (according to Olsson), but looking much more like the Tamiami fossils than had my specimens from Lehigh Acres. (I find this variation extremely interesting.) Once more there were great numbers of scallops, possibly from the sandy bottom of an ancient shallow sea. With them had lived fig shells, olives, lucinas, tellins, venus clams, bittersweet clams, cockles—a wealth of molluscan life, their past presence now marked by molds.

At the second rest stop I knew that I had come upon another great oyster bed, possibly from a Miocene patch reef such as I have pictured earlier. Little else was here save for a few broken pieces of pectens and one fragment of a turret shell, and the oysters probably dominated the scene, eight or ten million years ago, even as their fossils do today. This was all in Collier County. When we crossed over into Broward, the fossils were obviously Pleistocene—the many white fragments in brown rock that is characteristic of the Fort Thompson.

There is another story to be told about the geology of Florida, an that is the tale of how its fossils came to be studied and its strata assigned to the three major epochs: Miocene, Pliocene, and Pleistocene. This work is still in progress and a major battle has occurred along the way, for scientists are anything but the bloodless creatures they are sometimes pictured to be, and the proper dating of a fossil shell can engender quite as much heat, say, as business or social feuds in the nonacademic world.

Much of the geological charting of our country was done during the second half of the last century, but southern Florida was seemingly overlooked until 1886, probably because it was supposed to be mostly coral. In 1886, however, Professor Angelo Heilprin was sent down by the Wagner Free Institute of Philadelphia. (Their names appear in Heilprin's miter and the Wagner ark, both mentioned earlier.) Equipped with a schooner, Professor Heilprin set out to investigate what was then, geologically-speaking, virgin territory—west Florida from Tampa south. What he found was not a foundation of coral, but marl and limestone dating from the Miocene down through the Pleistocene. His greatest discovery—and it was a momentous one for geologists—was the fact that there was Pliocene strata with a rich molluscan fauna along the banks of the Caloosahatchee River. Until then it had been assumed that the only Pliocene fossils in our country lay west of the Rockies. The nearest known Pliocene sites were in Trinidad, and the Caloosahatchee beds rapidly gained world recognition as one of the most productive Pliocene areas ever found. (Since then, fossils of the same age have been discovered in North and South Carolina—the Waccamaw beds.) Professor Heilprin described and named many of the specimens, for a large number were new to science. His initial exploratory trip was followed a year later by that of William Dall, also from the Wagner Free Institute, and, during the next few years, Mr. Dall made a systematic and comprehensive study of all the Caloosahatchee fauna, publishing the results in a monumental work. Dall also added various other localities, principally exposures along Alligator and Shell creeks (tributaries of the Caloosahatchee), and along the Myakka River. Later geologists extended the reaches of the Caloosahatchee strata to Putnam County on the east coast and to Pinellas County on the west. The formation was assumed to be about ten million years old.

Most recently, Dr. Axel Olsson has been working on Pliocene

fossils discovered in the Saint Petersburg area—although that site has now been covered up—in Highland County, and at Pinecrest in the Everglades for late Miocene. One of the books that I depend upon for identification is Olsson and Harbison's *Pliocene Mollusca of Southern Florida* published by the Academy of Natural Sciences in Philadelphia in 1953.

The same year that the Olsson monograph appeared, a graduate student from Kansas University, Jules DuBar, raised the first serious question as to the correct dating of the Caloosahatchee. His argument against a Pliocene date rested principally upon a tooth of *Equus leidyi,* a late Pleistocene horse, found *under* Caloosahatchee fossils which had become more or less solidified in a mass of marl and limestone.

In view of Florida's history of erosion, of land buried again and again beneath the ocean waves, it seemed highly possible that the tooth had been washed into a gully or hole which took it into earlier strata. Then when the seas returned, they carried shells and marl into the hole, and the new material solidified to appear as if it had been there from the beginning. For years I was satisfied that this had to be the answer because, under the DuBar theory, all the Caloosahatchee was *late* Pleistocene, and this seemed most unlikely in view of the fact that over half of its mollusks were extinct, and those that were not often had living relatives in the Pacific, but not in the Gulf or Atlantic. No great catastrophe in the late Pleistocene would explain such mortality, and there was no way in the Pleistocene for Gulf shells to reach the Pacific. On the other hand, as I said earlier, the events of the late Pliocene, with the land bridge breaking the waterway between the two oceans and the upheaval of land in much of the Gulf, do provide the explanation that is needed.

In 1968, in an attempt to resolve this conflict, the Miami Geological Society organized a field trip through Broward, Glades, Palm Beach, Collier, and Hendry counties to study the formations in question. Their guide for the field trip, *Late Cenozoic Stratigraphy of Southern Florida—A Reappraisal,"* included among the seven articles a reprint of one by Dr. DuBar and new papers by Dr. Axel Olsson and Dr. H. Kelly Brooks.

Dr. Brooks set forth here, for the first time in print, the conclusions he had reached after eleven years of work in this field. He disagreed with both Olsson and DuBar, having determined that the lower part of the original "Caloosahatchee" was late Pliocene and early Pleistocene, instead of early Pliocene (Olsson) or late Pleistocene (DuBar). To the layman the difference seems slight; to a geologist it's a matter of five or six million years, and at this point no one can say who is right.

The wealth of fauna, however, that so excited the world of the nineteenth and early twentieth centuries is still here. We have simply moved some of it into the Miocene (for the Pinecrest was once thought Pliocene) and a lot into the early Pleistocene. If this revision is correct, the Waccamaw beds in the Carolinas will be affected, too.

Answers will probably be forthcoming in the next decade. There will be more uranium and thorium datings (so far these have not been too helpful, but they should be in the future); we shall have Druid Wilson's paper on "Unit A"; more vertebrate bones will be found; more careful studies made. For all this, those of us who are not professionals will have a ringside seat. And while we watch the geologists at work, we can still pick up fossils: Tamiami from the Tamiami Trail and Route 29; Pinecrest from the place of that name on the old Loop Road (Route 94) off the Trail, from Alligator Alley (within Collier County), from Lehigh Acres and Buckingham in Lee County, and from Highland County; probable Pliocene from Clewiston, La Belle, Fort Denaud, and a few other places along the Caloosahatchee; "Unit A" from Belle Glade in Glades County and probably elsewhere; and definite Pleistocene from a widespread area. Fossils of the last 100,000 years or so can be gathered on the Keys, on Key Biscayne, in Miami, in the Everglades, along the Broward stretches of Alligator Alley, in Naples, along the Caloosahatchee, and probably throughout much of southern Florida. It may be a shell, a piece of coral, a bryozoan. It may be a mangrove root. Whatever such remnant of the past happens to be, it almost certainly had its being long before man set foot on this continent. It's a reminder of a far distant time and a very different scene.

Common and Scientific Names

Prehistoric mammals (a few characteristic genera and species are indicated):

Pliocene

antelopes, prong-horned: *Hexameryx*
bears: *Agriotherium*
camels: *Procamelus, Megathylopus*
dogs and wolves: *Osteoborus, Pliogula*
glyptodonts: *Glyptodon*
horses: *Hipparion, Neohipparion,* and *Nannipus*
mastodons, mammoths: *Serridentinus, Gomphotherium*
peccaries: *Prosthennops*
rhinoceros, hornless: *Teleoceras proterus* (Leidy)
sloth, giant: *Megatherium* sp.
tapirs: *Tapirus*

Pleistocene

armadillos: *Chlamytherium, Dasypus*
bears: *Ursus, Tremarctos*
beaver, giant: *Castortoides*
bison: *Bison*
camels: *Camelops, Tanupolama*
capybaras: *Neochoerus, Hydrochoerus*
deer: *Cervus, Odoceilus*
dogs, foxes, and wolves: *Canis, Vulpes, Urocyon, Aenocyon*
elephants and mastodons: *Mammuthus, Mammut*
glyptodonts: *Boreastracon*
horses: *Equus*
opossums: *Didelphus*
peccaries: *Mylohyus, Platygonus*
pumas and saber-toothed tigers: *Felis, Panthera, Smilodon*
raccoons: *Procyon*
squirrels and rabbits: *Sciurus, Sylvilagus*
tapirs: *Tapirus*

Invertebrates - Miocene, Pliocene, and Pleistocene

barnacle: *Balanus concavus* Bronn
calusa venus: *Anomalocardia caloosana* (Dall)
crown melongena: *Rexmela subcoronata* (Heilprin)
Everglades scallop: *Plagioctenium evergladensis* (Mansfield)
Heilprin's miter: *Mitra heilprini* Cossmann
horrid vase shell: *Vasum horridum* Heilprin
left-handed cone: *Conus adversarius tryoni* Heilprin
lightning whelk: *Busycon contrarium* (Conrad)

lion's paw: *Nodipecten collierensis* (Mansfield)
moon shell: *Polinices caroliniana* (Conrad)
notogilla: *Notogillia wetherbyi* (Dall)
oysters: *Pycnodonta haitensis* (Sowerby), *Ostrea disparilis* Conrad, *Ostrea sculpturata* Conrad (all three are large oysters)
pear whelk: *Busycon pyrum floridanum* Olss. & Harb.
problematical cowry: *Siphocypraea problematica* (Heilprin)
quahog: *Mercenaria campechiensis* (Gmelin)
queen chank: *Xancus regina* (Heilprin)
rose murex: *Murex rubidus* Baker
sand dollar: *Encope tamiamiensis* Mansfield
scallop: *Aequipecten tamiamiensis* (Mansfield) (with a riblet between the larger ribs)
sea urchin: *Rhyncholampas evergladensis* (Mansfield)
tulip shell: *Fasciolaria apicina* Dall
Wagner ark: *Arca wagneriana* Dall
West Indian murex: *Chicoreus brevifrons* (Lam.)
worm shells: *Vermicularia recta* Olsson & Harbison, *V. weberi* Olss. & Harb.

References

Brooks, H. Kelly, et al., *Miocene-Pliocene Problems of Peninsular Florida.* 13th Field Trip, Southeastern Geological Society. 1967.

Cooke, C. Wythe, and Mossom, Stuart. *Geology of Florida.* 20th Annual Report. Tallahassee, Fla.: Florida Geological Survey, 1929. 198 pp. O. P.

Cooke, C. Wythe. *Scenery of Florida Interpreted by a Geologist.* Florida Geological Survey Bulletin 17. Tallahassee, Fla.: Florida Geological Survey, 1939. 118 pp. O. P.

DuBar, Jules R. *Stratigraphy and Paleontology of the Late Neogene Strata of the Caloosahatchee River Area of Southern Florida.* Tallahassee, Fla: Florida Geological Survey Bulletin 40, 1958. 267 pp.

Heilprin, Angelo. *Explorations on the West Coast of Florida and in the Okeechobee Wilderness.* Philadelphia: Wagner Free Institute of Science, 1887. Reprinted, Ithaca, N.Y.: Paleontological Research Institution, 1964. 141 pp.

Mansfield, Wendell C. "Some Tertiary Mollusks from Southern

Florida." *U.S. National Museum Proceedings,* Vol. 79, Article 21. Washington, D.C.: Government Printing Office, 1931. 12 pp. O. P.

Martin, Paul S. "Pleistocene Overkill." *Natural History* LXXVI (No. 10, 1967).

Olsson, Axel A., and Harbison, Anne. *Pliocene Mollusca of Southern Florida.* Philadelphia: Academy of Natural Sciences, 1953. 457 pp.

Olsson, Axel A., and Petit, Richard E. *Some Neogene Mollusca from Florida and the Carolinas.* American Paleontology Bulletin 217. Ithaca. N.Y.: Paleontological Research Institute, 1964. 65 pp.

Parker, Gerald G., and Cooke, C. Wythe. *Late Cenozoic Geology of Southern Florida.* Florida Geological Survey Bulletin 27. Tallahassee, Fla.: Florida Geological Survey, 1944. 119 pp.

Perkins, Ronald D., compiler. *Late Cenozoic Stratigraphy of Southern Florida—A Reappraisal.* Second Annual Field Trip of the Miami Geological Society. Miami: Miami Geological Society, 1968. 110 pp.

Puri, Harbans S., and Vernon, Robert O. *Summary of the Geology of Florida and a Guidebook to the Classic Exposures.* Florida Geological Survey Special Publication No. 5. Tallahassee, Fla.: Florida Geological Survey, 1964. 312 pp.

Richards, Horace G. *Studies on the Marine Pleistocene.* Philadelphia: American Philosophical Society, 1962. 94 pp.

Simons, E. L. "Unraveling the Age of Earth and Man." *Natural History* LXXVI (No. 2, 1967).

*Thomas, M. C. *Let's Find Fossils on the Beach.* Venice, Fla.: Sunshine Press, 1962. 51 pp.

Part IV
Wild Areas:
Natural and Man-Made

Rock ledges at the northern end of Key Biscayne extend into Bear Cut. Ledges such as these with rock pools and sheltered inlets are often rich in marine life.

Previous page:
Our national bird, the bald eagle, looks out upon an increasingly unfriendly world. Preserving the eagle is one of the major aims of conservationists.

12

Mud Flats, Swamps, and Rocky Shores

Geographically, the mud flat, the rocky shore, the mangrove swamp seem closely akin to the ocean beach. Sometimes a mere sliver of land separates one from the other, but the difference is enormous. On a sunny, quiet day with blue sea stretching far to the horizon and white sand lying in gentle curves along the shoreline, the beach is a welcoming, pleasant place, and throngs of bathers attest to this fact.

The mud flat, on the other hand, looks dirty and forbidding, and it's rare to find a human being walking across its treacherous-looking surface. It may border a shallow lagoon or bay, with the flat broken into long interlacing fingers. Mangroves with odd exposed stilt roots may grow on its edge, but few other plants favor this sterile-looking shore. A stagnant odor is common. Even the shells have lost their color and taken on the uniform whitish-muddy appearance of the flat. How treacherous is the mud? Will it bear a man or woman? What of the mangroves? Could one break through them if there were need to flee? From what? This is a nameless, unreasoning fear, but somehow, from somewhere, comes the memory of O'Neill's "Emperor Jones" and what the mangroves and the mud meant to him.

The rocky shore is only slightly more attractive. Here are sudden holes that can twist an ankle, slippery stretches due to algae, stones that are rough to the touch because of barnacles, and, always, the tide pools that have to be circled unless one is prepared to wade.

Because the mud flats, the rocks, and the mangroves share so little of the atmosphere of the beach, I purposely excluded them from that section. These are places for birds, rather than for man. Many times they carry a feeling of the remote wilderness, but he who has a taste for undisturbed wild areas will welcome such sites. On the mud flats may be found shorebirds by the hundred, drawn up in great ranks. Here are companies of sandpipers, some feeding busily, some resting in long rows. There are lines of plovers, too—in the Old English phrase, a "congregation of plovers," just as one has a "bevy of quails" or a "pride of lions." Intermingled with them are gulls and black skimmers, while farther out in the shoals are herons and ibises.

One of the most memorable gatherings of shorebirds that I found in Florida was on the causeway running between Vanderbilt Beach and Fort Myers Beach. The scene is a typical one—flats of mud and marl bordering an inland lagoon for a distance, at a guess, of half a mile. Close to a quarter of a mile extends between water and road, with the birds lined up at the water's edge.

Leaving the car, I scramble over windrows of bleached and chalky clams, crunching them underfoot. The whole area is laced with winding channels of water and it's hard to tell whether some of the mud flats are islands or necks of land. Beyond lies the lagoon, with a mangrove forest on its distant shore. A white pelican is drifting in the water, and near the mangroves I can make out a great blue heron stalking purposefully through the shallows.

All around me is the curious fetid smell of the mud flat. The marl oozes around my bare feet (for I have discarded footgear), and from time to time as I sink too deeply into it, I have to backtrack to firmer ground. In front, pellets from the burrows of fiddler crabs cover the ground, and there are many empty shells of the horseshoe crab.

But dominating everything is the army of shorebirds. On the outer bars, black-bellied plovers stand in rows facing the water. Small "ring plovers"—the semi-palmated—run busily along an inward curve of the lagoon. I hear the piping plovers, but it's some time before I can distinguish them, even though they are close at hand. So perfectly do they blend with the sandy marl that it's only when I catch a sudden movement and turn my glasses on that particular spot that I see the bird. Killdeers belong to the plover group and are the last of the common four. They have two rings on their breasts instead of the single one of the semi-palmated or the broken one of the piping plover. Just one is here today, running inshore beyond the piping plovers, and I am surprised to see him because killdeers are more commonly found around inland pools and plowed fields.

Six different sandpipers are in this gathering. Big gray willets are feeding off to the left in a little group, not far from a band of dowitchers. The dowitchers are rather stocky sandpipers, about the size of a black-belly, but with a long bill, and they feed in a distinctive manner, pumping their heads up and down like a sewing machine as they wade belly-deep through an expanse of shallow water. In among the black-bellies are dunlins, definitely smaller, with long bills that have a slight downward curve. Dunlins used to be called "red-backed sandpipers" and in spring they have a bright rusty back and a black belly. Pity the poor birder who tries to make his identification in winter—in breeding plumage many sandpipers are distinctive, but in winter they are distressingly alike!

Two different "peeps" are running around at the water's edge, although each kind usually stays with his fellows. One is the sparrow-sized semi-palmated sandpiper with black legs; the other, the least sandpiper, very slightly smaller with yellow legs. The last of our group is a knot, another of the stocky, short-necked birds, about the size of a black-belly, but with a bill that's longer than a plover's, shorter than a willet's, dowitcher's, or dunlin's. There are only half a dozen knots here as against twenty to fifty of most of the other species.

A constant flow of sound comes to me from the gathering. The plaintive whistle of the black-belly mingles with the piping call of the smallest plovers, and the sweet note of the ring-necks. I hear shrill peeps, a ringing "whee-wee-wee" from the willets, and the low trill of the dunlins. Every so often a flock rises abruptly into the air, whirls out over the water, dipping and twisting in beautiful arabesques, now showing white, now dark, and finally coming to rest just a few feet from where it started.

Most of the larger birds, with the exception of the dowitchers, are resting. Some have turned their heads around and laid them on their back feathers. Some are preening themselves. One knot is bathing himself vigorously, splashing water in all directions. But most of the running and active feeding are done by the peeps and the two little plovers.

To an inland dweller, the number and variety of the water birds is at first bewildering. I found it helpful, however, to sort them into their orders (there are nine of them) and this at least points up relationships. The nine are:

1. Grebes
2. Loons
3. Penguins
4. Tube-nosed Swimmers—the albatrosses, shearwaters, and petrels)
5. Pelicans and their allies (including cormorants, anhingas, and frigatebirds)
6. Herons and their allies (including storks, ibises, spoonbills, and flamingos)
7. Waterfowl: swans, geese, and ducks
8. Cranes, rails, and their allies (including limpkins, gallinules, and coots)
9. Shorebirds, gulls, and auks (including sandpipers, plovers, skimmers, terns, stilts, and avocets)

Two of these orders obviously do not concern us. It would be as surprising to find a penguin on a Florida mud flat as to see an albatross soaring overhead. Loons are sometimes seen during the winter months, swimming in the ocean and in saltwater lagoons, but in general we are dealing with six orders, all of which could have at least one representative in a swamp or mud flat. By showing what is likely to be around, the task of identification—for those who want names—may be eased.

From the great assemblage on the causeway to Fort Myers Beach, let us go southward to another mud flat—that at Chokoloskee, an islet near Everglades City that came into being as an Indian shell mound. Standing in the roadway which borders the shore, I hear the crabs before I see them, and for a moment I am puzzled at the sharp crackling ahead of me. Then as I break through the hedgerow, I look out on fiddlers by the thousands running over the sandy mud. Many are retreating into the mangroves, and their numbers are such that it's hard not to step on them.

Beyond the fiddlers is a bay so shallow that only a few inches seem to cover its entire bottom. No wave disturbs that flat surface; no duck paddles here; no heron wades. Only the shorebirds are huddled in a great multitude on the exposed flats—many of them the same ones that we saw on the causeway: black-bellies, ring-necks, dunlins, least sandpipers, a willet or two. Mangroves encircle much of the bay, and a yellow-crowned night heron is sitting motionless on one of the branches. This gray heron has a heavy body and a short thick neck, with black and white markings on his head. The "yellow crown" is not visible. A favorite article in his diet is the fiddler crab, which, of course, explains why he is here. Willets also like fiddlers, but, fortunately for these crabs, most of the common shorebirds find them too big to deal with. The other herons generally prefer fishes, although they also eat frogs and some crustaceans.

What vast quantities of animal life must swim, crawl, or burrow in this shallow water and in the mud below it! The plovers and sandpipers throng here because of the abundance of food: worms, insects, mollusks, and small crustaceans. Millions of tiny shrimps (ghost, snapping, and others) must lie in this soft ooze. Marine worms of many kinds must be burrowing through the mud. Amphipods (the order to which beach fleas and sandhoppers belong) are undoubtedly here, along with aquatic insects that live in or near brackish water. As I work my way carefully over the flats, I can see empty chalky macoma shells everywhere and I wonder how many of these have been eaten by the shorebirds.

A shallow bay or lagoon provides a very different home for marine life from that of the sandy or rocky coast, with its constant pounding of surf. On the ocean shore, many forms of life survive only by burrowing into the sand or by attaching themselves firmly to the rocks. Normally, the sheltered bay or lagoon has no such violent encounters with the tide, and its animal life can move about more freely. Minnows and invertebrates are usually abundant, but the species are not always the same as those of the beach. Most mollusks, for instance, have very specific requirements as to the amount of salt water they must have. Some can tolerate a degree of brackish water, some even do better when sea water is mixed with fresh, but many require the true oceanic currents. A sandy versus a muddy bottom also makes a great difference, with even closely related species showing marked preferences. What is true of shells is also true of other forms of marine life, and, in short, we have come back to ecological niches.

Looking out over the bay, I am suddenly aware that this scene could have been reproduced almost exactly 50 to 60 million years ago. As in the cypress swamp, I am again in an ancient world, for plovers and sandpipers had achieved a form very close to their present one at the beginning of the Cenozoic. Herons have an early ancestry, and the fiddler crab goes way back into antiquity. Three of the four mangroves have existed since the Eocene, so if I turn my back on the grasses and weeds by the roadside, I can easily imagine that I have stepped far back into the past.

As a matter of fact, all of the nine orders of water birds were much more abundant during other epochs than they are now. The pelicans, cormorants, anhingas, etc., were at their peak in the Paleocene, 70 to 60 million years ago, and have dwindled to a mere fraction of their former numbers. The same is true of the crane, rail order, and of the shorebird, gull group. Waterfowl are way down from their best periods during the Miocene and Pliocene, and the other orders show a similar decline. Only some of the land birds have increased during the last million years, with perching birds making a truly spectacular jump. Oliver L. Austin, Jr., in his *Birds of the World,* refers to "the steady decline of the more primitive non-passerine orders," and says that "numerically speaking, the perching birds are the heirs of the avian ages and should eventually inherit the birds' share of the earth, or whatever the dominant vertebrate, man, eventually leaves for them."

Shorebirds have definite flats that they frequent. On some of these muddy shores they may have been gathering long before Columbus sighted the New World. Other flats are recent, having been built by man, but man has also destroyed some of the favorite haunts of the water birds. I used to look for the sandpipers and plovers in an arm of the sea that came into Naples, until the land was taken over by developers and the shoreline was dredged out for boats. Marco Island lost many of its land and water birds because of spraying. On the other hand, shorebirds flock along the man-made Courtney Campbell Causeway between Tampa and Clearwater (Route 60). At low tide they can be seen along the causeway between Miami and Virginia Key, although the best spot for them, here, is behind the Marine Stadium, where there is often a magnificent assemblage that includes black skimmers, terns, and laughing gulls, along with the shorebirds, and, wading in the water, white and scarlet ibises.

There are variations on the mud flat theme. I saw a gathering of shorebirds on Lower Matecumbe, standing on a marly point facing the ocean. There was another collection of them around an inland pond on the Shark River loop road. In the first group, terns and skimmers mingled with the plovers and sandpipers; in the second, there were many yellowlegs and a common lake duck, the blue-winged teal. Shorebirds assemble on Sanibel on the muddy shores of Tarpon Bay, and it was here in the mangroves that I first saw that eerie creature, the anhinga. There, too, were night herons, almost lost to sight in the mangrove jungle. Plovers and sandpipers fed on the unwholesome-looking mud, and there, too, covered with slimy algae and marl, were some of the most beautiful of all shells—the crown melongenas.

Still a fourth setting can be seen at Flamingo, with a stony, muddy shore facing Florida Bay. Black skimmers often dominate the scene, and their early morning flight across the bay, with lower bill just cutting the water, is spectacular. There are shorebirds, of course, as well, along with many herons, and it was at Flamingo that I first saw a reddish egret, that dark heron, a little larger than the Louisiana and little blue, that is usually identified by his seemingly absurd antics. Frequently he runs through the water with wings outstretched. He may flap them, or he may hop around, having a method of feeding that calls for remarkable activity. The reddish egret is an uncommon heron, found only on saltwater flats, which explains in part why we are meeting him here for the first time.

The great congregations of shorebirds occur on wide mud flats, those that lie along a fair-sized body of water. But there is another kind of mud flat with few birds and a very different atmosphere, one that I first discovered on Sanibel. In a little pool, hemmed in by mangroves, a single snowy egret stepped gingerly through the thin layer of water, showing the "yellow slipper" at the end of his black leg with each deliberate footfall. The scene was hushed, secretive and timeless.

Virginia Key has a larger pond on the road behind the Marine Stadium. It, too, has that feeling of secrecy and remoteness. The water lies dark beneath the overhanging mangroves, and hardly a sound disturbs the quiet. But then, as I intrude upon this hidden world, there is an eruption of noise. A yellow-crowned night heron squawks loudly and flies, still complaining, into the mangrove forest. A kingfisher shrills in protest, and a greater yellowlegs takes off uttering his familiar "whew-whew-whew." I've disturbed an osprey as well, who must have been fishing in the pond. With a loud cry, he mounts up into the sky, a majestic creature with his white head, white belly, and hawk wings. Finally, a white ibis drifts across the lagoon, and, he, too, is berating me with harsh words.

I look at them all like a child who has just broken the best teacup. Really I meant no harm! But in spite of that, nothing is left on the near shore. Only in the distance can I see a great blue heron wading through the shallows, intent upon his dinner.

Now I am aware again of the pervasive rotting smell of mud flats. Skeletons of dead mangroves stand out against the sky and on one of them I discover the white ibis watching me intently. Vultures are circling—it's the kind of landscape in which vultures belong—but no other birds are to be seen.

The flats in front of me are broken by what seem to be thousands of short wands set upright into the ground. Actually they are the pencillike roots of black mangrove—properly called "pneumato-phores." Just as the cypress sends up "knees," so the black mangrove produces leafless stems, or breathing roots, from its heavy mass of underground roots, and these pneumatophores, most of them about a foot in height, have spread like an army over the mud flats, stopping only where the red mangrove begins. So dense is their growth that I can hardly walk through them, and I also sink ankle-deep into the mud, so I turn back to firmer ground.

Black mangrove trees line the near shore of the pond, coming up to the roadway from which I entered, but they are really only bushes here, not more than a few feet high. Their upturned leaves show pale green, almost silvery, undersides, and some are coated with salt crystals. When I see this I know for certain that I have the black mangrove, often called "salt bush" because of this peculiarity.

Up to now, I have spoken generally of "mangroves" without distinguishing the four species, and for the most part I meant red mangrove when I used the word. It's the red mangrove that forms a heavy background for the pond, its dark leathery leaves making great masses that seem to brood above the water. Its prop roots—grayish underpinnings, like stilts—are barely visible between the leaves and the surface of the pond. Close at hand, the great arching roots can be seen coming out of the trunk several feet above the ground and curving downward into the mud. Other roots descend from the branches and thicken into stems, and the whole makes an impenetrable thicket. The chief requirement of the red mangrove is water—salt or fresh—so that its roots do not dry out.

Both black and white mangroves grow a little farther back from the shore, but they, too, must be close to water in order to survive, and sometimes, as here, the pneumatophores of the black mangrove extend right into the water, too. The last of this group, the buttonwood, is not dependent upon close proximity to the sea. While it may be found with the red mangrove, it occurs most frequently farther inland with the black mangrove.

Only two of the mangroves, the white mangrove and the buttonwood (or button-mangrove), are related. The other two belong to separate families and it's better, botanically, to speak of a "mangrove habit." What characterizes the mangroves is their ability to grow in salt water and to build new land. The prop roots of the red mangrove, the pneumatophores of the black mangrove, and to a lesser extent of the white mangrove (which produces these roots much less frequently) catch and hold debris, and by this means play an important part in extending land seaward and in building new islands. The buttonwood (which, of course, is not related in any way to our northern sycamore or buttonwood) is a soil builder, too, but it operates in a different way.

Charles T. Simpson in *Florida Wild Life* gives an excellent description of this, saying that the buttonwood starts life as a tall tree but is soon knocked over by a storm, when it sends up straight shoots from the tip. "Again the erect growth is overthrown by storm and the tall, upright branches are prostrate. These send up other more or less straight trunks which in turn are blown over until the whole becomes a confused, straggling growth, sometimes reaching for more than a hundred feet from the place of starting." It's this sprawling thicket that again acts as a trap for leaves, branches, dirt, and debris washed in by storms.

There are other resemblances among the four. All have great underground root systems which hold the land against torrential rains and high tides. All have leathery dark green leaves, heavy wood, and bark rich in the tannic acid that is used for tanning leather. The water around them is often stained brown from this chemical and because of it the shipworm never bores into mangrove wood. The first three produce embryos or radicles that are fully grown and ready to put out roots or leaves as soon as they touch upon a muddy bottom. Since the live seedlings are often carried great distances by the current, and will start growing whenever they come to rest upon a sandy or muddy bar, they create many new islands. Before long, the Ten Thousand Islands are expected to be dry land with most of the intervening channels filled, all due to the mangroves. Whenever you see such a seedling on the beach, know that you are looking upon a mangrove on the move—and that its pioneering role may add fresh room for man's ever-expanding population.

I shall touch only briefly upon the differences between the four The red mangrove has oval leaves and prop roots, and attains tree size around Miami more frequently than the others. Red and white mangroves are so similar that I found a botanist checking the glands on the leaf petiole of the white to be sure of his identification, and at that point I gave up trying to say which was which, although I admit the glands do appear as easily spotted little bumps if one wants to go that far. The trunk of the black is a dark brown with orange-red showing through where the outer bark has peeled off, that of the white is reddish-brown. Leaves of both are elliptical and dark green with lighter undersides.

I have never found a buttonwood behaving in accordance with Simpson's description, but I am sure this is only because I haven't seen enough of them. Red mangroves and black mangroves are common, and probably the white mangrove is, too. I had to hunt for the buttonwood, though, at Fairchild, finally discovering a clump of small stems much like that of a lilac that has been allowed to send up many suckers. The leaves are alternate instead of being opposite as with the other three, and they are pointed at the tips, lanceolate in shape. Leathery dried fruits with a buttonlike look are conspicuous at the tips of the branches, and I'm told they were actually used as buttons in the early days on the Keys. Later I found a few bushy clumps on Key Biscayne and the gnarled, twisted trees that I mentioned earlier in the park on Virginia Key. A shrubby cultivated variety with silvery-gray leaves is often used on lawns and parkway plantings.

The mangroves that cover the Ten Thousand Islands, the islets in

Florida Bay, and most of the southwestern shore of Florida, including much of the Everglades National Park, make up the largest mangrove forest in the world. The four trees which we know in Florida are all tropical—Tampa is the northernmost limit of the red mangrove—but they spread southward through the West Indies, Mexico, and Central American to South America, and all but the red mangrove also appear on the coast of Africa. (The latter has relatives in Japan, tropical Asia, and Australia.) How they have managed such a wide distribution is something of a mystery. The seedlings seem designed for transportation by water, and yet somehow they crossed the Isthmus of Panama, before there was a canal, to make an appearance on Pacific shores. In a favorable climate and location some of the mangroves achieve tremendous height, but here on Virginia Key, the red mangrove wall around two-thirds of the pond is only about thirty feet high and there are many small trees close at hand that are mostly prop roots, with only a foot or so of trunk and leaves.

Before me on Virginia Key a muddy stretch goes down to the water and every inch, it seems, is covered with the holes and pellets of fiddler crabs. No fiddlers are in sight, however, today, and the only so-called crab is limulus, the horseshoe crab. With great interest I watch a female moving deliberately through the shallow water with a smaller male clinging on behind. Empty shells of limulus lay on the beach when I walked there and on some of the mud flats, but this is the first time I have seen the living creature. Because of my great interest in prehistory, I have commented often here on survivors from the past—on animals and plants that give us a glimpse of what it was like in far-distant periods of time. Such an animal is limulus. With his big, oddly-shaped front shield—more like a horse's foot than a shoe, the small triangular middle section, and the long, spikelike tail, he is unmistakable. Females may be as long as twenty inches, but even the smaller males are very noticeable, for the animal has a definitely archaic look.

There is much of interest about the horseshoe crab. In spite of the name, he isn't a crab—in fact he isn't even a crustacean, but belongs properly with the spiders. Limulus has certainly been with us in his present form for a good 175 million years. There has been a tendency in the last decade to push him well back into the Paleozoic as new evidence comes to light, but we will content ourselves here with picturing him in the Jurassic, crawling over the sandy floor or floating bottom up as he does today, while ichthyosaurs, those fellow reptiles and contemporaries of the dinosaurs, fished in the very same seas. Ever since then—while the dinosaurs multiplied and then died away, while mammals came to dominate the land, and finally, during man's emergence, limulus has gone his unchanging way, feeding on small clams, worms, dead fishes and seaweeds, chewing his food not with his jaws, but with the spiny base of his walking legs—an odd arrangement, to say the least, but one he shares with his extinct relatives, the ancient eurypterids of the Silurian period, some 400 million years ago.

The horseshoe crab is by no means the oldest form of life, though he is sometimes described as such. Many invertebrates are much earlier and even some fishes, such as the sharks, probably came before him, but he provides a clue as to what an extinct and rather important group, the Silurian eurypterids, were like. And he is a remarkable sea animal quite on his own. Today the horseshoe crabs are mating, even though it's only January, and I watch them moving through the shallow water with their oddly rolling gait until they are out of sight.

At my feet, whitened shells lie in little piles and windrows with strange-looking spikes of saltwort and glasswort shooting up among them. The glasswort looks primitive—as archaic as limulus—for its leaves have been reduced to scales, but this is a case of a modern plant that appears to have gone backward—retrograded—to fit its niche. Saltwort has a rather similar look with fleshy club-shaped leaves. Both live on salt flats, and this is their adaptation to an inhospitable terrain.

Beyond the glasswort, a large puddle is covered with a green sickly-looking scum. Leaves blow across the upper flats with a hollow rustle and I feel the ground giving again under my feet. A few years ago, a boy sank deeply into this mud not too far away and had to be rescued. Thinking of this, I turn back to the higher roadway.

Let the ibises and the night heron come back! Let the osprey fish in peace. Let the yellowlegs feed in these shallows. I shall disturb them no more. This is a secret world—and to my fancy a somewhat fearful one. I shall leave it to the birds and to all of the hidden inhabitants of the holes.

The mangroves on Virginia Key are small. One needs to go elsewhere to sense the true magnitude of the mangrove forest. Giant trees reaching seventy feet in height used to grow behind Cape Sable, and the forest here apparently was an extraordinary sight before it was damaged by Hurricane Donna. I never saw it, but I have gone through the winding channels of the Ten Thousand Islands in a motorboat, and have traveled by the same means through the mangroves off Key Largo. Both times I felt as if I were in a maze: the islands, the channels, were so incredibly the same, it was amazing that anyone could find a path through that jungle. Little else grows with the mangroves. For mile after mile, one island duplicates another, often with no land visible above the waves. It's an endless world of low green trees spreading over the sea, with water lapping constantly against the arching roots. I wondered how many men—before there were channel markers—were lost, and perhaps died here, unable to find a way out.

Another picture of mangroves comes to mind. In Matheson Hammock, the road winds through a magnificent growth with an impenetrable jungle of prop roots. This is the thicket at its most impressive and to me it has an awe-inspiring as well as a terrifying quality. Its very wildness, however, offers protection for many species. The mangrove swamps and islands have generally been a haven for nesting birds. Here breed herons, white ibises, pelicans, and the lovely roseate spoonbill.

And now before we leave these wilder areas, let us look briefly at the seaweeds and invertebrates of bay and rocky point. Bear Cut is the channel that lies between Key Biscayne and Virginia Key, and it was given the name because bears were once indeed seen on its shores. The northern end of Key Biscayne has been described in a very interesting booklet, "Littoral Marine Life of Southern Florida" by Frederick M. Bayer. Guide in hand, let us walk along this shore, for it's an excellent example of what lies beside a typical subtropical bay.

Sandy mud is underfoot, as we would expect, and there are crescent-shaped beaches with mangroves coming out into the water at the points. At the very outset my eye is caught by a dozen or more small black chimneys protruding from the sand in the very shallow water. On Marco I found one such chimney washed in by the waves, but here is a living colony of plumed worms. Just once have I seen the owner of a tube—on a muddy shore at Saint Croix in the Virgin Islands. The worm put out its head and its spectacular red plumes waved in the currents—a beautiful sight! A sea hare (that odd creature I also saw at Marco) lies stranded above the tide line, dark purple spots standing out against the yellow-green of its shapeless body.

An abundance of sea life, some of it living, much of it dead, is characteristic of a bay shore. The quieter waters here provide a home for many marine plants and animals, creatures that might not have survived in the ocean surf. As a result, a heavy tide wrack stretches behind me full of smelly sponges: orange tethyas, vase and tube sponges, branching haliclonas and verongias, hard, crusty axinellas, and crumbling dysideas. There are sea plumes and sea whips, too, buried under the mass of turtle grass.

Shells—mostly small ones—are strewn all over the shore. In an hour's time I pick up forty species, about what I had on the ocean side in an equal time, but with many differences. One shell is that of a young measled cowrie which, like melongena, is peculiarly a mollusk of the bay. So is the eastern oyster, and another is a West Indian bubble shell which belongs where I've found it—on a mud flat. Jasper cones are numerous, and so are common nassas. The lovely angel wing should be here, but isn't, perhaps because this isn't pure mud. It, like the pen shell, burrows into the floor of its watery home, but while pen colonies may be found in pure sand as well as in sandy mud, the angel wing lives only in soft mud and the shell may be as much as one to two feet below the surface.

Looking out over the bay, I can see long patches of turtle grass making purple bands in the greenish water. Dr. Bayer points out that there is manatee grass as well, here, and that the patches offer shelter to ark shells, tulip shells, star shells, pens, cockles, turban shells, murexes, young conchs, the spotted sea hare, and the variegated sea urchin. At low tide, the holes of worms and ghost shrimps can be seen, while near the high tide line are the burrows of the ghost crab. This is probably very much like the world that we saw in fossil form at Lehigh Acres.

Still following the guide, I go on to the first clump of red mangroves. This is another ecological niche with a definite community of its own. I should find live coon or mangrove oysters clinging to the roots by the curious hooked fingers of their shells. The mangrove periwinkle should be here and mangrove crabs should be visible, possibly in the upper branches. A tufted seaweed (bostrychia) ought to be growing on the roots, but not a plant or animal is to be seen. Raccoons and melongenas both feed on the oysters. Are they responsible for their absence, or has man disturbed the whole community, for this is a favorite picnicking and bathing area? Or pollution may be the answer. It's almost as interesting to find a niche unfilled as it is to find it properly tenanted. All that the roots hold today are broken shells, bottles, sponges, and pieces of wood, but at least this is land-building in a concrete form.

A stream runs down to the water on the other side of the point. I cross this and inspect another clump of mangroves but it, too, is barren of life. The muddy sand beyond, however, is strewn with seaweeds, some with curious forms and easily recognized. Conspicuous among them are halimedas, stiffened white seaweeds in the form of kidney-shaped wedges, strung one above the other. The merman's shaving brush, a tuft of stiff white hairs on a short stem, is also here. (Both of these were green when alive.) And finally I pick up a brown peacock's tail, looking like a rounded fan with concentric circles. It has the delightful name of *Padina sanctae-crucis*—Padina of the Holy Cross. These three seaweeds were common at Montego Bay in Jamaica when I first collected there in the early thirties, and they bring back a flood of memories. The merman's shaving brush is a characteristic plant of the warm bay, and the padina and this particular halimeda belong to sheltered areas.

To landward in the sand of the upper beach, I notice a meandering trail, two grooves with a fainter line between them, and know it for the mark of a young horseshoe crab. I've come almost half a mile, now, and the scene is changing, for at the northeast end of Key Biscayne, where bay and ocean meet, there is a rocky point made up of the fossilized roots of the black mangrove. Its surface is extremely rough, not only because of the roots, but because the shelf is broken by an endless number of holes. Inlets, fingers of water, also reach into the point, and tide pools are numerous.

As I near the point there are more tracks, but these are small and it takes only a few minutes to find out who is responsible—a tiny mollusk, the false cerith, with a black and white shell. The little animals are gathered by the thousands on the mud flats just before the shelf, and on the ledges themselves. They tell me at the very outset that I have come into a community of living things. Standing on the dark rocks and looking out over the shallow rock-encircled pools, I can see the evidence of life on every hand. Minnow-sized fish dart out from a sheltering rock and disappear in a miniature forest of seaweeds. Some of the weed is sea lettuce attached to the sandy bottom. Some are the reddish tufts of ceramium. Mermaid's hair grows on the rocks and there are clumps of brown padina, the peacock's tail. Wedge-shaped halimeda, bright green now in its living form, stands out among the flimsier sea lettuce and mermail's hair.

Shells move purposefully over the floor of a nearby pool. I pick one up and find, as I'd guessed, that it is the home of a hermit crab. All of the moving shells—and there are many of them—belong to the hermits. True crabs scuttle over the bottom, too, and the sands, like the ledge, are covered with false ceriths.

The simplest way to get out to the end of the point is to wade, and I do so, with bits of floating turtle grass and broken sea lettuce brushing against my ankles. On the larger masses of rock, the mangrove roots are clearly visible. I kneel down on one of these and discover the massive barnacles that I found near the Royal Biscayne Hotel. Honeycomb worms have built their encrusting tubes all over the fossil mangroves, and there are great numbers of neritas clinging to the rock just above and below the water's edge. Limpets are here, too, and off the point I can see the gelatinous fronds of caulerpa. This is all the familiar rock community, with the additional riches of the tide pool added to it.

The guide says I should find anemones and creeping comb jellies (vallicula), but if they are here, I can't spot them. What I do have is a group of venus girdles, transparent ribbons each an inch wide and perhaps ten inches long, drifting through the pool in wavy folds—resembling pale, nearly colorless chiffon as it might look if soaked with water. The venus girdle (there are a dozen or more) is also a comb jelly and it's the first I have ever seen. A close relative of vallicula, it is considerably more impressive, but this is an old story to every naturalist. What he goes for is often missing; what is there many times is much more interesting.

As I stand up, a scarlet ibis flies up Bear Cut, making a brilliant splash of salmon against the sky. A willet and a black-belly stand on the ledges not too far away, and a merganser bobs in the water of the bay some twenty-five feet offshore. The birds and the sea life make this a wonderful spot, but I wonder how much longer it will remain as wild as it is.

Because of the rough footing, few people come to the point on weekdays, and one can watch its wildlife free from noise and other disturbances. Places that offer such a wilderness feeling are only too rare today and we need them in our overcrowded world. And the point has another very special value, for, except on the Keys, rocky shores and tide pools are seldom found in southern Florida. The opportunity they provide for observation of near-shore life is almost unequalled, and as we learn to appreciate the community and its importance, places such as the point at Bear Cut should be set aside as areas that we can't afford to lose.

Common and Scientific Names

black mangrove: *Avicennia nitida* Jacq.

bostrychia: *Bostrychia montagnei* Harvey (a seaweed found on red mangrove roots)

buttonwood: *Conocarpus erecta* L. (var. *sericea* Forster ex DC - silver buttonwood)

comb jelly: *Vallicula multiformis* Rankin

common nassa: *Nassarius vibex* (Say)

constricted macoma: *Macoma constricta* (Gmelin)

coon oyster: *Ostrea frons* Linné

crown melongena (Florida crown conch) *Melongena corona* (Gmelin)

false cerith: *Batillaria minima* (Gmelin)

fiddler crab: *Uca pugnax* (S. I. Smith) (the most common fiddler crab)

ghost crab (sand crab): *Ocypode arenaria* Say (*Ocypode albicans* Bosc)

ghost shrimp: *Upogebia affinis* (Say) (this would seem to be the likely callianassid here)

glasswort: *Salicornia perennis* Mill.

halimedas: *Halimeda tuna* (Ellis & Sol.) Lamouroux, *H. opuntia* (L.) Lamouroux (wedge-shaped seaweeds common in Biscayne Bay)

hermit crabs: *Clibanarius* sp. (*C. antillensis* Stimpson, *C. tricolor* (Gibbes), and *C. vittatus* (Bosc) use smaller shells and are all found here)

horseshoe crab: *Limulus polyphemus* L.
mangrove crab: *Aratus pisonii* (H. Milne Edwards)
mangrove periwinkle: *Littorina angulifera* (Lam.)
measled cowrie: *Cypraea zebra* L.
merman's shaving brush: *Penicillus capitatus* Lam.
peacock's tail: *Padina sanctae-crucis* Borg
red mangrove: *Rhizophora mangle* L.
saltwort: *Batis maritima* L.
tessellate nerite: *Nerita tessellata* Gmelin
venus girdle: *Cestum veneris* (Lesueur)
West Indian bubble: *Bulla occidentalis* A. Adams
white mangrove: *Laguncularia racemosa* Gaertn. f.

References

Bayer, Frederick M. "Littoral Marine Life of Southern Florida." A Guidebook for the Geological Society of America Convention: November 1964; Field Trip No. 7. Geological Society of America. 1964. 21 pp. O.P.

Davis, John H., Jr. "The Ecology and Geologic Role of Mangroves in Florida." *Papers from the Tortugas Laboratory* XXXII. Washington, D.C.: Carnegie Institution, 1938.

*Hall, Henry M. *A Gathering of Shore Birds.* New York: Devin, 1960. 242 pp.

Matthiesen, Peter. *The Shorebirds of North America.* New York: Viking, 1967. 270 pp.

Rathbun, Mary J. *The Brachyuran Crabs of Porto Rico and the Virgin Islands. Scientific Survey of Porto Rico and the Virgin Islands,* Vol. XV, Part I. New York: New York Academy of Sciences, 1933. 121 pp.

Schmitt, Waldo L. *Crustacea Macrura of Porto Rico and the Virgin Islands. Scientific Survey of Porto Rico and the Virgin Islands,* Vol. XV, Part 2. New York: New York Academy of Sciences, 1935. 137 pp.

13
Man-Made Jungles
and a Game Preserve

Small jungles have been created in several of the parks of South Florida, but the theme has been given most attention in the commercial "jungles." Three of these in the Miami area are outstanding, the Monkey Jungle, the Parrot Jungle, and the Orchid Jungle. All three make use of existing hammocks on the limestone ridge that extends south from Miami to Long Pine Key in the Everglades National Park. (This is that ancient rim along the eastern edge of the Glades that also reaches up to Fort Lauderdale.) All have kept much of the existing vegetation, adding exotics to accord with the popular idea of a jungle setting; and all benefit from the fact that the interior of these hammocks is frost-free.

The oldest of the three, the Monkey Jungle, was started in 1933 on a fifteen-acre piece of ground, twenty miles south of Miami, with twelve monkeys from Senegal as the chief popular attraction. These animals—they were crab-eating macaques—were set free in the hammock and allowed to roam at will within a good part of the fifteen acres. Much is made of the fact that they settled down so well that the present population is now almost entirely Florida-born. Macaques, however, happen to be among the most adaptable of all primates. They normally breed in zoos, so it was not too surprising that they were able to accept the climate of the warmest part of Florida. Their native habitat is the mangrove swamps of Indonesia, so the greatest change was to a dryer terrain and away from the crabs that are their preferred food.

The band now numbers seventy-five and the chief problem turned out to be not one of keeping the monkeys in good health but of getting them to accept human visitors. Their resentment was so great, in fact, that an enclosed walk had to be provided to protect the public. Publicity for the Monkey Jungle stresses the point that visitors are caged, while the monkeys are free.

Macaques are ground-dwellers, closely related to African baboons and among the common monkeys of southern Asia. The rhesus monkey, used for biological experiments (RH negative-type blood is named for him), is a typical macaque. The crab-eater is moderate-sized with short, rather heavy arms and legs, and grayish-brown hair. He fits exactly our idea of a "normal monkey."

Those in the Monkey Jungle seem to have a restless, fretful temperament. Of course in such a large band, they are of all ages and their tempers are not all the same. Here are older domineering males; wizened, dried-up females: young monkeys, including infants; timid individuals that back away from the bullies. As we walk along the enclosed boardwalk, an old hag (there is no better word for her) moves along on top of our cage, extending a skinny arm and clawed hand for peanuts. She has a basket on a chain which she lets down for food, drawing it up with an impatient rattling of the chain.

Macaques, like baboons, have an organized social life, with a chieftain or dominant male at the top of the hierarchy. Their aggressiveness and their battles for place mark these two groups out from the other much more peaceable primates. Their belligerency, however, comes from a terrestrial life. Tree-dwellers usually flee from predators, but the macaques and baboons often stand their ground and fight. It's also likely that the monkeys here, with a population of seventy-five, are overcrowded and that this has produced tension and irritability.

They seem to be "on stage" most of the time. Near the entrance, a pavilion looks across a small pool to the feeding area. Here the monkeys gather several times a day for fruit and other food, and at all times they are performing: jumping restlessly up and down, snatching food from each other, chattering. Some enter the pool for oranges, even diving down for the fruit.

The setting for the macaques makes use of the standard jungle ingredients, drawing upon many parts of the tropical world. The fishtail palm actually comes from their native land. Senegal date palms, Indian banyans, crotons, and bananas are also "right" in this sense, besides being among the classical exotics for jungle atmosphere. The rest of the vegetation is a little jarring to a naturalist, but it's obviously too much to ask that Asian animals be exhibited among Asian plants.

Philodendrons and heliconias are South American. Mexico or Central America is responsible for oyster plants, blue agave, and monstera. The hibiscus is from China, and a rather startling-looking palm, with long black needles all the way up its trunk, is probably a gru-gru from Argentina. These are set among coconut palms, strangler figs, ferns, and the other native growth of the hammock, and I must admit the whole blends together surprisingly well, creating a satisfactory "jungle" for North American eyes. Gaping sinkholes in the coral limestone add a bizarre note, but are not too out of place, and alligators are kept in one of these.

When the Indian monkeys proved a success, quite a number of other primate species were added. Their number was once forty; it may be greater now. Most of these are in cages: the larger gorillas, orangutans, chimpanzees, gibbons, mandrills, and other baboons; and many smaller and very attractive monkeys—spider, owl, diana, de Brazza, patas, and others—as well as macaques, langurs, and marmosets. But some—South American monkeys—roam freely in another enclosed section of the hammock. Some of the chimpanzees are dressed up and trained to perform on bicycles, in toy cars, with a guitar—according to the flyer given visitors, but I didn't take time to watch the show. For me the South Americans were by far the best part of the jungle and I would have been well content to have spent all my time with them.

Once again, native hammock forms the basis of the setting, with the reddish muscular arms of gumbo-limbo conspicuous among the green leaves. A blurb in "Greater Miami Attractions" refers to "the Amazonian Rain Forest where six species of South American monkeys live in a specially re-created tropical rain forest with thousands of exotic trees, palms and plants from their own jungle."

This picture undoubtedly pleased a publicity agent, but it has obvious flaws, which brings us to what the jungle is really like. There are jungles and jungles, of course, just as there are different kinds of rain forests. Some ecologists will have it that the only true rain forest is that growing on a humid mountain slope such as is to be found on the eastern slopes of the Andes. I have seen such a rain forest on El Yunque in nearby Puerto Rico. Clouds brushing across it spill rain every half hour or so with the result that leaves and ferns are constantly dripping. This is the proper habitat of the tree fern; they were abundant on El Yunque.

More broadly speaking, tropical rain forests spread across a large part of South America, covering much of the upper third to half of the continent. At one time this area was an immense inland sea, and much of it is still under water during that half of the year when there are heavy rains and the rivers flood. Rain clouds sweeping in from the Atlantic are blocked by the Andes and this also accounts for the excessive moisture. At all times it is a damp, very humid region, and "the steaming forests of the Amazon" is an apt, if overdone phrase. The temperature is fairly constant, the mean varying only about five degrees and averaging close to eighty the year around. In this warm wet world, plants grow so abundantly that there is an everlasting battle for existence. Their variety is also amazing, with as many as 3,000 different trees and shrubs in one square mile. It is true that since the ground under the dense canopy is mostly in deep shadow, vegetation is sparse, but floor upon floor of heavy greenery rises into the air in the upper levels. Most birds, insects, and monkeys are to be found only in the treetops.

If one could re-create the Amazon jungle in Florida, it would probably be uncomfortably damp and the monkeys would be invisible, so it's just as well that it hasn't been done. Among other things, towering forest trees are a feature of the rain forest, and there hasn't been the time nor the optimum growing conditions to produce such giants. In the Amazon basin, the average tree reaches over 100 feet, with an occasional monarch rearing its head to 200. To support this height, massive buttresses such as those we saw on the kapok tree are common.

What has been done to make the South American monkeys feel at home and to lend atmosphere is to the good, even if it isn't a re-creation of their native habitat. The chief additions in this section are heliconias, with their bananalike leaves and bright red and yellow bracts, and a great number of lianas. Philodendrons—some with cut leaves, some with solid heart-shaped leaves—are common. Woody ropes of these and other climbers twine around the trees and hang in coils and loops, perfectly designed for the tree-dwelling acrobatic primates of South America. My only regret is that no advantage was taken of the many Brazilian trees and shrubs (a really colorful array) that could have been secured right in Florida.

About half of the common groups of South American monkeys are represented here. I saw squirrel monkeys, three kinds of marmoset, and a red ouakari. Red howlers were present, but keeping out of sight. The most conspicuous of the missing species was the capuchin (the common organ-grinder monkey), and his absence is curious; but some of the others: tamarins, callimicos, titis, and sakis probably couldn't adjust to the much colder and dryer climate. A sakiwinki was included, and died; the attendant spoke of it with as much sorrow as if it had been a pet dog. Some that belonged here in the rain forest were in cages outside and obviously didn't get along well when given so much freedom.

Actually the New World monkeys are unlike the macaques in almost every respect. I was glad to have seen the Asiatic monkeys because the contrast was so vivid. Of course there are major physical differences between Old and New World primates. A number of the latter have prehensile tails which Old World monkeys lack; there is a wider partition between the nostrils, which are directed sideways—those of the Old World go forward and down—and the Old World monkeys often have bare rumps, which is never the case with the New World primates. Perhaps most important is the fact that many of the South American simians are such beautiful creatures.

Unlike the macaques, the South Americans make no objections to our entering their realm, and we have no need of protection. (I should note, however, the fact that many Asiatic and African monkeys are also very gentle—macaques and baboons being the exception.) Inside the gate there are identifying pictures, and the advice to speak quietly, move gently, and not offer the monkeys food.

At first I can see nothing but the leaves, the vines, and the ferns of the hammock. Then gradually, as I stand still and look, faces peer out of the mass of foliage. Here is a squirrel monkey, an impish creature with yellow legs, white face, staring black eyes, and a black nose and lips. Huddled up on a limb on the other side is a red ouakari, looking like a little old man with a mournful expression. His face is red and naked, while the rest of his body is covered with long silky reddish hair. Beyond is a golden lion marmoset, again with a naked face, framed in a silky lion-like mane. He is clinging to a vine and his bushy golden tail hangs down below. I see more squirrel monkeys watching me, with curious intelligent faces—in fact, the hammock that had initially seemed so empty is alive with them. It's like one of those picture puzzles I had as a child, when the game was to find all of the hidden objects. Recently, the golden-lion marmosets have been removed from the "Rain Forest," and cotton-top marmosets are no longer there.

A narrow path covered with wood chips winds through this small forest. Because it isn't the Amazon rain forest, shrubs and low trees lean across the path and give shelter to the monkeys. Some of the watching animals are so close it seems as if I could touch them, but I know that such an action would only startle them. These are shy retiring creatures; some of them probably believe they are unseen; none ask for food.

A little way along I see a true marmoset, for the maned marmosets belong to a different genus. This one is the cotton-top, and his brown gnomelike face, with its pointed ears, looks out of a mass of thick pale fur almost as if he had pulled part of a bearskin around him and was peering out of it. He gives an odd little chirp as I pass; the cotton-top has deceived many people into thinking he was a bird because that is just the way he sounds.

As the path crosses a boardwalk, I look down into a gully with tree ferns, a brook, a waterfall, and misting sprays of water directed into the trees. Here the monkeys are fed seven times a day, the attendant summoning them with a bell. There are many kinds of feeding stands—some on the ground, some in the trees—and a variety of food is put out. Most of the monkeys will eat some fruit, seeds, and nuts, although the red ouakari has to have protein to survive, and in nature the squirrel monkeys live mostly on butterflies and other insects, while the marmosets normally feed on insects and eggs.

The only real vegetarian is the howler, and I am sorry that he has stayed away. Normally, he lives in the upper reaches of the tree canopy, and he has also been hunted so much that he is suspicious of humans. In addition—unlike the other American monkeys—he doesn't associate with other species, so that his absence is hardly remarkable. I had read so often of the howling choruses at dawn—the sound is described as bloodcurdling and earsplitting—that I wanted very much to see one of the vocalists that produced it. Howlers are fairly big monkeys, slow, somewhat surly, and retiring; the red howler has heavy red fur and a bushy red beard.

A white-lipped marmoset appears, however, and squirrel monkeys, by the score, swing themselves in from branch to branch, squealing as they come. For a moment, there seem to be monkeys all around us, and the attendant claims that the squirrel monkeys number between two and three hundred. The owl monkey, or douroucouli, with a truly owllike face belongs here, but the only specimen was caged. He, alone of all primates, is nocturnal, and during the day remains curled up in his "den"—out of sight and asleep. The spider, green, ring-tailed, and woolly monkeys are also caged although they, too, are part of the South American jungle. Spider monkeys are extraordinary creatures, with their elongated legs and arms, and their completely prehensile tails, so sensitive that they can pick up peas. I am sorry none have been allowed to run free and that I can't watch them swinging from branch to branch, using their four limbs and tail quite indiscriminately. Possibly they were too big for the "jungle." With the exception of the howlers, the primates in the rain forest are all small. Marmosets are no bigger than squirrels and, in Elizabethan times, court ladies used to carry them in their sleeves.

Every now and then I stumble upon something so delightful or so interesting that I wish time would stand still: that I could hold the passing moments and spread them out to an hour or two. This is the way I felt as I watched the monkeys coming in to feed in their Florida "rain forest." They don't belong in this natural setting any more than the exotic plants that are so widespread. But if one is going to re-create a jungle scene, it seems reasonable that some of the animal life of that jungle—parrots, as well as monkeys, should also be on view.

When a Miamian, Franz Scherr, looked at the Monkey Jungle in 1936, he complained that the trees and plants were not identified. (I quite agree with him: I would like to have seen more names.) The story goes that the answer he got was, "Go build your own jungle if you don't like ours! " And this was what he did. As with the owners of the Monkey Jungle, he turned to the ridge south of Miami—that choice area for tropical plants—and bought twenty acres of hammock land on Red Road near the Fairchild Tropical Garden. Here he established the Parrot Jungle and developed a parrot show, just as a monkey show was created in the earlier jungle.

Franz Scherr had grown up in Europe, and his Germanic background probably helped in the careful scientific study he set for himself. His plants were going to be named, and accurately so, and for this purpose he spent long hours at the United States Plant Introduction Center, pouring over the various species. The results are obvious. Not only does he have a remarkable selection of tropical exotics—one to delight any botanist—but there are names everywhere.

In one way it's a pity that the two jungles couldn't be combined, since macaws are fully as much a part of the Amazonian rain forest as monkeys. The result, however, might not be desirable. What would the monkeys make of such a constant shrieking and squawking as the macaws are guilty of? In such close quarters they could hardly escape the racket. And in another way, the atmosphere of the two places is entirely different.

In the Parrot Jungle, the emphasis is on color—brilliant, striking hues such as those of the gold and blue macaw, the hyacinth macaw, the yellow-headed Amazon (all three from the Amazon basin), the scarlet macaw, and the military macaw (common in Mexico), and of parakeets from the Indo-Malayan region. Flamingos are part of the picture and many beautiful flowering plants, from hibiscus (100 varieties), to bougainvillea, allamanda, flame vine, thunbergia, heliconias, unusual aechmeas, begonias, and orchids. There is almost too much to look at in the Parrot Jungle, and it comes, quite frankly, from the tropics (and near tropics) all around the world. In the Monkey Jungle it might have been possible to group South American and Asiatic plants separately and develop the idea of proper habitats for their animals. But in the Parrot Jungle, the planting is a melange of native and exotic plants and must be accepted as such.

Nonetheless, the Parrot Jungle is a triumph of design. In a small space it creates a dream jungle that gives a feeling of remoteness and enchantment. Mr. Scherr was fortunate in his choice of location. His hammock (a cypress head, actually) followed part of the original bed of Snapper Creek, and he made use of this to provide waterways all through his jungle. A meandering path winds around them with planting that creates one lovely scene after another.

Let us ignore the parrot show, and follow the jungle path. At the outset, it is bordered by the shiny green leaves of wild coffee, a native plant that I first learned to recognize here. That one label added to my pleasure in the many, many coffee shrubs I encountered throughout southern Florida.

A pond beside the walk has carp—orange, silvery, and gold—and an island with seven brilliant macaws resting among the heart-shaped leaves of a giant philodendron. Many of the parrots are unrestrained. They fly—often with loud screeching—all through the hammock and even beyond, but food and the sense of home territory bring them back. The seven today—three scarlet macaws, three gold and blue, and one military—make a brilliant picture. Many of the less common parrots are chained to perches or kept in large cages. One such, just a little farther along, is the sulphur-crested cockatoo (snowy-white with a yellow crest), from Australia. Nearby are Lear's macaw, one of the hyacinthine macaws, and a blue-fronted Amazonian, both from South America. I prefer my birds and monkeys roaming free, however, and shall turn my attention to the plants.

The first striking exotic is hunter's robe, closely related to philodendron and monstera, with a tremendous vine and heavy leaves. This one is from the Solomon Islands and is to be found again and again along the path. The leaves are heart-shaped and blotched with yellow, and there's no denying that for a jungle effect of smothering exuberant growth, little can equal the vines of this family.

Now we have the nun's hood orchid, one of the loveliest flowers I know, with waxy-white blossoms tipped with purple, while the undersides and tube are of brownish-peach. Nearby is the beautiful pink shell ginger from East Asia, looking like an orchid with red and brown markings on its yellowish lip. Also close at hand, offering a complete change of form and mood, are the swordlike leaves of traveler's tree and heliconia. Heliconias belong with the macaws and have the same garish appearance, for their flowering stalk is often clothed with brilliant red and orange bracts. For one more variation, here is African umbrella grass growing at the edge of a pool, with black and gold fish swimming beneath its flattened umbrellalike tops. Umbrella grass is a sedge related to papyrus.

Water, as I have said, is all through the jungle and we are seldom out of sight of it. Pool follows pool. Here is one with a black bottom, bordered by philodendron and backed by cypress. Another has water falling over great ledges and white vanda orchids with dangling racemes of flowers nearby. A low-growing ixora adds its scarlet color to the scene. Pandanus arches above a third pool; a fourth has two fountains. I am aware that as the path weaves back and forth, I may have looked at the same pool twice, seeing it from a different view. Where the waterway narrows to a stream, I bend over a low wall of coral rock, its crannies filled with ferns, and begonias in its larger pockets. Across the way, on the other side of the stream, are tilted moss-covered boulders, with more ferns growing in their cracks. Once again, umbrella grass bends above the water. A last pond is given over to alligators. Here, a fantastically sprawling coco plum arches over the water, crossing it four or five times. Its great horizontal limbs bear any number of epiphytes, among them *Aechmea mariae reginae,* named for the Queen of Heaven. The aechmeas are South American bromeliads with long, straplike leaves that are often curiously banded and blotched. This one has a showy spike, with reflexed crimson bracts. Another aechmea (there are quite a few in the Parrot Jungle) looks artificial, with pink bracts and silvered dark green leaves. These were new to me and I found them most impressive. A related bromeliad is guzmania, with a strange reddish-orange blossom.

There can't be as many plants as at Fairchild Tropical Garden, but what is here is effectively displayed. Set against the dim light and the pervasive green of the hammock, a guzmania, an aechmea, a heliconia can be quite startlingly brilliant. The setting emphasizes the cool waxy white of a vanda, the orchid shade of a cattleya, the delicate beauty of the nun's hood orchid.

Some of the nonflowering epiphytes are also striking. There is a staghorn fern on a cypress, and elkshorn farther along. The names are descriptive—there is no problem in learning them and almost everything is labeled. Here is a resurrection fern riding upon the limbs of a live oak, while high in the upper branches, a blue and yellow Amazonian surveys me coolly and critically. I was surprised to learn that parrots are not only highly intelligent but also extremely temperamental: responsive to human moods, capable of affection, jealousy, and vanity.

Beyond the junglelike hammock, the scenery changes with setting after setting designed for photographers. Much of it takes on the landscaped artificial look of Cypress Gardens, but there is no denying that it's dramatic. The approach to this section is under a pergola overgrown with blue thunbergia. With its three-inch flowers in azure blue, this is my favorite of all climbers. Next comes one of the unbelievable specimens of the plant world—the sausage tree—bearing long pendulous brown fruit in a sausage shape. The flowers of this tree open only at night and are pollinated by bats. Moving from one spectacular sight to another, we pass under a massive banyan, 100 feet in diameter, growing on both sides of the walk and arching above it in a solid canopy. Beyond is a group of tree ferns close by a pond that is full of water lilies and backed by umbrella grass.

A little farther on the left we look down over a wall and stony bank into the cactus ravine, with one of the best collections of desert plants to be found in the southeast. Giant saguaros rise like sentinels on either side, and between them, set in among the rocks, is an array of queer shapes: spiny golden barrel, cow's horn and candelabra plant (two spiny euphorbias), flattened bunny ears (an opuntia), Turk's cap, sand dollar, inch worm, and woolly torch. Crown of thorns, lavender scallops, and other succulents sprawl over the ground, with the sharp leaves of agave and the six-foot pillars of Spanish bayonet standing out in contrast.

From these fantastic plants and their other-world scenery, we turn to the pièce de résistance. Just across from the cactus garden is a large pergola with a showy covering of flame vine, yellow allamanda, and pink pandorea. Standing under this flowery ceiling, we look down upon a theatrical setting: sweeping greensward, a lake, and close to a hundred flamingos. The whole is in a kind of bowl, with a scenic background of variegated crotons, offset by coconut palms and a screen of bougainvillea, allamanda, flame vine, and other tropical vines. Behind this, casuarina forms the third tier of plant growth.

On one shore of the lake is a bank of Spanish bayonets. The water surrounds an island with a giant cactus and some of the more colorful birds, both native and exotic: spoonbills, wood ducks, mandarin ducks, scarlet ibis, and African crowned cranes. The Parrot Jungle boasts 500 parrots, of which 117 are macaws. It also has 200 other birds, including those we have mentioned as well as black cockatoos, mynahs, the giant crowned pigeon of New Guinea, golden and Lady Amherst pheasants, silver pheasants from Tibet, and peacocks. It's a showy array.

The show's finale comes as we stand looking down on the lawn and lake. The parrots have performed, the crowd has gathered as directed on the overlook, and now an attendant rounds up the flamingos and sends them squawking and flapping–some hundred strong–in front of the spectators. Cameras whir, everybody exclaims–it's the high point of the day.

The Orchid Jungle is the newest of the group, opening as a commercial venture in the late forties, although an orchid collection had been established there in the twenties. It, too, is on one of the hammocks on the ridge, and it, too, like the Monkey Jungle, is not far from Homestead. The largest of the three, it has thirty acres of land, twenty-five of them in the so-called jungle.

The property was bought by Thomas Fennell's father. Father and son shared a great interest in orchids (the family had been growing them, as a matter of fact, since 1886), and Thomas Fennell took part in their cultivation whenever he was in the area. For a time he was superintendent of the U.S. Plant Introduction Center at Coconut Grove (where Franz Scherr learned his plant names). Then he became Chief of Operations at the National Agricultural Research Center in Beltsville, Maryland. Still later, he worked as an agricultural expert for the Haitian government and in the same capacity in Puerto Rico. In other words, plants were his business, so it was hardly surprising when he returned to Florida in 1949, intending to start an enterprise of his own, that this business should turn out to be orchids.

The Orchid Jungle has no performing animals. It offers simply the atmosphere of a tropical hammock, with orchids by the thousand growing out-of-doors as they would in their natural habitat. Some of the eighty-eight species native to Florida are included, but most of the plants come from the far parts of the tropical world, with such orchids as epidendrum, cattleya, and oncidiums from Central and South America; cymbidiums, dendrobiums, phalaenopsis, vandas, and others from Malaya, tropical India, and the Philippines. Taken all together, they make this the world's largest outdoor orchid garden.

The climate of South Florida, even at its southernmost end, isn't really right for the monkeys of the Amazon basin. The orchids of South America, on the other hand, are not at their best in the steaming jungle. They prefer a cooler, less moist climate, and the location of the Orchid Jungle suits them very well. Some of these plants have grown in place on their trees for twenty-five or thirty years, and are still thriving.

Live oaks are the principal tree of the hammock and three-fourths of a mile of trails wind through them in the Orchid Jungle. Walking along the crushed coral paths, it is very pleasant under these spreading limbs, and I can see orchid plants everywhere, even though the first week in March is early for bloom. Today there are quite a number of cattleyas (the big flower of the florists), but I prefer a white vanda, a delicately spotted phalaenopsis, a crimson broughtania, or a greenish-brown epidendrum with many small flowers on a long spray. Here and there I find one of these beauties; a few oncidiums are in bloom; and I am entranced by "Little Indian Chief," a variety of *Epidendrum radicans* that the Fennells, I believe, developed, for the other half of their business is breeding and propagating orchids.

Orchids, however, are not the only things to be seen here. Philodendrons wind around the trees, not just haphazardly, nor for jungle atmosphere, but because they, too, are on display as a collection of many varieties. Monstera is here, of course, and there are many cycads and bromeliads (Spanish moss, wild pine, aechmea, and guzmania all belong to this group). The ferns, the sinkholes, the occasional black pool of the Florida hammock are all here, and much botanical information is supplied along the way. Altogether the Orchid Jungle is a delightful place.

Lion Country Safari near West Palm Beach is a more recent attempt to bring another type of animal world to Florida. Here in a 640-acre wild game preserve, a remarkable collection of animals has been assembled, for the most part roaming freely within large enclosures. Cars can enter the preserve and explore most of it by winding roads. It is indeed a "safari," the nearest thing to such an adventure that I have seen in this country.

Within the first part of the area one comes upon ostriches, African crowned cranes, long-legged secretary birds, Barbary sheep, and antelopes with fantastically varied horns. Zebra browses beside ostrich; cranes mingle with gazelles; and all go about their business of feeding and living, it seems, with little regard for the passing cars. I look with amazement at the array of antelopes; at the spiral horns of addax, eland, and kudu; at Thompson's gazelle and Beisa oryx with long, imposingly straight horns; at the regal headgear of the water buck; at the gracefully curving armature of springbok, impala, sitatunga, and sable antelope. There is hardly a false note in the gathering. This is Africa—as far as the animals are concerned.

The scenery is Florida pine flatlands. And it fits surprisingly well, just as Florida hammock was made to do for the Amazonian monkeys. Knowing what the African plain should be like, I would have been pleased with a true African thicket placed here and there in the preserve to give a suggestion of the actual plains setting. It's possible, though, that the effort to match plants with animals would hardly be justified today. One can only hope that before long, as we begin to associate flora with fauna, there will be a demand for the whole community—the truly right habitat.

You pass through one gate for the zebras, ostriches, and antelopes. A second admits you into lion country—300 acres, in which over a hundred of the great beasts roam more or less at will, hindered only by occasional moats. Zebras, giraffes, and gnus (wildebeests) share their territory, unmolested by the lions, apparently because the latter are well-fed and have no need to hunt. Even so, zebra beside lion tenses the atmosphere. The ungainly giraffe belongs in the landscape and at the same time looks oddly vulnerable.

I look out at the great cats lying by the roadside in groups of six to twelve and realize what an astonishing experience it is to pass within barely a few feet of these magnificent but dangerous animals. One or two are wakeful: they act as sentinels for the pride. The rest are stretched out, somnulent, relaxed, beautiful specimens of sleeping power. It's been suggested that their listlessness is due to drugs, administered to protect visitors, but lions are by nature creatures of the night. When well-fed, sleep comes naturally to them, and they bask even so on the African plains in lazy catlike attitudes, undisturbed by the blazing heat of the sun. There is little shade here. Cypresses are still leafless; pines provide scanty shelter. As I've said, the lions hardly need protection, but some of the scrubby growth of Africa would have done much to make the picture more complete.

The road through lion country meanders to such an extent that almost every part of the preserve comes into view. I might add that guards are stationed in jeeps near every pride, and car windows have to be closed so that no danger is connected with the drive. The beasts are normally indifferent to cars, but it's impossible to count on their behavior—hence the strict precautions. Even so, the motorist is probably much safer in Lion Country than if he drove alone through one of the great African preserves.

Waterways thread the enclosure, encircling the whole area (to provide double protection with the heavy fence), and looping through it to create a number of islands. On one such island are chimpanzees; on another, four young African elephants with an older Indian animal; on a third, a white rhinoceros (I didn't see it, but it was undoubtedly there). The moats protect the monkeys and elephants, while making them appear to be an integral part of the landscape. Just a small flaw in the picture was the lack of woods for the chimpanzees. Their islet held only some leafless palms (it's possible the monkeys had torn off the fronds) and a rocky cave. Since these are forest primates, they should have had at least one well-grown tree in their domain (ideally, of course, one that had originated in Africa or Madagascar).

I was pleased with the game preserve; the balance of Lion Country, however, was something of a disappointment, offering a mixture of mammals, reptiles, and birds from all over the world. The reptiles and many of the mammals were caged, and water birds were crowded into a fenced-in pond. I was also bothered by animals that looked out of place on the "jungle cruise": camels on one tiny island, a sandhill crane on a second, more chimpanzees on a third. Only the South American anteater was right in this setting. Camels and sandhill cranes just don't seem to belong on islands, particularly when those spots are very small and surrounded by a great deal of water. The African part had been so well done; had that idea been maintained throughout with African birds and reptiles, Lion Country would be outstanding. As it is, the second part seems commercial and ordinary with one exception. The Curio Hut carries the same note of authenticity as does the game preserve. Here is native African handicraft: beadwork, skin drums, blankets, wood carvings, weapons, pottery, batiks—all of high quality and all for sale. Such a fine collection of folk art is worth looking at, even if one has no desire to buy any of it.

The latest attempt to bring exotic animals to Florida in their proper setting is Jungle Larry's Safari Land at the Caribbean Gardens in Naples. The new owner acquired the gardens in September of 1969 and now advertises an Amazon Jungle Expedition, a Congo Safari, and a Tropical Asian Shikar.

For many years the Caribbean Gardens has been home to an outstanding collection of water fowl with ducks, geese, and swans from all parts of the world. As I've said, the birds used to wander freely throughout the garden, swimming in two large lakes and following visitors to beg for peanuts. Unlike the waterfowl exhibits at Lion Country or at Crandon Park Zoo, there was no sense of overcrowding, and I have always felt that this was one of the more successful displays of exotic wildlife.

All of this has been changed. The lakes are now fenced in, few of the birds wander outside the enclosures, and many of their islets are occupied by mammals. The result, as one might expect, is again a feeling of too little space for too many wildfowl. The Fleischmann collection, however, was not sold with the gardens and its eventual fate is still uncertain, the birds remaining where they are merely on a temporary basis.

Turning from what has been lost to what is gained, I found much of great interest. The jungle or wildlife exhibit of the future, I am certain, will emphasize the living community and its natural habitat. In the first lagoon devoted to the Amazon jungle, this has been done exceptionally well. Tapirs now wade in the shallow water, looking entirely at home. A giant anteater roams around one island; agoutis, spider monkeys and a capybara, are on others; and on still another, a two-toed sloth hangs upside down in a mahoe. All of the islets have trees and there are generally grasses and leather ferns as well. Scarlet, and gold and blue macaws perch on one tree, and, as with the plains section in Lion Country, the animal assemblage is right. I feel as if I could be looking at a stream in the Amazon country if I ignore the fact that there is no dense rain forest on its banks. As we have seen, though, it would be impossible to bring the true rain forest to Florida, and the new management, I understand, means to do everything it can to suggest the proper habitat for each group of animals. A South American grassland community is planned to round out the presentation of the life of this continent.

I was less happy about some of the other new features. While in the South American section, I passed jaguars in a small cage, and caged king vultures. Going on to the Asiatic part, I came upon a mournful-looking, though beautiful, Bengal tiger—also confined—and to some rare hybrids, the offspring of a lion and a tiger, called "tiglons." Great hornbills were caged, as were mynahs, and in the African section, cheetahs, African lions, black leopards, and diana monkeys filled more cages.

There's no question that the big cats hold a strong appeal for the public and I admit that they are properly placed in the right continents. It's also true that the atmosphere is still one of a beautiful tropical garden, with only an occasional caged animal. It's far from being a zoo—at least at the present time. But I would greatly prefer it if every small cage or enclosure could be removed and only those animals displayed that can be shown in large enclosures.

One such exhibit is evidently planned for a hillside beyond the "tiglons." Here, at the present time, African ostriches and cranes roam with Indian gazelles and black bucks from Asia. Will it eventually be African or Asian? One can't tell.

Wildfowl also have not yet been separated according to their respective continents so that in the Amazon jungle I look down upon Canada geese, a colorful New Zealand shelduck, bar-headed geese from central Asia, and a European rosy-breasted pochard. Egyptian geese are here, too, and a magpie goose from Australia. Only the flamingos (and there is a small colony of these beautiful birds) can be said, in any sense, to belong—and they wouldn't really be found in the Amazon jungle.

The final disposition of the waterfowl collection, however, has not yet been settled, and the other wildlife displays are in the process of being worked out. Much of it is good. I had been fearful that the Caribbean Gardens as I knew them were gone forever and that I would be unhappy in the new Jungle Larry's Safari. Instead I found the Amazon lagoon a good addition and the essential quality of the gardens unchanged. What was more, the men in charge of the various sections have an interest in the wildlife community—in placing animals in their proper setting.

It would be exciting if a similar kind of interest could be developed elsewhere. I would like to see the Monkey Jungle concentrating on South American life in a setting as nearly right as could be achieved. Or possibly on the rain forest and a good reproduction of Malayan wildlife and habitat. I would like to see Lion Country limited to

Africa with more of the proper vegetation of that country and no caged animals. Possibly a third center could be entirely devoted to Asiatic life. Then all of these areas could well be tied together for publicity purposes and the four offered as a round-the-world tour. This would provide a stimulating adventure, and a valuable educational experience as well.

Common and Scientific Names

aechmeas: *Aechmea fasciata* (Lindl.) Baker, *A. mariae reginae* Wendl.
broughtonia: *Broughtonia sanguinea* B. Br.
bunny ears: *Opuntia microdasyus* Lehm.
candelabra plant: *Euphorbia lactea* Haw.
cattleya orchids: *Cattleya* sp.
cow's horn euphorbia: *Euphorbia grandicornis* Goeb.
epidendrum orchids: *Epidendrum atropurpureum* Willd., *E. radicans* Pav. var. Indian Chief
flame vine (orange trumpet vine): *Pyrostegia ignea* (Vell) Presl. (*Bignonia venusta* Ker)
giant saguaro: *Carnegiea gigantea* Britt. & Rose
golden barrel (golden cactus): *Echinocactus grusonii* Hildm.
gru-gru: *Acrocomia totai* Mart.
guzmania: *Guzmania lingulata* Mez
heliconias: *Heliconia angustifolia* Hook, *H. espirito sanctos* (Holy Spirit heliconia), *H. psittacorum* L. f.
hunter's robe (pothos): *Rhapidophora aurea* (Lind. & André) M. R. Birdsey
inchworm cactus: *Kleinia pendula* DC
lavender scallops: *Kalanchoe fedtschenkoi* Ham. & Per. var. *marginata*
microcoelia: *Microcoelia* sp.
nun's hood orchid (nun's orchid): *Phaius grandiflorus* (Lour.)
sand dollar cactus: *Astrophytum asterias* (Zucc.) Lem.
sausage tree: *Kigelia pinnata* (Jacq.) DC
shell flower: *Alpinia speciosa* (Wendl.) K. Schum.
Turk's cap cactus: *Melocactus intortus* Mill.
umbrella grass: *Cyperus alternifolius* L.
vandas: *Vanda lamellata* Lindl. var. *Boxalli*, *Vanda* sp.
woolly torch: *Cephalocereus palmeri* (Rose)

References

*Bates, Marston. *The Land and Wildlife of South America.* Life Nature Library. New York: Time, Inc., 1964. 200 pp.

*Carr, Archie F. *The Land and Wildlife of Africa.* Life Nature Library. New York: Time, Inc., 1964. 200 pp.

*Eimerl, Sarel, and De Vore, Irven. *The Primates.* Life Nature Library. New York: Time, Inc., 1965. 200 pp.

Muir, H. "Gaudiest Things that Fly: The Parrot Jungle." *Saturday Evening Post* 223 (April 21, 1957):40-1.

Shelford, Victor E. *The Ecology of North America.* Urbana: University of Illinois Press, 1963. 610 pp.

Wylie, Philip. "You, Too, Can Grow Orchids." *Saturday Evening Post* 224 (September 15, 1951): 38-9

A deer peers out of protecting vegetation, safe in the surrounding wilderness. Some of this wilderness must be preserved both for animal life and for human beings.

Conclusion:
Preserving the Present

As I write of the natural scenery and wildlife of southern Florida, I wonder constantly how many of the areas I have described will be gone before my book appears in print. Many changes have taken place since this work was begun.

On my sea lane, a towering apartment house—eleven stories high—now stands where, a few years ago, were pithecellobiums, palms, sea grapes, and Spanish needles. It is surrounded by cement and not a blade of the original vegetation is left. I knew that the sea lane was doomed, but I tried to take heart from the fact that this wasn't the only good spot for wildlife; almost as many birds and insects could still be found in a small hammock right in the center of Key Biscayne. Here, too, there was a mixture of native and exotic plants, and the latter reminded me once again of Dr. William J. Matheson who started a coconut plantation here in 1909 and brought in many trees which he had collected from the tropics and subtropics of the whole world. His handiwork could be seen in a magnificent kapok with its buttressed trunk, in a glorious African tulip tree with yellow-fringed, orange blossoms, in a hedge of reclining pandanus, and in a bronzy-leaved pongemania from Australia. I came to the place often just to admire these beautiful trees. With them were mingled pithecellobiums, coconut palms, mahoes, strangler figs, and geiger trees. Spanish needles covered the ground, and native vines such as bullbrier and matrimony vine (Christmasberry) clambered over the underbrush. The place was so obviously attractive to wildlife that it was given special mention in Richard L. Cunningham's *Field List of South Florida Birds* as "a good spot for migrating or wintering land birds."

When I came back to the island in the winter of 1969, I was dismayed to see that the hammock had been destroyed, too, and in its place were coconut palms. As a result I could hardly find a warbler that year, other than the ever-present palm warbler, on the island. Gone were the butterflies and moths that had given me so much pleasure: I discovered barely a few scattered strays during my three-month stay. Other real estate developments shared the blame for losses. Mergansers, willets, and sanderlings had left the beach, disturbed, probably, by the construction racket, for in addition to the apartment house on the sea lane, and various buildings inland, a large hotel was going up along the shore. Its lot had once been a favorite spot for painted buntings. More butterflies and birds were around later, however, when heavy construction stopped.

Mollusks were also dwindling. Each year Bear Cut at its eastern end has fewer and fewer interesting shells, and other marine life seems to be decreasing as well. Pollution may be partly responsible, but much is due to constant commercial collecting.

With two parks on the island—Crandon and Cape Florida State—it would seem as if ample space had been left for wildlife. Cape Florida, though, has been taken over by casuarinas, and since little will grow under these trees (particularly in a thick stand), few weedy patches remain—not enough for an abundant insect life. Where insects are scarce (and they seldom occur on the Australian pines, themselves), the birds that feed on them are also rare, and this is the story of the state park. Crandon Park has little more in the way of wildlife, which puzzles me because there is native growth here among the exotics, particularly at the northern end, but for some reason it fails to attract many birds or insects. During the summer months, when mosquitoes are a problem, there is heavy spraying, and this may account in part for the steady drop in birds.

Another loss has been the pond behind the Marine Stadium. It was here that I found an osprey, a great blue heron, a white ibis, and a greater yellowlegs. Why it was drained I don't know, unless it just seemed a "useless" stretch of water. Beyond that vanished lagoon, shorebirds still congregate in great numbers, but they, too, will disappear if a causeway is built, as planned, from Virginia Key to Fisher's Island.

At Naples a lonely and beautiful beach once lay just north of Doctor's Pass, and it was a prized spot for shellers. Wide mud flats extended inshore, and here, too, could be found a spectacular gathering of shorebirds. This is now a city of hotels and apartment houses, with few feet of open space left. Most of this has happened since 1968.

Marco Island is another example of a lost wild area. When I first saw it in 1965, the developers were just starting work and the southern end had not yet been affected by their activities. Pulling off the road near Caxambas Pass, my ears were assailed by bird calls: warblers, vireos, and woodpeckers—feeding in thickets much like those of the sea lane. Several calls were unfamiliar, and I would start after one only to be distracted by another nearer to hand. While I pursued the birds, it's true that I was pursued by mosquitoes. I wished for some insect repellent, but this was a small matter beside such riches. It was one of those moments dear to every birder. Near the center of the island, an inlet afforded the rare sight of sandwich terns dipping and wheeling over the water. Other terns were diving as well, and not far away was the nest of a great horned owl. At that time, *A Field List of South Florida Birds* said that Marco was often "one of the best birding areas in South Florida."

A year later there were no mosquitoes (almost certainly the result of spraying) and the Caxambas Pass thickets were completely silent. The nest of the great horned owl was empty, and dredging and road-building had driven away the terns. By 1969 the few birds left were ordinary species—nothing one would come any distance to see. The Marco developers, aware of the island's past fame as a wildlife Eden, tried to maintain its reputation by having it included in the Bald Eagle Sanctuary Program. But then they ignored the guidelines laid down to protect nesting eagles, and the chief nest was deserted. Like the eagles, the shellers gave up, too. By 1969 the parking area near the famous beach held only a handful of cars, and it seemed clear that they, also, had finally become discouraged.

Wildlife is being threatened elsewhere in South Florida. In 1969 there was nationwide concern over the jetport whose construction was actually begun near the Everglades National Park. According to a federal report, the jetport was likely to doom the Park, and it was agreed that another location should be sought. We can only hope that a satisfactory one will be found. On the shores of Biscayne Bay a thermonuclear plant promised more trouble. A year or so ago the existing electrical plant at Turkey Point was already discharging so much hot water that it was overheating the bay. Serious damage to underwater plant and animal life in a 670-acre area was the result, and for a time—under Secretary Hickel—the federal government opposed any enlargement. Now it seems possible that the thermonuclear plant will be built, in spite of the danger to the marine world. Biscayne Bay is already so badly polluted from sewage that bathing is forbidden, and this pollution is probably affecting its wildlife, too.

These examples will illustrate some of the problems that face not only southern Florida, but the state and the world. The overriding problem—man's possible destruction of his whole environment—is currently receiving so much attention that I shall not go into the larger aspects of air and water pollution, or of overpopulation. Our concern here is mostly with the preservation of wildlife.

Throughout the world today we are losing plants and animals at a wholesale rate—partly as the result of hunting, overcollecting, and poisoning; partly because of destruction of habitat. In Florida a century ago, herons and ibises nested in unnumbered thousands. Their flocks darkened the sky, and their extinction seemed impossible. Plume hunters took their toll first; this was followed by the drying out of the Everglades. Wood storks are down from 150,000 in 1900 to a bare 7,000 to 10,000 now, and there has been a noticeable decrease in most of the larger birds (herons, ibises, etc.) just since the 1930s and 1940s. Alligators were estimated at a million in the last century. They number now about 10,000. Key deer reached an estimated low of 25 to 50 animals in the mid-1940s. In 1967 it was believed that a million fishes in Florida died from pollution.

Until recently we were convinced that a man's right to do what he wanted with his property was almost paramount—and his right to kill the birds and animals around him something to be restricted only when absolutely necessary for their survival as a species. The Florida Wilderness Committee summarized the change in the *Florida Naturalist* of April 1969:

In a big state like Florida, the past philosophy was to let every man do whatever he wanted, or could, for his own pleasure or benefit. The wilderness was endless and hostile—something to be tamed, exploited, to make a buck out of (if he were smart enough), a place to dump trash or to shoot anything that moved, for fun or profit or to eat.

That system had some defense when Florida had only 10,000 or 100,000 or maybe even 1,000,000 people, but it's not working now. We're approaching 10,000,000 on the same stretch of land, and there are some good changes in thinking.

Potential losses (complete extermination, that is, of many species) go far beyond the concern of a few naturalists who must do without some favorite flowers, birds, reptiles, or shells. Many insects are beneficial—we need bees, for instance, for fruit and vegetable pollination. Birds still provide a better control of pests than most insecticides. Dredging and pollution endanger the fish and shrimp industries, and finally there is that intangible need that people in general have for open space, plants, and wildlife. Tourism is vitally important to Florida, and visitors come, according to the Florida Development Commission, first for beaches and relaxation, secondly for natural scenery, fishing, and hunting.

What has been done to halt the drain on wildlife falls into two parts: first an effort to stop intentional destruction of animals and plants through excessive hunting, collecting, and timbering; and second, an effort to stop unintentional destruction through damage to wildlife areas and the spread of pesticides and other forms of pollution. Many national organizations such as the National Audubon and Wilderness Societies, The Sierra Club, Friends of the Earth, and others, are playing an important role in helping to preserve our natural scenery and wildlife. And Florida is also fortunate in the many local agencies (both public and private) that are engaged in the fight. Florida Audubon has been active in conservation since the turn of the century and is now joined with many other groups in a strong Conservation Council. The governor, most Florida legislators, many county commissioners, and the present Flood Control Commission are concerned about the problems that confront wildlife.

Aside from the initial action against plume hunters and the ban on collecting liguus snails, attention for a good many years centered upon acquiring parks and refuges. The National Everglades Park was created in 1947; Corkscrew Swamp Sanctuary in 1954. The Key Deer Act of 1954 authorized a federal sanctuary for these tiny deer. Of the others in South Florida, Pelican Island National Wildlife Refuge near Sebastian offers protection to pelicans and other water birds. Created in 1903, it was the first national wildlife refuge in our country. The John Pennekamp Coral Reef State Park (moving down around the southern tip of the state) is intended to save corals from commercial collectors and reef fishes from spear divers. Great White Heron National Refuge speaks for itself. Sanibel National Wildlife Refuge provides sanctuary for herons, ibises, spoonbills, and water birds generally. Three smaller National Wildlife Refuges—Island Bay near Charlotte Harbor, Passage Key, and Pinellas in Tampa Bay—were established for the same purpose. Biscayne National Monument, authorized by Congress and now in the process of being acquired, will protect marine life in general, and a National Monument in the Upper Keys, Islandia, dedicated to the same purpose, has also been approved. In addition there are many state parks as well as Audubon and private sanctuaries.

Many of the refuges were greatly needed and have proved effective. The Key deer herd has recovered, and pelicans were saved from destruction by fishermen who believed—quite mistakenly—that the birds were a danger to nets and to commercially valuable fish. The great white heron has made a good comeback. Cypresses at Corkscrew and mahoganies in the Everglades have been protected.

But it's becoming evident that sanctuaries and preserves are not enough. One island rookery (a refuge) was wiped out when nearby dredging took its marine food. Pelicans are suffering from DDT taken in through the fish they feed upon. Alligators continue to be killed in the Everglades Park although they are supposedly protected both by the refuge and by Florida law. Drainage and the redirection of water flow outside the Park endanger that whole area. So does pollution from fertilizers and pesticides washed down from truck farms to the north. Until recently there was the possibility of heavy air traffic above the Park and training flights over it still go on. Many parks dare not label their orchids because this seems to be an invitation to collectors to take them. Most of Florida's rarer plants, although protected by law, are in danger of being exterminated.

What is the solution? More laws such as banning the sale of alligator products? Stronger sanctions? More education? The latter should play a part. We need to recognize the fact that our affluent society, with its many hobbies and its ability to afford luxuries, is taking too great a toll of the natural world.

Mollusks offer an obvious example. When I was young, the supply seemed limitless, but at that time we collected only the empty shells on the beach. Before long, however, shell societies grew up and it became a serious game. Dead shells were no longer good enough; the real collector had to have live mollusks, and he went out at night with a flashlight, or used a dredge and a boat or diving equipment for his work. He also took more than he needed of any good species in order to have extras for trade or sale. Because there were so many collectors, shell shops became abundant, offering species from Florida as well as from the rest of the world. Manufactured shell ornaments became a big business and appeared on every souvenir counter. Then we noticed that dead shells were no longer appearing in any normal numbers on some beaches. Sanibel has gone way down, as I said earlier, and while other causes were at work, overcollecting was an important one. A trio of commercial collectors worked over Bear Cut one year and the handsomer gastropods are now missing along that shore.

If we could put some rein on our appetites—in the interest of leaving some of this natural world to our children—it would make a big difference. Individual effort (multiplied a thousandfold—as it could be) could stop the alligator hunting by refusal to buy alligator products. Mollusks might recover if we stopped buying shell ornaments. Sea turtles would be given a chance if we gave up eating their meat and soup. If plant collectors would observe the law (for while the single specimen that's taken doesn't seem enough to make a difference, again it's multiplication that does the damage)—*if* some of these things could be done, posterity would benefit.

And now for the other side—the incidental destruction of wildlife. Today the main battle is concentrated here, and we are concerned about the loss of living quarters and food supply as well as the contamination of water, food, and air.

Currently no one questions the fact that DDT and its like are endangering many birds. First to be affected were the predators (eagles, ospreys, and most other hawks) and bluebirds. Recently brown pelicans have been added; they have disappeared from Louisiana (where they are the state bird) and from Texas. The cause is now well known: poisons build up from insects and worms through small birds to predators, and from plankton through fish to pelicans, ospreys, and eagles. By the time it reaches the larger birds, the dosage may be a destructive one, with sterile eggs or overly fragile eggshells as an initial result; adult mortality in later stages. Bluebirds are more directly affected, but here, too, sterile eggs are the first sign of trouble. Fortunately there has been worldwide concern over the cumulative effects of DDT and other persistent pesticides and the damage they are doing. Some states have already banned the use of DDT (Florida's public agencies stopped using it for mosquito control as far back as 1951) and conservation groups here are now urging a statewide ban on *all* broadcast use of the persistent pesticides (DDT, chlordane, lindane, heptachlor, dieldrin, aldrin, and endrin), and the substitution of nonpersistent and specific dusts and sprays.

Biological controls are often very effective, as Sanibel discovered. This island once had a major mosquito problem. It holds the world's record for the number of mosquitoes—a third of a million—caught in one trap on one night. This was September 15, 1950. Since that time mosquitoes have been practically eliminated on the island, and without the use of sprays. The method used is described fully in the *Florida Naturalist* of April 1969, and consisted of flooding the areas where mosquito eggs were laid and then providing enough top minnows and killifishes to dispose of the larvae. On Sanibel the mosquitoes have gone; the birds remain. In fact their bird population has risen, thanks to the Ding Darling Sanctuary and the fact that many birds driven from Marco and the Everglades seem to have sought refuge there.

Pesticides are one part of the story, but equally important is loss of habitat, and the changes here creep up on us insidiously. Development now seems such a normal part of life—we think we have to have more housing, roads, causeways, golf courses, and channels for boats. And there is still so much wilderness in Florida—so much sea bottom. Why can't the birds, reptiles, and shellfish go somewhere else? Unoccupied space is often hard to find, if they survive the original breakup of their homes. And when they disappear (from death or dispersal), they leave a blank that people are beginning to notice.

Habitat destruction, originally, came from cutting timber and clearing land. Next there was the drainage described in Chapter Nine. Then widespread fires swept over the Glades since the dried-out peat burned like tinder, and birds, mammals, reptiles, fishes, and insects perished by the thousands. When flood control areas were established, water was diverted from the Everglades (creating drought conditions there and widespread mortality), and the overflow from Lake Okeechobee was channeled out to sea by means of the Caloosahatchee and the Saint Lucie Canal. On the east coast this brought damage to wildlife because of silt and excessive fresh water flow.

The entire country has, at long last, been aroused to the dangers threatening the Everglades National Park, and in June of 1970 Congress finally guaranteed the necessary water in an omnibus flood control act for Florida that made the entire appropriation dependent upon the release of a sufficient flow to the Glades. As a further step we hope the state of Florida will take a good look at the overall supply and use of water in the whole region. The biggest threat is that, with continued industrial development on the southeast coast, there simply won't be enough water to go around. At some point Florida should say: "This is the limit for industrial and residential development in the southern part of our state. Anything beyond this will result in water shortages for everyone concerned."

On the southwest coast, too, there is a danger of general shortages if the Big Cypress watershed is drained, and developers are now at work in that area. Part of the Big Cypress adjoins the western half of the Park, and its drainage or any damming of the water flow will also hurt the Park. The best answer is probably private or public purchase of as much of the land as is available to bring it under Park control, with restrictions on the building of canals in the section claimed by developers.

Earlier I mentioned the jetport that was to have been built in the Big Cypress Swamp not far from the Park. One runway for training flights had actually been completed when public outcry stopped all further work. The objections were numerous and ranged from excessive noise, bird kill, and air and water pollution (jet fuel, oil, and gas from runways, and roads, sewerage, and pesticides) to—most serious of all—the fact that an enormous city was expected to rise around the airport. It was agreed then that as soon as a new jetport had been built, the training facilities would be moved, and that in the meantime a team of University of Miami scientists would study the effects of the flights on the ecology to be certain they were not harming the Park.

Collier County also imposed a two-year moratorium on zoning changes in the area surrounding the jetport. No trailer parks or commercial enterprises were to come in while further studies were being made, but apparently some have done so, in spite of the moratorium. As desirable land becomes less and less available, developers are turning to the wetlands, and the pressure for clearing and draining some of the watershed is bound to be very strong.

Because of their loss of habitat, some Florida animals have been hard-pressed. One of these is the bald eagle, our national bird, and it's not certain now that the efforts to save him will prove successful. For a time it looked as if Florida Audubon had an answer with its Bald Eagle Program. In this project, cooperating landowners agree not to cut down the trees (most often pines) in which these great birds nest, and not to allow burning or bulldozing around the site while the nest is occupied. Hunters are forbidden to come within range of the birds because many eagles are shot each year, even though it's illegal. Three million acres are now covered by this agreement, with ranchers, foresters, and national and state parks involved. Until recently our national bird seemed to be holding its own in Florida. Of course, as soon as young birds moved away from protected territory, they ran into gunners, pesticides, and destruction of nesting sites, but at least the eagles remaining in the sanctuary grounds were safe. There was no increase, but there were no losses. Then, however, a new problem arose. Pollution, washed down from the north, entered Everglades National Park, which holds the largest colony of eagles. Because of this new danger, the eagles' fate in Florida is again in doubt.

Protecting all birds of prey would be an important step. To many gunners an immature eagle looks like a hawk, and hawks, being predators, are supposed to be undesirable. If we could only realize the importance of the *whole* community, hawks would no longer be killed—and immature eagles would be saved as well. Each link in the chain of life has its place. Hawks play their part—an important one—in controlling rodents. When they take smaller birds, they are likely to catch the weak and sickly and thus often stop the spread of disease. Other kinds of predators are also needed in the natural scheme of things. Alligators serve to keep fish such as gar within bounds. There are too many squirrels and rabbits in eastern North America because we have destroyed most of the foxes and bobcats that kept them under control. (These two predators are still abundant in Florida.) All native animals belong in the picture and we normally hurt the community when we remove any major group.

The sea world has troubles, too, for man pollutes the water, destroys the food, and disturbs the bottom land. The term "pollution" covers many things. Water can be polluted through human and industrial wastes, through oil from tankers and undersea wells, through pesticides, through overheating, through the entry of salt water into freshwater areas, and vice versa, and through oversilting. Rivers are very likely to become polluted, and there is a particular hazard here because river mouths provide great natural nurseries for many kinds of sea life. In southern Florida they are the breeding ground for shrimp, shellfish, and many valuable commercial fish, and one of the essential factors is the brackish quality of the water—that is the right mixture of salt and fresh. When too much fresh water and silt are released, as in the Saint Lucie Canal, the damage can be severe. Rivers must also be kept free from poisons. Feeder canals from the Saint Lucie run out through farmland and fruit groves. Commercial spraying is done throughout this area and when pesticides are washed into the Saint Lucie, heavy fish kills may result.

The greatest breeding ground for shrimp, shellfish, and fish is in Florida Bay, particularly in the brackish waters of the Shark River-Whitewater Bay area. When fresh water flow is cut down because of drought or the actions of the Flood Control District, too much salt water enters the river and bay, and it also rises into the estuaries and inlets throughout southern Florida, endangering not only marine nurseries but our supply of drinking water as well. Salt water is also pushing into the interior through cuts in that limestone rim which surrounds the Everglades—this natural barrier having been broken at many points to allow boats to go inland. Earlier I mentioned the Turkey Point plant and its overheating of south Biscayne Bay.

These are some of the problems. Man acts often without meaning to harm water life, but he injures it just the same. Fortunately many Florida officials are now alert to the dangers and are trying to guard against them as much as possible. The hot water pollution will probably be stopped, if not at the present time, within two or three years. Dams have been built along the limestone rim to hold back the salt water. The Army Engineers sent more water into the Saint Lucie to dilute the pesticide as soon as they heard of the fish kill. But had the feeder canals been banked, it wouldn't have happened in the first place.

We also disrupt the aquatic world by dredging and fill. Again man's wants seem reasonable. Waterfront property is tremendously valuable. Why not build out the land? A double job can be done by digging out a channel for boats, and then using the sand and gravel taken out to create new land, holding it in place with bulkheads. This was done at San Francisco where dumping of garbage and refuse also added to the available sites for building—until that city realized that half of its bay had disappeared!

Such building destroys the sea's natural link with the land—most often beach, marsh, or swamp. A developer sees the marsh only as "waste land"—something to be reclaimed—and many of the rest of us are only just beginning to understand the true importance of wetlands. One great function is slowing down fresh water as it enters a bay or river so that no sudden outpouring (as from the Saint Lucie) can damage marine life. A marsh with its widespread sheet flow is also a barrier to salt water, and freshwater marshes help maintain the ground water table. Adding lakes would make our drinking supply even more assured.

Marshy areas are important food-producing regions. Fabulous amounts of minute vegetable and animal matter are developed here, and, during heavy rains, much of this is washed seaward into bays and river mouths to feed sea creatures. Because of this influx, the shallow water of bays can support an astonishing amount of marine life—both fauna and flora.

Another way in which man disturbs the sea world is by altering the sea bottom. Life zones depend a good deal upon depth. Many plants and animals live only between the tides; other forms are found just beyond the low tide line; still others need deeper water. The turtle grass at a depth of a few feet shelters a tremendous community.

Whenever sea bottom is covered up, whenever channels are dug out for boats, the sea life that belonged there dies. Birds, too, may be affected by these changes. When the intertidal area is taken away, herons, ibises, spoonbills, and shorebirds lose their feeding grounds. Many of the eastern American shorebirds pass through Florida (some of them winter here) so this affects more than the Florida residents.

Suppose, however, that we ignore for the moment the plight of birds and marine life. A salt marsh is drained; the shoreline is built out with dredging and fill, the new line held in place by bulkheads. A community springs up with houses lining the water's edge, crowding close to the boating channels. It's a typical Florida development, and it stands defenseless against hurricanes and tidal waves. While the marsh was there, it absorbed the worst of the big waves; it took the initial shock of the storm. Man's flimsy dwellings are often crushed like match boxes when exposed to the full force of a hurricane.

Again, Florida is taking action in the interest of both men and wildlife. The state would like to see a mean high tide bulkhead line in force. Under this, bulkheads would not be built beyond the normal high tide line and dredging would not be allowed on the seaward side. Several counties have followed this (it's the line favored by conservationists), but Dade County (where Miami is) generally uses the mean low tide line, although a mean high tide line is provided for its mangrove section. Residents of Dade County are all too familiar with the results of the low tide line. It means that barriers can be built out onto the beach making it impossible to walk freely between the tide lines.

The high tide bulkhead line doesn't mean a ban on all boat channels or marinas, but it does mean that man's interests are being weighed against the destruction of marine life, and where the former are not of overwhelming importance, ecological values are being considered. The same reasoning is being applied to freshwater lakes where bulkhead lines are also likely to be established. Not long ago a project to mine Lake Okeechobee for limestone was stopped because it would disturb the lake bottom to an unreasonable degree.

This kind of balancing took place when a causeway was proposed between Elliott Key and the mainland. Developers wanted the causeway. But, every structure of this kind disturbs the marine world not only because of the dredging and filling required to build it, but because it forms a wall against food-bearing currents and the normal distribution of life. When water is overheated or otherwise polluted, a causeway seriously interferes with the dissipation of heat or pollution.

The weighing isn't only man versus nature; it's also man against man. The Big Cypress site for a jetport was chosen, it's been said, to aid Miami; one farther north might divert some of the winter visitors to other cities. But Miami already has crucial problems with housing and traffic during the winter season. It might be a good idea to let some of the incoming flow go elsewhere. Can the other cities take it? Will there be enough water for the cities of the southeast and southwest coasts if the drainage of the Everglades and Big Cypress Swamp continues? This is what has to be considered, along with the effect on wildlife.

In making such decisions, an effective, full-time commission on land-use and environment is all-important. Such a commission might have regional divisions with a sufficient staff to survey every acre within its jurisdiction and to keep abreast of all undesirable changes. Had we had an agency of this kind, the Dade Port Authority would probably have been saved its tremendous outlay for the initial training jetport. (The federal government is having to foot the bill for any loss involved there.) Florida Power and Light would not have built its long cooling canal from Turkey Point to Card Sound. And to go from these major problems to the other extreme, my small pool on Viriginia Key might not have been drained and the bird hammock on Key Biscayne might have been preserved. Residents of Key Biscayne are upset about their loss of open space and wildlife—the changing look of the island. Had they realized its importance, they might have bought the hammock before it was destroyed. But they (like many other members of the general public) need guidance as to when to protest, when to try to get action. Something as small as an acre or two of weeds and shrubs, carefully selected for bird and insect life, might do a great deal for both Crandon Park and Cape Florida State Park.

On Marco, the developers would obviously like to maintain the island's fame as a place for birdlife. Had they been shown how to control mosquitoes without heavy spraying, they might have followed Sanibel's example. Instead, when the birds left and as the shellers dwindled, they began to advertise wildlife figures that any naturalist would question. For instance, they claim to have 430 different species of shells—and this is a wildly improbable figure! They say that 15,000 to 20,000 birds (curlew, ibis, heron, crane, and others) are seen daily at the rookery. Every birder knows that the long-billed curlew (the only possible one) is rare in South Florida, is a shorebird, and would not be found in a rookery. The sandhill crane belongs on the prairie—I'm sure it has never been seen at Marco. The number of birds is quite hard to believe. I have never seen a rookery on the island, although herons and ibises use the mangrove islets offshore. In short the flier seems full of misstatements. Similar misstatements are put forth about many Florida attractions, and I can't believe that they really help either the places involved or the state. It would be better—if natural scenery and wildlife are such potent drawing cards—to make the facts fit the dreams of tourists and newcomers, rather than to throw out false lures.

The land-use commission that I would like to see functioning would advise against (and, where necessary, control) private disposition of land that was not in the public interest. And it would also have some control over public agencies. Road-builders are only too fond of running superhighways through parks and refuges. The U.S. Army Corps of Engineers has built many a canal and dredged out many a river against the advice of conservationists. The actions of the federal Predator Control Bureau are often ill-advised, but we are up against the desire of an entrenched government agency to keep busy. Often what is needed is more control of its agencies by state and federal governments.

One more threat I touched on earlier. This is the foreign plants and animals that are "going wild." Casuarinas are one of the worst offenders. Not being subject to native insects or diseases, they have an edge on native plants. When Hurricane Betsy took the coconut palms on Cape Florida, casuarinas moved in—and since they are unattractive to insects, they offer little food for birds. The same is true of melaleucas, which are also highly resistant to fire. Brazilian pepper flourishes for the same reasons (although birds do like its berries)—and all three are making inroads into the Everglades.

English sparrows and starlings (both introduced) have long been a problem. Should we welcome newcomers such as the scarlet ibis, the red-whiskered bulbul, the spotted-breasted oriole, the marine toad, the Cuban tree frog, the Bahamian anole, the catfish from Thailand?

How much will they compete with native birds and other animals? Many naturalists think that all such exotics should be discouraged, and they may be quite right. The most recent pest is the voracious African snail, released in Miami in 1966 and already numbering over 20,000 individuals. This foreigner feeds on citrus plants, grass, and tree bark, and since he, like other non-natives, is not subject to natural controls, he is likely to go on multiplying at a frightening rate.

With the inroads made by dubious foreigners and the destruction of native alligators and plants, with the costly effect of pesticides and the elimination of wildlife areas both on land and sea, Florida has her hands full. We who enjoy her climate and scenery, her wildlife and wilderness, can make a small return by understanding the problems and by helping wherever our aid may be effective. Florida has become one of the great recreation areas of our nation. She offers the only tropical wilderness in the mainland United States, and it would be a great pity if what means so much to all Americans should ever be lost.

References

Allen, Robert Porter. "Our Only Native Stork, the Wood Ibis." *National Geographic* 125 (No. 2, 1964).

Brooks, Paul. "Superjetport or Everglades Park? " *Audubon* 71 (No. 4, 1969).

*Dasmann, Raymond F. *A Different Kind of Country*. New York: Macmillan, 1968, 276 pp.

Gottschalk, John S. "Wetlands, Wildlife and the Army Engineers." *Audubon* 68 (No. 2, 1966).

Glooschenko, Walter A., and Glooschenko, Valerie A. "Thermal Pollution." *Florida Naturalist* 42 (No. 1, 1969).

Florida Wilderness Committee. "We'll Get What We Deserve." *Florida Naturalist* 42 (No. 2, 1969).

Idyll, C. P., Tabb, D. C., and Yokel, Bernard. "Conservation in Biscayne Bay." *Florida Naturalist* 40 (No. 3, 1967).

Laycock, George. "Where Have All the Pelicans Gone? " *Audubon* 71 (No. 5, 1969).

McCluney, William Ross, ed. *The Environmental Destruction of South Florida.* Coral Gables, Fla.: University of Miami Press, 1971. viii, 134 pp.

*McClung, Robert M. *Lost Wild America: The Story of our Extinct and Vanishing Wildlife.* New York: William Morrow, 1969. 239 pp.

Provost, Maurice. "Man, Mosquitoes and Birds." *Florida Naturalist* 42 (No. 2, 1969).

Raftery, John C. "Adverse Environmental Influences on Everglades National Park." *Florida Naturalist* 42 (No. 3, 1969).

*Teal, John, and Teal, Mildred. *Life and Death of the Salt Marsh.* Boston: Little, Brown & Co., 1969. 278 pp.

Trumbull, Stephen. "The River Spoilers." *Audubon* 68 (No. 2, 1968).

Williams, Lovett E., Jr., and Larry L. Martin, "Can We Solve the Brown Pelican's Problem? " *Florida Naturalist* 42 (No. 3, 1969).

Index

(Italicized page numbers refer to lists of common and scientific names)